UNHOLY WAR

Also by John L. Esposito

Author

The Islamic Threat: Myth or Reality?

Islam: The Straight Path

Women in Muslim Family Law

Islam and Politics

Makers of Contemporary Islam (with John O. Voll)

World Religions Today (with Darrell J. Fasching and Todd Lewis)

Islam and Democracy (with John O. Voll)

Editor

The Oxford Encyclopedia of the Modern Islamic World

The Oxford History of Islam

The Oxford Dictionary of Islam

Political Islam: Revolution, Radicalism, or Reform

Voices of Resurgent Islam

Islam in Asia: Religion, Politics, and Society

The Iranian Revolution: Its Global Impact

Muslims on the Americanization Path?
(with Yvonne Yazbeck Haddad)

Islam, Gender, and Social Change (with Yvonne Yazbeck Haddad)

Religion and Global Order (with Michael Watson)

Islam and Secularism in the Middle East (with Azzam Tamimi)

Muslims and the West: Encounter and Dialogue
(with Zafar Ishaq Ansari)

UNHOLY WAR

Terror in the Name of Islam

John L. Esposito

OXFORD
UNIVERSITY PRESS

OXFORD
UNIVERSITY PRESS

Oxford   New York
Auckland   Bangkok   Buenos Aires   Cape Town   Chennai
Dar es Salaam   Delhi   Hong Kong   Istanbul   Karachi   Kolkata
Kuala Lumpur   Madrid   Melbourne   Mexico City   Mumbai   Nairobi
São Paulo   Shanghai   Taipei   Tokyo   Toronto

First published by Oxford University Press, Inc., 2002
First issued as an Oxford University Press paperback, 2003
198 Madison Avenue, New York, New York 10016

www.oup.com

Oxford is a registered trademark of Oxford University Press

Library of Congress Cataloging-in-Publication Data
Esposito, John L.
Unholy war : terror in the name of Islam / John L. Esposito.
p. cm.
Includes bibliographical references and index.
ISBN 0-19-515435-5 (cloth)   ISBN 0-19-516886-0 (pbk.)
1. Terrorism—Religious aspects—Islam.
2. Jihad. 3. Islam and world politics.
4. Anti-Americanism. I. Title.
HV6431 .E76 2002
322.4'2'0882971—dc21   2001058009

1 3 5 7 9 8 6 4 2
Printed in the United States of America

For John and Mary Esposito
in honor of their 87th and 90th birthdays

Contents

Preface to Paperback Edition

I wrote *Unholy War: Terror in the Name of Islam* both to explain why 9/11 occurred and to place the attacks within their broader context. This understanding is now even more important because of what has happened since 9/11: the continued threat of terrorism internationally and domestically, the American-led war against terrorism, and the exponential growth of anti-Americanism and hatred of America globally.

Since the initial publication of *Unholy War*, many have continued to equate the religion of Islam with global terrorism. At the same time, American statements and policies have reinforced in Muslims the conviction that the American-led war is in fact a war against Islam.

The White House and Pentagon apologized for the early use of such inflammatory terms as "Crusade" and "infinite justice." Subsequently, however, the code name "the green front" (green is the symbolic color of Islam) was employed for raids by government officials on Muslim organizations and homes in Northern Virginia and Georgia. But more than rhetoric, it was the trajectory of American policies in the war against terrorism that reversed international sympathy for America after 9/11 and fueled widespread anger and anti-Americanism. Among the key factors were the broadening of the American-led military campaign's scope beyond Afghanistan, talk of second frontiers and in particular the "axis of evil" countries (e.g., Syria and Iran), America's continued "pro-Israel" policy during the second intifada in Israel/Palestine and failure to effectively pressure Israel to halt Israeli military action in the West Bank and Gaza, and President Bush's unilateral approach to the war in Iraq. One-sided American rhetoric and policies not only in Israel/Palestine but also India/Pakistan (regarding Kashmir) and Russia/Chechnya also fed anti-American sentiment among mainstream Muslims and hatred of America among militant extremists.

Anti-Americanism is also fed by leaders of the Christian Right such as Pat Robertson, Jerry Falwell, and Franklin Graham (who offered the prayer at President Bush's inauguration), who have denounced Islam as an evil religion and labeled Muhammad a terrorist and pedophile. Belief grew among many Muslims that despite his public statements that Islam must be distinguished from Muslim extremism, President George W. Bush was nevertheless deeply influenced by the Christian Right. The association of the president and members of his administration and of Congress with the Christian Right strengthened the conviction of most Muslims that American foreign policy is anti Islam and the Muslim world. Post 9/11, given the nature of the American media's focus on the Robertsons and Grahams and on the continued terrorist threat, many Americans see Islam and the Muslim world through explosive headline events, failing to distinguish between the religion of Islam and mainstream Muslims and the extremists who hijack Islamic discourse and belief to justify their acts of terrorism.

This deadly radical minority remains a threat to Muslim societies as well as to the West.

As became evident in the debate over the American-led war against Iraq, anti-Americanism became a broader-based phenomenon among many in Europe and other parts of the world who fear an "Imperial America" bent on creating what has come to be called a "New American Century." The anger and frustration with American foreign policy is especially strong and widespread in Arab and Muslim societies, expressed by government officials, diplomats, the military, businessmen, professionals, intellectuals, and journalists alike. Many admire the fundamental principles and values of the West—political participation, human rights, accountability, and basic freedoms of speech, thought, and the press. But they believe that there is a double standard—these American principles and values are applied selectively or not at all when it comes to the Muslim world.

In the post–Iraq war period and the continuation of the war against global terrorism, understanding the politics of the Muslim world as well as the sources of radicalism and extremism is more important than ever before. The Bush administration remains challenged to remember that this is as much a political war as a military war, to recognize more fully that while military force is important, in the long term the most effective weapon will be public diplomacy, the conduct of American foreign policy. America will need to join with its partners in the international community, addressing the root causes of terrorism, in this confrontation between the civilized world and global terrorists who engage in an unholy war.

Preface

Terror in the Name of Islam

The tragedy of September 11, 2001, brought Americans together as a nation, united in grief and in resolve. At the same time, Americans from every walk of life began asking some hard questions about America, global terrorism, and the Muslim world. More than a decade ago, in the wake of the fall of the Soviet Union and Saddam Hussein's call for a jihad against the West in the 1991 Gulf war, I wrote *The Islamic Threat: Myth or Reality?*, responding to the growing propensity among senior government officials, political commentators, and the media to see a new "evil empire" replacing the communist threat.

Sadly, more than a decade later, the same questions about Islam and the Muslim world are still being asked: Why do they hate us? Why is Islam more militant than other religions? What does the Quran have to say about jihad or holy war? Does the Quran condone this kind of violence and terrorism? Is there a clash of civilizations between the West and the Muslim world? Yet it is now more important than ever that we educate ourselves about Islam and the roots of terrorism.

Master terrorist Osama bin Laden, like other religious extremists, is the product of his upbringing and experiences in life, of the religious world he inherited and which he reinvents for his own purposes. As in the history of every world religion, violent struggles have been a part of Muslim history. Bin Laden and other terrorists

exploit the authority of the past (Muhammad, the Quran, and Islamic history) for the religious rationale, precedents, and radical
interpreters to justify and inspire their call for a jihad against Muslim governments and the West; they legitimate warfare and terrorism, and they equate their suicide bombings with martyrdom. An
understanding of the religious and historical sources for their beliefs, values, tactics, and actions becomes imperative. Have they
hijacked Islam for their own unholy purposes, or do they, as they
claim, represent a return to the authentic teachings of the faith?

In some sense, bin Laden and al-Qaeda represent a watershed
for contemporary Islamic radicalism. Although in the past the
Ayatollah Khomeini and other major Islamic activist leaders had
called for a broader Islamic revolution, both violent and nonviolent, the focus and impact of most extremist movements from
North Africa to Southeast Asia had been at the local or regional
level. Osama bin Laden and al-Qaeda represent the next major
step, jihad international, that not only declares jihad against governments in the Muslim world and attacks Western representatives and institutions in the region but now makes America and
the West a primary target in an unholy war of terrorism.

America's wars of the twentieth century were fought on the soil
of other countries. Now, the battle has been brought to our own
shores and to the symbols of our economic and political power.
The stakes have risen for everyone. The attacks against America
on September 11 have rightly been seen as a clarion call to recognize our danger and respond to an enemy that threatens all—all
the countries, cultures, and peoples of the world.

The twenty-first century will be dominated by the global encounter of two major and rapidly growing world religions, Christianity and Islam, and by the forces of globalization that will strain
relations between the West and the rest. It is not a time for pro-
voking a clash of civilizations or for the self-fulfilling prophecy
that such a clash is inevitable. It is rather a time for global engagement and coalition building, for the active promotion of coexistence and cooperation. Amidst pressures to win the global war

against terrorism at any cost, how we understand Islam and the Muslim world will affect how we address the causes of terrorism and of anti-Americanism and whether we preserve our American values at home and abroad. We must be able to move beyond political rhetoric, beyond the world of black and white, of unadulterated good versus evil invoked not only by bin Laden and those like him but by his opponents as well.

I have written this book for the vast majority of people in the West, non-Muslims as well as Muslims, whose lives and communities in the twenty-first century are inextricably intertwined. The Muslim world is no longer "out there"; Muslims are our neighbors, colleagues, and fellow citizens, and their religion, like Judaism and Christianity, rejects terrorism. Never before have soft phrases like "building bridges of understanding" been more critical in a war that ultimately cannot be won simply by military power. Understanding and action go hand in hand for Muslims and non-Muslims alike. All of us are challenged to move beyond stereotypes, historic grievances, and religious differences, to recognize our shared values as well as interests, and to move collectively to build our common future.

Of all the books I have written this has been the most difficult, because of the horrific occasion that precipitated it and the range and selection of coverage. As a result, I am especially indebted to those who assisted me and worked under severe time constraints. Natana De Long-Bas is in every sense my senior research assistant. Her work on this project as on others reflected consistent excellence. Her commitment is captured in a picture I have of Natana in labor in the hospital delivery room, working on her research for this book! Juliane Hammer came late to the project but at critical points provided much-needed quick and thorough research. My work has been made infinitely easier due to two remarkable people, Clare Merrill, Assistant Director, and Thomas Jordan, Administrative Assistant, of the Center for Muslim-Christian Understanding at Georgetown, whose intelligence, energy, and results-orientation are invaluable.

I am indebted to several scholars—Ahmed Rashid, Tamara Sonn, James Piscatori, and John O. Voll—who read all or portions of the manuscript, often providing key insights. Cynthia Read, my long-time editor at Oxford, played an especially important role with this book, carefully reviewing each chapter and providing invaluable feedback. The most important person in writing this book was Jean Esposito, my wife, partner, and best friend. While she always managed to balance her own career and interests with substantial involvement in all my books, for this book she was a pivotal force as we determined its structure, contents, and text, and when I was ready to pull the plug, she convinced me to continue. *Unholy War* is in every sense of the words as much her book as mine.

1

The Making of a Modern Terrorist

Osama bin Laden seems like the last person destined to be a global terrorist. His journey from a life of wealth and privilege, as the scion of a multibillionaire Saudi family with close ties to the king and royal family, to the caves and military training camps of Afghanistan sounds more like the stuff of fiction than reality. What happened to transform a quiet, shy, serious, and wealthy Saudi young man into the world community's most wanted criminal? How are we to understand a man who has been described as "an Islamic zealot, a military genius, a poet, and an impassioned enemy of the United States"?[1]

Osama bin Laden was born in Riyadh, Saudi Arabia, in 1957, the seventeenth (the seventh son) of fifty-two children. His father, Muhammad bin Laden, had come to the Kingdom from South Yemen around 1930 as an illiterate laborer. He started a small construction business and went on to become one of Saudi Arabia's wealthiest construction magnates. He developed ties to the royal family and was awarded exclusive contracts. In the 1950s, Osama's father designed and built the al-Hada road, which permitted Muslims from Yemen to make the pilgrimage to Mecca (*hajj*), one of the five basic religious requirements of Islam, more easily. His company also received a multibillion dollar contract to restore and expand the Grand Mosques of Mecca and Medina, raising his company's prestige throughout the Muslim world and setting the stage for the company's expansion beyond Saudi Arabia. The bin Laden family established a large industrial and financial empire, the Bin Laden Group, which became one of the largest construction companies in the Middle East.[2] Ironically, given Osama's recent outrage at the Saudi-American alliance and the presence of American forces in the Kingdom, the Bin Laden Group built many military support facilities in the Kingdom, including those used by U.S. forces during the Gulf War.

The relationship between the bin Laden clan and the royal family goes beyond business ties to include friendship and intermarriage. The bin Laden sons have attended the same schools as numerous princes of the royal family in Europe and America and have studied at and/or given money to some of the best universities, including Harvard, Oxford, and Tufts.[3]

Osama's father was a strong, hard-working, dominating, pious man who insisted on keeping all of his children in one household and raised them according to a strict moral and religious code. The family home was open to many Muslims, especially during hajj, and Osama was able at an early age to meet Muslim scholars and leaders of Islamic movements from all over the Islamic world.[4] Like many in the Arab world, bin Laden's father is said to have felt passionately about the Palestinian-Israeli conflict. This appears in an anecdote that has the elder bin Laden seeking to contribute to the liberation of Palestine. One day, as the story goes, he demanded that his company's engineers convert two hundred bulldozers into tanks for the purpose of attacking Israel. Told that the task was impossible, he decided instead to produce as many sons as possible and convert *them* into fighters. But out of all the bin Laden sons, Osama became the only fighter.[5]

Information on Osama bin Laden's youth is limited and at times contradictory. Some maintain that he was a religiously committed young man protected from corruption by his early marriage to a Syrian girl.[6] Other sources report that, like many wealthy youths of his time, he visited Beirut in the early 1970s, where he enjoyed the nightlife and women of this cosmopolitan city, known at that time as "the Paris of the Middle East."[7] Like most young people, he would find or begin to define himself at university.

Bin Laden was educated in Medina and Jeddah, earning his degree in public administration in 1981 at Jeddah's King Abdulaziz University, where he studied management and economics. During his studies, he became more and more religiously oriented, influenced by his university experience and unfolding events in Saudi Arabia and the wider Muslim world. Osama's religious worldview was shaped both by Saudi Arabia's deeply conservative Wahhabi interpretation of Islam and by the revolutionary Islam that began to spread in the 1970s. Each of these influences would be formative in the development of his jihadist vision, mission, and strategy.

The Islamic Vision

Islam emphasizes action, performing the will of God. It more closely resembles Judaism with its focus on following the law than Christianity with its emphasis on belief. Muslims are enjoined to act, to struggle (*jihad*) to implement their belief, to lead a good life, to defend religion, to contribute to the development of a just Islamic society throughout the world. The life and experience of the early community provide the model for the spread and defense of Islam through *hijra* and jihad. When Muhammad and his Companions suffered unremitting persecution in Mecca, they emigrated (*hijra*) to Yathrib, later renamed Medina, "the city" of the Prophet. Having regrouped, established, and strengthened the community at Medina, Muhammad then set about the struggle (jihad) to spread and defend God's Word and rule. This pattern of hijra and jihad in the face of adversity, coupled with the concept of the *ummah* (the worldwide Islamic community), which stresses a pan-Islamic unity, has guided Muslims throughout the ages, including bin Laden and many terrorists today.

Jihad and the Creation of Saudi Arabia

Osama bin Laden's worldview was very much influenced by the religious heritage and political climate in Saudi Arabia and the

Arab world in the 1960s and 1970s. Key influences included the environment of Saudi Arabia, a self-styled Islamic state with a rigid, puritanical, Wahhabi brand of Islam, the militant jihad ideology of Egypt's Sayyid Qutb, whose disciples had found refuge and positions in the kingdom, and the devastating Arab defeat in the 1967 Arab-Israeli war.

The kingdom of Saudi Arabia from its earliest beginnings has relied on the blending of religion and political power. Its origins stretch back to the eighteenth century when an Islamic revivalist and theologian, Muhammad ibn Abd al-Wahhab, formed an alliance with a local tribal chief, Muhammad ibn Saud of Dariyya (a town near modern-day Riyadh), to create a religiopolitical movement, Wahhabism. The movement swept across central Arabia, capturing Mecca and Medina and uniting its tribes in what its followers believed was a re-creation of Islam's seventh-century beginnings under the Prophet Muhammad. Athough the movement was crushed by the Ottoman Empire, a descendant of the House of Saud, Abdulaziz ibn Saud (1879–1953), reasserted the family's claims to Arabia and led a religious and political movement that resulted in the establishment of modern-day Saudi Arabia.

The Wahhabi religious vision or brand of Islam, named after Muhammad ibn Abd al-Wahhab, has been a staple of the Saudi government, a source of their religious and political legitimation. It is a strict, puritanical faith that emphasizes literal interpretation of the Quran and *Sunnah* (example) of the Prophet Muhammad and the absolute oneness of God. The Wahhabis denounced other tribes and Muslim communities as polytheists or idolaters. Anything the Wahhabis perceived as un-Islamic behavior constituted unbelief (*kufr*) in their eyes, which must be countered by jihad. Thus jihad or holy war was not simply permissible: to fight the unbelievers and reestablish a true Islamic state was required.

Abdulaziz framed the development of Saudi Arabia using stories and symbols drawn from the life and struggles of Muhammad. He recruited Bedouin tribesmen to join the brotherhood of believers and, like Muhammad's community, engage in a process of hijra

and jihad. Like Muhammad and the early community, they emigrated to new settlements where they could live a true Islamic life
and be trained religiously and militarily. They combined missionary zeal, military might, and a desire for booty to once again spread
Islamic rule in Arabia, waging holy wars approved by their religious leaders. Abdulaziz used the banner of the puritanical Wahhabi
to legitimate fighting other Muslim tribal leaders and seizing Mecca
and Medina. As in the Christian tradition, death in battle merited
martyrdom and eternal bliss in paradise; likewise, as in the Christian Crusades, victory meant not only the triumph of virtue but
also the rewards of plunder and booty. Wahhabi history and paradigms were an essential part of Osama bin Laden's religious faith
and sense of history, a heritage he would turn to in later life for
inspiration and guidance.

During the 1970s many Islamic activists, both Saudi-born and
foreigners, were to be found in the Kingdom. Among Osama's
teachers at King Abdulaziz University was Dr. Abdullah Azzam,
who would later become prominent in Afghanistan. Azzam, a Jor-
danian member of the Palestinian Muslim Brotherhood and re-
portedly a founder of Hamas, had strong academic and Islamic
activist credentials.[8] Trained at Damascus University in theology,
he earned a doctorate in Islamic jurisprudence at Egypt's famed al-
Azhar University. Azzam was an advocate of a militant global jihad
ideology and culture, seeing it as a duty incumbent on all Muslims. Sometimes described as the Emir of Jihad or Godfather of
global jihad, Azzam was a captivating speaker who preached a clear
message of militant confrontation and conflict: "Jihad and the
rifle alone: no negotiations, no conferences, and no dialogues."[9]
Azzam's jihad was global in scope, aimed at recouping the glories
and lands of Islam. "This duty will not end with victory in Afghanistan; jihad will remain an individual obligation until all other
lands that were Muslim are returned to us so that Islam will reign
again: before us lie Palestine, Bokhara, Lebanon, Chad, Eritrea,
Somalia, the Philippines, Burma, Southern Yemen, Tashkent and
Andalusia [southern Spain]."[10]

Dr. Muhammad Qutb, a famous scholar and activist, was another of Osama's teachers. He was a brother of Sayyid Qutb, a leader of the militant wing of the Muslim Brotherhood who was executed in 1966 when Gamal Abdel Nasser's government crushed and outlawed the Brotherhood. Sayyid Qutb is widely acknowledged as the father of militant jihad, a major influence on the worldview of radical movements across the Muslim world, and venerated as a martyr of contemporary Islamic revivalism. Qutb's writings and ideas provided the religious worldview and discourse for generations of activists, moderate and extremist. For those Muslims who, like bin Laden, were educated in schools and universities with Islamist teachers, Sayyid Qutb was a staple of their Islamic education.

Bin Laden was educated at a time when Islamic movements and religious extremist or jihad movements were on the rise in the broader Muslim world and within Saudi Arabia. The disastrous and humiliating defeat of the Arabs in the 1967 Six-Day Arab-Israeli war, in which the combined forces of Egypt, Syria, and Jordan were beaten within hours by "tiny little Israel," was a major turning point in the history of contemporary Islam. It generated deep soul-searching about what had gone wrong with Islam, the modern failure and impotence of a Muslim world that for centuries after its creation had experienced unparalleled success and power. What came to be called The Disaster was countered in 1973 by a jihad against Israel fought by Anwar Sadat. Its code name was Badr, symbolizing the first great and miraculous victory of the Prophet Muhammad over a superior Meccan army. This was followed by another significant event in the world of Osama bin Laden. The Arab oil embargo, with its crippling impact on the West, gave Muslims a new sense of pride. The Arab world and the heartland of Islam seemed to reemerge as a major economic power after centuries of subservience to European imperialism.

The 1970s also witnessed an increase in the power and visibility of internal Islamic opposition and reform movements. In Egypt the Muslim Brotherhood along with a series of radical groups reemerged as a major oppositional force. Iran's Islamic revolution came as an inspirational rallying cry for Islamic activists across the Muslim world. Saudi Arabia itself was rocked by the seizure of the Grand Mosque in Mecca in 1979 by militants who called for the overthrow of the House of Saud. Many of these militants were well-educated, pious activists who denounced the wealth and corruption of the "infidel" regime and the corrosive impact of the West on religious and social values. They wanted to purify and return to traditional Islam, re-creating a true Islamic state and society. While bin Laden does not seem to have sided with Saudi extremists, he could not help but be strongly affected by the activist mood of the 1970s in Saudi Arabia and beyond.

Jihad in Afghanistan:
The Making of a Holy Warrior

A major turning point in Osama bin Laden's life, the beginning of his journey toward becoming a *mujahid,* or warrior for God, occurred with the 1979 Soviet invasion and occupation of Afghanistan. As bin Laden would later say, "What I lived in two years there, I could not have lived in a hundred years elsewhere."[11] By the 1970s Afghanistan had become overwhelmingly dependent on the Soviet Union's patronage for its survival. Marxist and Maoist parties thrived while Islamist parties and movements were repressed. In July 1973 Prince Muhammad Daud, a former prime minister and cousin of the Afghan King Zahir Shah, overthrew the government, abolished the monarchy, and proclaimed himself president of Afghanistan. Five years later the People's Democratic Party of Afghanistan staged a coup and established a new communist government. This was followed by the direct intervention and occupation of Afghanistan by the Soviet Union in 1979. The occupation galvanized Afghanistan's diverse tribal and religious leaders and movements in a popular jihad. Afghanistan's tribal society had a fragile unity offset by the realities of its multiethnic tribal society comprising Pashtuns, Uzbeks, Tajiks, and Hazaras divided religiously between a Sunni Muslim majority and a minority of

Shii Muslims. Soviet occupation, however, provided a common enemy and mission. The call for a jihad offered a common, though transient as history would prove, Islamic religious identity and source of inspiration. The *mujahidin* holy war to liberate Islam and Afghanistan from Soviet (atheistic) communist occupation would eventually drive out the Soviet military, defeat the Afghan communists, and lead to the establishment of an Islamic state in 1992.[12]

When the anti-Soviet jihad began, bin Laden was among the first to rush to the Afghan refugee camps in Peshawar, Pakistan, to meet with mujahidin leaders, some of whom he had already come to know during hajj gatherings at his home in Saudi Arabia. From 1979 to 1982 he collected funds and materiel for the jihad and made intermittent visits from Saudi Arabia to Pakistan. In 1982 he finally entered Afghanistan, bringing large quantities of construction machinery as well as funding, and becoming a full participant in the Afghan jihad. By 1984 increasing numbers of Arab mujahidin were arriving in Pakistan to join the holy war. Bin Laden responded by establishing a guesthouse in Peshawar for Arabs on their way to the front in Afghanistan. In 1986 Osama became more directly involved in the war, setting up his own camps and commanding Arab mujahidin forces who became known as Arab Afghans in battle. He subsequently created al-Qaeda (the base), to organize and track the channeling of fighters and funds for the Afghan resistance. Six-feet five-inches tall, with a long beard and piercing eyes, the wealthy and powerfully connected bin Laden was well on his way to becoming a poster-boy for the jihad, at first as a hero and later as a global terrorist.

Bin Laden's activities were applauded by the Saudi government, which, along with the United States, had made a heavy commitment to supporting the jihad against the Soviet Union. For America, this was a "good jihad." Ironically, although the United States had been threatened by Iran's revolutionary Islam and the violence and terrorism committed by jihad groups in Egypt, Lebanon, and elsewhere, our government was able to cheer and support Afghanistan's holy warriors, providing considerable funding as well as

Central Intelligence Agency (CIA) advisers. Everyone was in agreement. For Osama bin Laden, as for Saudi Arabia and indeed Muslims worldwide, the Afghan jihad to repel foreigners from Islamic territory was eminently in accord with Islamic doctrine.

Bin Laden proved himself to be a selfless and dedicated mujahid, or holy warrior. Still young, he was more comfortable as an activist than as an ideologue, focused primarily on the jihad in Afghanistan rather than on Muslim international politics and activism. Ahmed Rashid, expert on the Taliban and al-Qaeda, writes of bin Laden:

> Arab Afghans who knew him during the jihad say he was neither intellectual nor articulate about what needed to be done in the Muslim world. In that sense he was neither the Lenin of the Islamic revolution, nor was he the internationalist ideologue of the Islamic revolution such as Che Guevera was to the revolution in the third world. Bin Laden's former associates describe him as deeply impressionable, always in need of mentors, men who knew more about Islam and the modern world than he did.[13]

The Radicalization of a Saudi Elite

How did Osama bin Laden, member of the Saudi elite, mujahid, and hero of the war in Afghanistan, become radicalized? After Soviet troops withdrew from Afghanistan in 1989, bin Laden returned to Saudi Arabia and a job in the family business. Though initially received as a hero, speaking at mosques and to private gatherings, he was soon at loggerheads with the royal family, vociferous in his warning of an impending Iraqi invasion of Kuwait. Saudi Arabia, along with Kuwait and the United States, had for many years, in particular during the Iraq-Iran War, been strong supporters of Saddam Hussein's Iraq, seeing it as a check on the Ayatollah Khomeini's Iran. When Iraq did invade Kuwait in August 1990, bin Laden quickly wrote to King Fahd, offering to bring the Arab Afghan mujahidin to Saudi Arabia to defend the kingdom. Instead, the deafening silence from the palace was shattered by news that American forces were to defend the House of Saud. The admission and stationing of foreign non-Muslim troops in Islam's holy land and their permanent deployment after the Gulf war, bin Laden would later say, transformed his life completely, placing him on a collision course with the Saudi government and the West. He spoke out forcefully against the Saudi alliance with the United States, obtained a *fatwa* (legal opinion) from a senior religious scholar that training was a religious duty, and sent several thousand volunteers to train in Afghanistan.

Like other Arab Afghans who returned to their home countries, in Afghanistan bin Laden had enjoyed the freedom to think and act and to engage in a religious mission to overcome injustice and create an Islamic state and society. In Saudi Arabia he found himself bound within the confines of a regime whose policies and alliances he more and more came to despise as corrupt and un-Islamic. While many of the Arab Afghans who returned to Egypt, Algeria, and elsewhere quickly became involved in radical opposition movements, bin Laden continued to struggle within the system. The government restricted his movement in an attempt to silence him. Finally, in April 1991 he escaped to Afghanistan via Pakistan. When he arrived, however, he found himself not in the Islamic state for which the jihad had been fought but in one mired in the religious and ethnic warfare of its aftermath.

Within a brief period after the Soviet withdrawal, the great Islamic victory had collapsed into interethnic and sectarian warfare, fueled by foreign patrons. The net result was chaos and the devastation of Afghanistan as various warlords vied to set up their own fiefdoms.

Despite the Afghan victory, the jihad had failed to develop a coherent ideology or basis for political unity. The United States walked away from an Afghanistan whose countryside was devastated by a ten-year Soviet occupation that had cost more than one million lives. Mujahidin groups, many of which today make up the Northern Alliance that with U.S. backing fought and defeated the Taliban, represented competing ethnic, tribal, and religious groups. The country was gripped by a civil war that pitted the majority Pashtun population in the south and east against the ethnic minorities of the north—Tajik, Uzbek, Hazara, and Turkmen. The conflict was further compounded by the intervention and competing agendas of outside powers. Pakistan and Saudi Arabia supported Sunni mujahidin groups while Iran backed an alliance of Shii minority organizations. The majority of Afghans found themselves caught in the middle of a prolonged civil war marked by heavy fighting, lawlessness, pillaging, rape, and plunder. Bin Laden was frustrated by his inability to contribute to the resolution of the problems of chaos and lawlessness. In 1992, after several months amidst the inter-mujahidin squabbling and fighting over succession after the collapse of the pro-Soviet regime, bin Laden moved to Sudan.

Sudan and the Entrepreneur-Mujahid

In January 1989, in a coup led by Colonel Omar al-Bashir, the National Islamic Front (NIF) had come to power in Sudan and established an Islamic republic. Bashir had enlisted the help of Hasan al-Turabi, the Sorbonne-educated leader of the NIF, regarded by many as one of the most brilliant and articulate of the Islamic activist leaders of political Islam internationally. Al-Turabi became the ideologue of the regime, holding a number of political positions, including speaker of the parliament. NIF members provided the backbone and infrastructure for the new government. The government, in a relationship that proved mutually beneficial, welcomed bin Laden. Bin Laden found a refuge and invested his wealth in much-needed construction projects as well as farms and other businesses in the fledgling Islamic state. During these years Sudan, with its open borders, was increasingly condemned by America and Europe for its links with revolutionary Iran and for harboring international terrorists and their training camps. In 1993 Sudan was placed on the State Department's list of countries that sponsor terrorism. bin Laden was among those individuals whom U.S. intelligence identified as sponsoring terrorist training camps. Although he denied direct involvement and was never formally indicted, bin Laden voiced his approval for the World Trade Center bombing in 1993 and the killing of U.S. troops in Mogadishu, Somalia. American officials were divided as to whether he provided training and arms to those responsible.

Bin Laden's final break with Saudi Arabia came in 1994 when the Kingdom revoked his citizenship and moved to freeze his assets in Saudi Arabia because of his support for fundamentalist movements. From that point on, bin Laden became more outspoken in his denunciation of the House of Saud. Now pushed to the fringe, he joined with other dissident activists and religious scholars to create the Advice and Reform Committee, founded in Saudi Arabia but forced subsequently to move to London. This political opposition group strongly criticized the Saudi regime but did not overtly advocate violence.

By 1995, a series of events and accusations had catapulted the previously obscure bin Laden to center stage. U.S. intelligence sources claimed that he had established extensive training operations in northern Yemen near the Saudi border.[14] Investigators charged that Ramzi Yousef, the captured mastermind of the World Trade Center bombing, had stayed at a bin Laden–financed guesthouse and had financial links to bin Laden. Bin Laden sent a letter to King Fahd advocating guerrilla attacks to drive the U.S. forces out of the Kingdom. Some charged that he was linked to an unsuccessful assassination attempt in Addis Ababa, in June 1995, against President Hosni Mubarak of Egypt. When five Americans and two Indians were killed in a truck bombing in Riyadh in November 1995, bin Laden denied involvement but praised those who committed the attack.[15] Responding to mounting international pressure, especially from the United States and Saudi Arabia, in May 1996 Sudan expelled bin Laden. Ironically, Sudan offered to extradite him to Saudi Arabia or America; both refused to take

him. Though some had urged the United States to take advantage
of the tentative overtures that the NIF government was making,
the Clinton administration chose otherwise.

Bin Laden fled back to Afghanistan.[16] Shortly after, in June, a
large truck bomb tore apart the Khobar Towers, a U.S. military
residence in Dhahran, Saudi Arabia, killing nineteen servicemen.
Investigators were initially divided between placing the blame with
bin Laden or with a militant Saudi Shii organization.[17] Bin Laden
praised those behind the Riyadh and Dhahran bombings but denied direct involvement: "I have great respect for the people who
did this. What they did is a big honor that I missed participating
in."[18] In June 2001 thirteen members of Saudi Hizbollah, a Shiite
group from the Eastern province of Saudi Arabia, were indicted in
the United States for the Dhahran bombing.

The Taliban and bin Laden

In 1996, Afghanistan witnessed the rise of an improbable militia
that would go on to unite 90 percent of the country and declare
the Islamic Republic of Afghanistan. After almost eighteen years
of Soviet occupation followed by civil war, a seemingly endless
cycle of carnage and chaos was abruptly reversed by the astonish-
ing success of a new Islamic movement.

Late in 1994, as if out of nowhere, the predominantly Pashtun
Taliban, a band of *madrasa* (seminary) students (*taliban*) who had
been living as refugees in Pakistan suddenly appeared. Initially
the Taliban were portrayed as having no military background. In
fact many of their *mullahs* (religious leaders) and students were
veterans of the Afghan-Soviet war who had returned to the
madrasas after the departure of the Soviets. Within two years they
swept across the country, overwhelming the Northern Alliance of
non-Pashtun minorities. Denouncing the contending mujahidin
militias, the Taliban claimed the mantle of moral leadership as
representatives of the majority of Afghans who were victims of
the internecine warfare.

Taliban

At first the Taliban were hailed as liberators who promised to restore law and order, stability and security, and make the streets safe for ordinary citizens. They disarmed the population, cleaned up corruption and graft, and imposed *Shariah* (Islamic law). Initially, they enjoyed success and popularity as a reform movement. It was not until their capture of Kabul in 1996 that they revealed their intention to rule the country and to impose a strict puritanical form of Islam. With substantial support from Saudi Arabia and Pakistan, by 1998 they had subdued 90 percent of the country and driven the Northern Alliance into a small area of northeast Afghanistan.

The Taliban brand of Islamic radicalism has been significantly influenced by a militant neo-Deobandi movement in Pakistan. Ironically, the Sunni Deobandi began in the Indian subcontinent as a reformist movement. However, its political expression and ideology were transformed within Pakistan's Jamiyyat-i-Ulama-i-Islam (JUI), a religious party with a rigid, militant, anti-American, and anti-non-Muslim culture. Many of the Taliban were trained in the hundreds of JUI madrasas. Often run by semiliterate mullahs, these schools were first set up for Afghan refugees in the Pashtun-dominated areas of Pakistan, along the border with Afghanistan. Many were supported by Saudi funding that brought with it the influence of an ultraconservative Wahhabi Islam. Students received free education, religious, ideological, and military training. The Taliban teachers showed little knowledge or appreciation for their classical Islamic tradition or for currents of Islamic thought in the broader Muslim world today. They espoused a myopic, self-contained, militant worldview in which Islam is used to legitimate their tribal customs and preferences. The classical Islamic belief in jihad as a defense of Islam and the Muslim community against aggression was transformed into a militant jihad culture and worldview that targets unbelievers, including Muslims and non-Muslims alike.

When they came to power, the Taliban turned over many of their training camps to JUI factions, who in turn trained thousands of Pakistani and Arab militants as well as fighters from South and Central Asia and the Arab world in their radical jihad ideology and tactics. Assisted by military support from Pakistan and financial support from the Wahhabi in Saudi Arabia, with JUI mentoring and influenced by Osama bin Laden's evolving radical jihadist political vision, the Taliban promoted their own brand of revolutionary Islam. They imposed their strict Wahhabi-like brand of Islam on Afghan society. They banned women from school and the workplace, required that men wear beards and women *burqas*, banned music, photography, and television, and imposed strict physical punishments on deviators. Their intolerance for any deviation from their brand of Islam expressed itself in the slaughter of many of Afghanistan's Shii minority (10 percent of the population), whom they disdained as heretics, when the Taliban overran Shii areas such as Mazar-e Sharif in northwest Afghanistan.

Many Muslim religious leaders around the world denounced Taliban "Islamic" policies as aberrant. Muslim governments as diverse as Iran and Egypt, along with Western governments and international human rights organizations, condemned Taliban violations of human rights. Despite their control of most of Afghanistan, by the fall of 1998, neither the United Nations nor most of the global community acknowledged their legitimacy. The Taliban government was recognized by only three nations, Saudi Arabia, Pakistan, and the United Arab Emirates.

Nevertheless, bin Laden found the Taliban's Afghanistan a comfortable haven and useful base of operations. The Taliban leader, Mullah Omar, had been quick to offer sanctuary and express his admiration for bin Laden's sacrifices and dedication to jihad. Bin Laden skillfully cultivated and developed his relationship with Mullah Omar and the Taliban, providing financial support, building roads and other construction projects, and sending his Afghan Arabs to fight alongside the Taliban in critical battles.

Bin Laden's entourage and followers grew steadily. He attracted Arab and other Muslim dissidents, many of whom had had to flee their native countries. Among them were several prominent Egyp-

tian radicals: Dr. Ayman al-Zawahiri, a physician and a leader of
the banned Islamic Jihad in Egypt; Rifai Taha Musa, leader of Egypt's
banned Gamaa Islamiyya; and two sons of Shaykh Omar Abdel
Rahman, the blind Egyptian preacher indicted for involvement in
the assassination of Anwar Sadat, suspected of involvement in the
World Trade Center bombing of 1993, and later found guilty of
conspiring to blow up major sites in New York City. Omar Abdel
Rahman had visited Afghanistan several times during the war
against the Soviets, when he and bin Laden had first met. Of these
men, however, the one to wield the most influence over bin Laden
would be Dr. Ayman al-Zawahiri.

Ayman al-Zawahiri:
From Medical School to Jihad University

The story of Ayman al-Zawahiri is that of a gifted surgeon who
became a leader of an Egyptian terrorist group on the road to becoming Osama bin Laden's confidant, reputed mentor, and successor. Ayman al-Zawahiri was born in 1953 into a prominent and
conservative religious family. He grew up in Maadi, an upscale
suburb of Cairo inhabited by wealthy Egyptians and foreign diplomats. His grandfathers were the rector of al-Azhar University,
the Islamic world's oldest and most prestigious religious school,
and president of Cairo University, Egypt's leading modern secular
university.

Family and friends remember Ayman as a normal, well-adjusted
young man—an intelligent, well-read, polite student who went
on to become a physician. However, 1967 had been a defining
moment for him as it was for many in the Arab world. After the
disastrous Arab defeat in the 1967 Arab-Israeli (Six Day) war and
the disillusionment over Arab (secular) nationalism and socialism
that followed, al-Zawahiri turned to political Islam. He joined the
Muslim Brotherhood when he was only fourteen years old. By 1979,
he had embraced a radical option and joined Islamic Jihad, a violent extremist group composed of small clandestine cells. He quickly

became one of its leaders and by 1983 was recruiting members, organizing secret cells and underground operations. After the assassination of Anwar Sadat, Zawahiri was arrested along with hundreds of others. Though no direct link to Sadat's death could be established, he was tried and sentenced to three years in prison on charges of possessing weapons. After his 1984 release from prison, where like many others he had been beaten and tortured, he briefly returned to medical practice in a clinic. The political climate in Egypt and his radical past and prison record, however, prompted al-Zawahiri to emigrate and take a position in Saudi Arabia. Within the year he went to Afghanistan, where he worked as a surgeon, treating wounded Afghan and Arab fighters in field hospitals.[19] It was during this time that he met Dr. Abdullah Azzam, the Palestinian Islamist activist who had taught bin Laden at King Abdulaziz University in Jeddah, Saudi Arabia. Azzam had gone to Pakistan to make his contribution to the war in Afghanistan. After a short stint teaching at the Islamic University in Islamabad, Pakistan, he founded the Jihad Service Bureau, whose mission was the recruitment of Saudis and other Arabs through publications and other media. Azzam joined with bin Laden and Zawahiri in recruiting and training Muslims for the jihad against the Soviets. They formed a lasting friendship and alliance in their growing commitment to a global jihad. After the Soviet defeat in 1989, Zawahiri returned to Egypt and to his leadership role in Islamic Jihad.

Zawahiri played an important role during the 1990s, organizing underground operations and integrating former mujahidin into the ranks of Islamic Jihad. The violence and terrorism of Islamic Jihad were met with equal force by Egyptian military and police. Bloody confrontations were accompanied by the arrest, interrogation, torture, and imprisonment of thousands.

In 1992 Zawahiri moved to Sudan with bin Laden, and in 1996 both returned to Afghanistan. From there, al-Zawahiri continued to be involved in the jihad against the Egyptian state. He is believed to have been the mastermind behind terrorist attacks, including the massacre of fifty-eight tourists in Luxor in 1997, for which he was sentenced to death in absentia by an Egyptian court in 1999. He also merged Islamic Jihad with al-Qaeda and worked with Osama bin Laden to plot and execute their global jihad.

Many believed that Zawahiri possessed a deeper theological understanding and more international perspective than bin Laden, and that he was responsible for broadening bin Laden's vista for jihad beyond the Arab world to the wider Muslim world and to a jihad against America and/or the West. Hamid Mir, a Pakistani journalist who interviewed bin Laden, believes that al-Zawahiri also masterminded the September 11, 2001, attacks. Although only religious leaders can legitimately issue fatwas, bin Laden had nevertheless issued a fatwa allowing the killing of innocent people: "to kill Americans and their allies—civilians and military—is an individual duty for every Muslim who can do it in any country in which it is possible to do it." When Mir pressed him on how this was permissible in light of the fact that the Prophet Muhammad forbade Muslims to kill innocent civilians, he noted that bin Laden responded only after consulting with Zawahiri and checking some Islamic sources.[20] Others, however, contend that bin Laden has long had a global animosity toward America and Israel as well as the intellectual and financial means to pursue it, and that it is he who broadened the perspective of Zawahiri, who had spent the bulk of his formative years as a terrorist focused on toppling the regime and establishing an Islamic state in Egypt. Regardless of who influenced whom, the bin Laden and Zawahiri joint venture produced a powerful global ideology and agenda.

Afghanistan and bin Laden's
Declaration of Holy War

Safely entrenched in Afghanistan, Osama bin Laden assumed a more visible and vocal leadership role in international terrorism, calling openly for a jihad against America and its allies. In August 1996 he issued a Declaration of Jihad whose goals were to drive U.S. forces out of the Arabian peninsula, overthrow the Saudi gov-

Jihad

ernment, and liberate Islam's holy sites of Mecca and Medina, as well as support revolutionary groups around the world. In November, he again repeated his threat to wage holy war against the United States and its allies if Washington did not remove its troops from the Gulf.[21] By 1998, he seemed increasingly comfortable and astute in using the media to propagate his message and garner support in the Muslim world. From that time onward, his media appearances and statements were carefully crafted, emphasizing both his image and message.

In 1998 bin Laden announced the formation of the World Islamic Front for the Jihad Against Jews and Crusaders, an umbrella group of radical movements across the Muslim world, and issued a fatwa stating that it is the duty of all Muslims to kill U.S. citizens and their allies. The title of the organization summed up the man and his view of the world. Muslims were under siege, their lands occupied in a world dominated by their historic enemies, militant Christianity and Judaism. All true Muslims had an obligation to heed the call to a global jihad, a defense of the worldwide Islamic community. Global politics were indeed for bin Laden a competition and jihad, a clash of civilizations between the Muslim world and the West, between Islam and a militant Judeo-Christian conspiracy. Foreign influence and intervention in the Islamic world had once again underscored the traditional division of the world into the land of Islam (*dar al-Islam*) and the land of warfare (*dar al-harb*). Because of Western abuses, the entire world has been divided, he claimed, "into two regions—one of faith where there is no hypocrisy and another of infidelity, from which we hope God will protect us."[22] If bin Laden and al-Qaeda's attempt to mobilize the world of Islam for their jihad further convinced most Muslim and Western governments of the magnitude of the Islamic threat, it also seemed to contribute to bin Laden's attraction for a growing number of Muslims, particularly in the younger generation. Like Ayatollah Khomeini and Saddam Hussein before him, bin Laden seeks legitimacy and the mobilization of the "Muslim street" or general population through identification with many of the perceptions and grievances of mainstream as well as extremist Muslims. He hijacks Islam, using Islamic doctrine and law to legitimate terrorism.

The major issues and themes of bin Laden's message reflect both his Arab roots and a growing awareness of the broader Islamic community. His primary focus was at first the presence of foreign troops in the Arab peninsula, the overthrow of the Saudi regime, and the Palestinian-Israeli conflict. Bin Laden labeled America and Israel as crusaders and Jews and Zionists and condemned the Saudi regime as compliant and corrupt. He then extended his accusations to embrace the death of one million innocent Iraqis due to Western sanctions as well as struggles in Bosnia, Chechnya, and Kashmir.

Bin Laden played to the Muslim sense of historic oppression, occupation, and injustice at the hands of the West. After September 11, he charged, "What the United States tastes today is a very small thing compared to what we have tasted for tens of years. Our nation has been tasting humiliation and contempt for more than 80 years."[23] He paints a world in which Muslims and Islam are under siege:

> America and its allies are massacring us in Palestine, Chechnya, Kashmir, and Iraq. The Muslims have the right to attack America in reprisal. . . . The September 11 attacks were not targeted at women and children. The real targets were America's icons of military and economic power.[24]

The heart of bin Laden's jihad against America starts with his outrage at the injustice in his homeland—the infidel's occupation of sacred territory and its support for a corrupt un-Islamic government: "The call to wage war against America was made because America spearheaded the crusade against the Islamic nation, sending tens of thousands of troops to the land of the two Holy Mosques over and above its meddling in Saudi affairs and its politics, and its support of the oppressive, corrupt, and tyrannical regime that is in control."[25] Refusing to any longer recognize Saudi Arabia by name, bin Laden referred to the sacred territory it "occupies." Interestingly, King Fahd and the House of Saud some years earlier had taken to using the title "Custodian of the Two Holy Sites" of Mecca and Medina because they recognized their vulnerability to Islamic critics who insisted that monarchy is antithetical to Islam.

Bin Laden also connected Western presence in the Gulf with a more international concern: America's complicity in Israeli expansionism, its support for "Jewish and Zionist plans for expansion of what is called Greater Israel."[26] Contrary to what many said in the aftermath of September 11, Palestine is a primary issue for bin Laden. His messages have consistently spoken of Zionist and Jewish offenses against Muslims. His passionate statements on the plight of the Palestinians, who have been living under Israeli military occupation in violation of UN Security Council resolutions for over forty years, graphically describe, capture, and appeal to the outrage of many in the Arab and Muslim world toward Israeli policy and the complicity of the international community:

> For over half a century, Muslims in Palestine have been slaughtered and assaulted and robbed of their honor and of their property. Their houses have been blasted, their crops destroyed. And the strange thing is that any act on their part to avenge themselves or lift the injustice befalling them causes great agitation in the United Nations which hastens to call an emergency meeting only to convict the victim and to censure the wronged and tyrannized whose children have been killed and whose crops have been destroyed and whose farms have been pulverized. . . .[27]

Bin Laden holds the American people, who elect their president and Congress, responsible for Israeli oppression of Palestinians: "their government manufactures arms and gives them to Israel and Israel uses them to massacre Palestinians."[28] He charges that the Jewish lobby has taken America and the West hostage. He calls upon the American people to rise up against their government as they did during the Vietnam war and force it to give up America's anti-Muslim policies and massacre of Muslims. Muslims have the right, indeed the obligation, to defend themselves. He appeals then to the Islamic teaching that jihad in the defense of Islam and to correct an unjust political order is legitimate and required:

> We are carrying out the mission of the prophet, Muhammad (peace be upon him). The mission is to spread the word of God, not to indulge in massacring people. We ourselves are the target of killings, destruction, and atrocities. We are only defending ourselves. This is defensive jihad. We want to defend our people and our land. That is why we say, if we don't get security, the Americans, too, would not get security. This is the simple formula that even an American child can understand. Live and let live.[29]

In bin Laden's view, charges of "terrorism" are specious in a world of immorality and oppression within which ostensible acts of terrorism are sometimes necessary and justified. He paints the modern world in polarities, a world of belief and unbelief, within which the forces of evil, oppression, and injustice assault the forces of good. The Muslim world and Islam are under siege:

> They rob us of our wealth and of our resources and of our oil. Our religion is under attack. They kill and murder our brothers. They compromise our honor and our dignity and dare we utter a single word of protest against the injustice, we are called terrorists.[30]

Like a Muslim jurist, he legalistically distinguishes between "commendable" and "reprehensible" terrorism. To terrify the innocent is unjust; however, terrorizing oppressors is necessary:

> There is no doubt that every state and every civilization and culture has to resort to terrorism under certain circumstances for the purpose of abolishing tyranny and corruption. . . . The

terrorism we practice is of the commendable kind for it is directed at the tyrants, the traitors who commit acts of treason against their own countries and their own faith and their own prophet and their own nation. Terrorizing those and punishing them are necessary measures to straighten things and make them right.[31]

Osama bin Laden plays to a centuries-long tradition of reform in Islam, most of it aimed in the last one hundred years toward the struggle over Muslim oppression by the West. Why do his calls for a defensive jihad resonate as truth for mainstream Muslims as well as for extremists who live today in the Muslim world? This is the question we will examine in the next chapter.

Jihad and the Struggle for Islam

If you were watching a television special on *jihad*, with four Muslim speakers, you might well hear four different responses to the question: "What is jihad?" One might say that jihad is striving to lead a good Muslim life, praying and fasting regularly, being an attentive spouse and parent. Another might identify jihad as working hard to spread the message of Islam. For a third, it might be supporting the struggle of oppressed Muslim peoples in Palestine, Kashmir, Chechnya, or Kosovo. And for the final speaker, as for Osama bin Laden, jihad could mean working to overthrow governments in the Muslim world and attacking America. However different these interpretations are, all testify to the centrality of jihad for Muslims today. Jihad is a defining concept or belief in Islam, a key element in what it means to be a believer and follower of God's Will.

In the late twentieth and twenty-first centuries the word jihad has gained remarkable currency. It is used by resistance, liberation, and terrorist movements alike to legitimate their cause and motivate their followers. The Afghan mujahidin, the Taliban and the Northern Alliance, have waged a jihad in Afghanistan against foreign powers and among themselves; Muslims in Kashmir, Chechnya, Dagestan, the southern Philippines, Bosnia, and Kosovo have fashioned their struggles as jihads; Hizbollah, Hamas, and Islamic Jihad Palestine have characterized war with Israel as a jihad; Algeria's Armed Islamic Group has engaged in a jihad of terror against the government there, and Osama bin Laden has waged a global jihad against Muslim governments and the West.

The importance of jihad is rooted in the Quran's command to struggle (the literal meaning of the word jihad) in the path of God and in the example of the Prophet Muhammad and his early Companions. These are fundamentals of Muslim belief and practice. Jihad is a concept with multiple meanings, used and abused throughout Islamic history. Although jihad has always been an important part of the Islamic tradition, in recent years some Muslims have maintained that it is a universal religious obligation for all true Muslims to join the jihad to promote a global Islamic revolution.

Many Muslims today believe that the conditions of their world require a jihad. They look around them and see a world dominated by corrupt authoritarian governments and a wealthy elite, a minority concerned solely with its own economic prosperity, rather than national development, a world awash in Western culture and values in dress, music, television, and movies. Western governments are perceived as propping up oppressive regimes and exploiting the region's human and natural resources, robbing Muslims of their culture and their options to be governed according to their own choice and to live in a more just society. Many believe that the restoration of Muslim power and prosperity requires a return to Islam, the creation of more Islamically oriented states and societies. Some Muslims, a radicalized minority, combine militancy with messianic visions to inspire and mobilize an army of God whose jihad they believe will liberate Muslims at home and abroad.

If jihad has so many meanings, how are they to be understood? Which interpretations are correct? Which of the meanings promote positive improvements and reforms, and which have been exploited to justify extremism and terrorism? These questions are not new—they have been debated by Muslims throughout the ages.

The history of the Muslim community from Muhammad to the present can be read within the framework of what the Quran teaches about jihad. The Quranic teachings have been of essential significance to Muslim self-understanding, piety, mobilization, expansion, and defense. Jihad as struggle pertains to the difficulty and complexity of living a good life: struggling against the evil in oneself in order to be virtuous and moral, making a serious effort to do good works and to help to reform society. Depending on the circumstances in which one lives, it also can mean fighting injustice and oppression, spreading and defending Islam, and creating a just society through preaching, teaching and, if necessary, armed struggle or holy war.

The two broad meanings of jihad, nonviolent and violent, are contrasted in a well-known prophetic tradition. It is said that when Muhammad returned from battle he told his followers, "We return from the lesser jihad to the greater jihad." The greater jihad is the more difficult and more important struggle against one's ego, selfishness, greed, and evil.

Understanding the various ways in which jihad has been interpreted throughout Muslim history will enable us to distinguish between extremist organizations on the one hand and the majority of Muslims on the other.

When Osama bin Laden or the leaders of other terrorist groups speak today, like all Muslims they often consciously or unconsciously use the past to legitimate their agenda and tactics. They place themselves under the mantle of the Prophet. They also link their militant jihadist worldviews to famous earlier interpretations of jihad, for example, that of the prominent medieval theologian and legal scholar Ibn Taymiyya or that of Sayyid Qutb, the godfather of modern revolutionary Islam. Are they simply appropriating a tradition of holy war or are they reinventing their tradition to support their self-declared unholy wars of violence and terrorism?

The struggle for the soul of Islam going on today is the product of a rich and complex history. From the very beginning, jihad was used both by those in power and by those who challenged that power, by insiders and by outsiders. Early Muslim history provides the clearest antecedents and paradigms for what is going on today. And so to understand jihad, we must begin with the Prophet Muhammad and the Quran.

Muhammad's Jihad

Islam and the Quran, like all the great world religions and their scriptures, offer a universal message, a discourse that can speak to all times and places. Believers in every age and situation find teachings, principles, and values that give them meaning and guidance. Jews can look to the Hebrew Bible to find stories of Joshua and King David spreading and defending their faith and community by warfare, as well as passages that extol the virtues of peace. Christians look to a tradition that can support pacifism but also a just-war theory that legitimates warfare. Similarly, the Quran and the Sunnah, or prophetic example, provide a theology for peace, for living in a world of diverse nations and peoples. They also provide guidelines on how to fight the enemy as well as how to fight against corruption and oppression. As we shall see, the challenge in Islamic history has been to draw a careful line between self-defense and aggression, resistance and rebellion, reform and terrorism.

The world in which Islam emerged in the seventh century was a rough neighborhood where war was the natural state. Arabia and the city of Mecca, in which Muhammad lived and received God's revelation, were beset by tribal raids and cycles of vengeance and vendetta. The broader Near East, in which Arabia was located, was itself divided between two warring superpowers of the day, the Byzantine (Eastern Roman) and the Persian (Sasanian) Empires. Each had competed against the other for world dominion.

Seventh-century Arabia was critically located along the profitable trade routes of the Orient. As a result it was subject to the rivalry and interventions of its powerful imperial neighbors. The rise and spread of Islam was caught in both the local politics and fighting of Arabia and the imperial warfare of the Near East. Muhammad's preaching would add to this mix and would itself become a source of conflict.

Muhammad's reformist message posed an unwelcome challenge to the religious and political establishment, the priests, tribal leaders, and businessmen of the community. The new religious mes-

sage that Muhammad preached, like that of Amos and other biblical prophets before him, denounced the status quo and called for
social justice for the poor and the most vulnerable in society—
women, children, and orphans. Muhammad and the Quran condemned Arabian polytheism and put a spotlight on Meccan society's
unbridled materialism, avarice, and corruption, a condition of ignorance and unbelief called *jahiliyyah*. This is a very important
term, rich in meaning, that has been reappropriated and reinterpreted by fundamentalists today to describe and condemn Western society.

Muhammad's prophetic call summoned the people to strive and
struggle (jihad) to reform their communities and to live a good
life based on religious belief and not loyalty to their tribe. His
insistence that each person was personally accountable not to tribal
customary law but to an overriding divine law shook the very foundations of Arabian society. Muhammad's newly claimed status and
authority as God's messenger and his entreaties to believers to take
action against social corruption threatened the authority of powerful elites. Muhammad proclaimed a sweeping program of religious and social reform that affected religious belief and practices,
business contracts and practices, male-female and family relations.
The Quran rejected Arabian polytheism and insisted that there
was only one true God. It denounced the corrupt practices of many
merchants and the exploitation of orphans and their inheritance
rights. It condemned infanticide, spoke of the religious equality
of men and women, and expanded the marriage and inheritance
rights of women. To uphold this deeply challenging message and
mission, Muhammad and his followers would have to fight, wage
jihad, to stay alive.

The example of the original Islamic community has deep significance for reformers as the only model to be emulated. Sayyid
Qutb, writing in the mid-twentieth century, echoes those who came
before and after him and testifies to the continuing power of the
first Islamic community to inspire Muslims in all ages:

At one time this Message [the Quran] created a generation—the generation of the Companions of the Prophet (may God be pleased with them) without comparison in the history of Islam, even in the entire history of man. After this, no other generation of this calibre was ever again to be found.[1]

Hijra and Jihad: Response to Persecution and Conflict

The first decade of Muhammad's preaching met with resistance and persecution and produced limited results. The community remained small and under constant pressure. The experience of Muhammad's nascent community would provide the model for later generations, a guide for responding to persecution and rejection, to threats to the faith, to the security and survival of the community. The twin ideals of *hijra* (which means to emigrate from a hostile un-Islamic jahiliyyah environment) and jihad were established. Faced with ever-increasing threats and persecution, in 622 c.e. Muhammad and his followers moved (hijra) from Mecca to Medina, approximately 250 miles away, where he established the first Islamic community or city-state. The central significance given to this move can be seen in the fact that the Muslim calendar begins with the year of the hijra and the creation of the Islamic community, rather than earlier dates such as the year Muhammad was born or the year in which he received his first revelation from God.

Moving from the traditional safety of one's tribe and kinsmen in warring Arabia to form alliances with alien tribes based on a broader Islamic ideal and a collective surrender to the will of God was another of Muhammad's revolutionary concepts—one fraught with danger and potential strife. Therefore, it follows that what many refer to as "defensive jihad" appears in the earliest Quranic verses, revealed shortly after the hijra to Medina when Muhammad and his followers knew they would be forced to fight for their lives: "Leave is given to those who fight because they were wronged—surely God is able to help them—who were expelled from their homes wrongfully for saying, 'Our Lord is God'" (22:39). The defensive nature of jihad is reinforced in 2:190—"And fight in the way of God with those who fight you, but aggress not: God loves not the aggressors." Both mainstream and extremist movements and "holy warriors" like Osama bin Laden, who emigrated from Saudi Arabia to establish his movement and community with its training bases in Afghanistan, have selectively used the pattern of hijra and jihad for their own purposes.

Jihad for Defense and Expansion

From 622 c.e. until his death ten years later, Muhammad very successfully consolidated his power in Medina and united the feuding tribes of Arabia. At critical points throughout these years Muhammad received revelations from God that provided guidelines for the jihad. As the Muslim community grew, questions quickly emerged about who had religious and political authority, how to handle rebellion and civil war, what was proper behavior during times of war and peace, how to rationalize and legitimize expansion and conquest, violence and resistance. Answers to these questions were developed by referring to Quranic injunctions. The Quran provides detailed guidelines and regulations regarding the conduct of war: who is to fight and who is exempted (48:17, 9:91), when hostilities must cease (2:192), how prisoners should be treated (47:4). Verses such as Quran 2:294 emphasize proportionality in warfare: "whoever transgresses against you, respond in kind." Other verses provide a strong mandate for making peace: "If your enemy inclines toward peace then you too should seek peace and put your trust in God" (8:61), and "Had Allah wished, He would have made them dominate you and so if they leave you alone and do not fight you and offer you peace, then Allah allows you no way against them" (4:90). From the earliest times it was forbidden to kill noncombatants as well as women and children and monks and rabbis, who were given the promise of immunity unless they had taken part in the fighting. The Prophet's example (and Islamic law) also provide answers to questions about how the Muslim community should act. Stories about how the Prophet behaved are preserved in narrative traditions or *hadith*. They have been and continue to be used throughout the world to provide guidance for Muslim decisions and behavior.

Under the leadership of Muhammad and then his early successors, the Islamic community spread rapidly, creating a vast empire greater than Rome at its zenith and stretching from North Africa to India. Muslim armies—motivated both by economic rewards from the conquest of richer, more developed societies and by religious zeal, the promise of reward in heaven—successfully overran the Byzantine and Persian Empires, which had become exhausted from endless warring with each other.

The religious rationale (as distinct from the practical political and economic motives) for conquest and expansion was not to force conversion to Islam upon other faiths who had their own prophets and revelations—the Quran states clearly, "There is no compulsion in religion" (2:256)—but rather to spread its righteous order so that ignorance and unbelief could be replaced by just societies throughout the world. The religious justification made for a jihad to propagate the faith is connected to Islam's universal mission to spread the word of God and the just reign of God's will for all humanity: "So let there be a body among you who may call to the good, enjoin what is esteemed and forbid what is odious. They are those who will be successful" (3:104); and, "Of all the communities raised among men you are the best, enjoining the good, forbidding the wrong, and believing in God" (3:110).

Martyrs who sacrifice their lives to establish Islamic ideals or to defend those ideals hold a special place in Islam. The Quran has many passages that support the notion of martyrdom and that comfort those left behind. For example, "Were you to be killed or to die in the way of God, forgiveness and mercy from God are far better than what they amass" (3:157); and, "Never think that those who are killed in the way of God are dead. They are alive with their Lord, well provided for" (3:169). Both Sunni and Shii traditions value and esteem martyrdom in their beliefs and devotions. Sunni Islam has historically valorized martyrdom through veneration of the struggles (jihads) of the early community with the Meccan Arabs and within their jahiliyyah culture of unbelief, while Shii Islam celebrates annually the martyrdom of its early leaders who fought to reinstate the true values of Islam into their society.

Hadith literature also provides many affirmations of the rewards for those who die for Islam. Muslim tradition teaches that martyrs are distinguished from others in life after death in several ways: their self-sacrifice and meritorious act render them free of sin and therefore they are not subject to the post-mortem interrogation of the angels Nakir and Munkar; they bypass "purgatory" and proceed to one of the highest locations in heaven near the Throne of God; as a result of their purity, they are buried in the clothes in which they died and do not need to be washed before burial.

With the growth, expansion, and development of the Islamic community, concern about the power and lifestyles of rulers and the need to expound more fully and clearly what the Quran said about the "straight path of Islam" resulted in the emergence of religious scholars (*ulama*, the learned). The ulama developed the *Shariah*, Islamic law, seen as the ideal blueprint for Muslim life.

Over the ages, Islamic law and jurists became the primary authorities for the meanings of jihad, when to declare and when to restrict jihad. While Muslim rulers declared and conducted the jihad, legal experts, known as *muftis*, provided *fatwas* (legal opinions) that could be used either to legitimate or to challenge the legitimacy of a jihad, a practice that continues up to the present day. For example, during the Gulf war, Muslim rulers obtained fatwas to legitimate their participation in the American-led coalition against Saddam Hussein's declared jihad, and Saudi Arabia obtained a fatwa to legitimate the presence of non-Muslim American troops in the Kingdom.

Islamic law stipulates that it is a Muslim's duty to wage war not only against those who attack Muslim territory, but also against polytheists, apostates, and People of the Book (at first restricted to

Jews and Christians but later extended to Zoroastrians and other faiths) who refuse Muslim rule. Muslims gave these people two choices: conversion or submission to Muslim rule with the right to retain their religion and pay a poll tax (a common practice applied to outsiders, within and outside of Arabia). If they refused both of these options, they were subject to war. Muslim jurists saw jihad as a requirement in a world divided between what they called the *dar al-Islam* (land of Islam) and the *dar al-harb* (land of war). The Muslim community was required to engage in the struggle to expand the dar al-Islam throughout the world so that all of humankind would have the opportunity to live within a just political and social order. One school of law, the Shafii, posited a third category, the land of treaty (*dar al-sulh*), a territory that had concluded a truce with a Muslim government.

Other Quranic verses, sometimes referred to as the "sword verses," are quoted selectively to legitimate unconditional warfare against unbelievers and were used by jurists to justify great expansion. The argument, developed during the period under the early caliphs, a time when the ulama enjoyed royal patronage, was that the sword verses abrogated all the earlier verses that limited jihad to a defensive war: "When the sacred months have passed, slay the idolaters wherever you find them, and take them, and confine them, and lie in wait for them at every place of ambush" (9:5). Yet the full intent of this verse, if it is used in isolation, can be overlooked. It is followed by: "But if they repent and fulfill their devotional obligations and pay the *zakat* [tax for alms] then let them go their way for God is forgiving and kind"(9:5). Although this verse has been used to justify offensive jihad, it has traditionally been read as a call for peaceful relations unless there is interference with the freedom of Muslims. The same is true of the following: "Fight those who believe not in God nor the Last Day, Nor hold that forbidden which hath been forbidden by God and His Apostle, Nor hold the religion of truth (even if they are) of the People of the Book, Until they pay the tax with willing submission, and feel themselves subdued" (9:29).

Jihad: Sectarianism and Terrorism in Early Islam

From its beginnings the faith, unity, and very survival of the Islamic community were threatened by civil war, sectarianism, violence, assassination of its leaders, and terrorism. Disorder (*fitnah*) was and remains a primary political and social evil. The Quran and the example of the Prophet's community or state at Medina linked Islam with politics and society in the struggle (jihad) to implement God's will and to create a just social order. Islam was riven by deep divisions and conflicts revolving around leadership and authority. The community divided into two major and often competing branches, Sunni and Shii.

Although Islam is the second largest religion in the world, many in the West knew nothing about it until Iran's Islamic revolution catapulted Islam into the consciousness of the world. It is ironic that the West's contemporary encounter with Islam began with the actions of Islam's Shii minority, who make up only 15 percent of the Muslim community. Throughout the 1980s, the Western nations' primary experience of Islam was with the Ayatollah Khomeini's brand of radical Islamic fundamentalism. Fears of its export throughout the Muslim world dominated the corridors of power and media headlines.

In the United States, Shii Islam is identified primarily with the militancy, anti-Americanism, and terrorism of the Iranian revolution and of Hizbollah in Lebanon. This has obscured the richness of the Shii religious tradition and spirituality, its diverse branches and differing experiences of and attitudes toward war and peace. Shiism is a faith born out of the experience of oppression and tyranny. It is the official religion of empires and states in North Africa as well as in Iran and Yemen. It has fought jihads of liberation and of expansion and conquest. In modern times, its leaders have included a seminary-trained revolutionary like Ayatollah Khomeini and the cosmopolitan, urbane Harvard-trained Agha Khan, who uses his community's wealth for major educational and social welfare projects around the world. The road traveled by

Shii from their origins to the present reveals a rich legacy able to provide support for both reformers and revolutionaries.

The origins of Shii Islam go back to the death of Islam's charismatic prophetic leader in 632 C.E. The community was plunged into a crisis over who would succeed Muhammad. Should the successor be the most pious Muslim or a direct descendant of the Prophet? The seeds of dissent in the Islamic community were planted when the companions of the Prophet moved quickly to select Abu Bakr, Muhammad's father-in-law, an early convert and well-respected member of the community, as the Prophet's first successor or *caliph*. The caliph was to be the political leader of the community. Although not a prophet, a caliph enjoyed a certain religious prestige and authority as head of the community. He led the Friday congregational prayer, and his name was mentioned in the prayer. As the protector of Islam, the caliph led the jihad and was to govern the community by the Shariah (Islamic law). Those who accepted the choice of Abu Bakr, the majority of the community, became known as Sunnis (followers of the *Sunnah*, or example of the Prophet).

This transition of leadership set in motion a sequence of events that led to division, rebellion, and historic conflict. A minority of the community, the Shii (meaning the party or followers of Ali), took strong exception to the selection of Abu Bakr. They believed that before his death Muhammad had designated the senior male of his family, Ali, the Prophet's cousin and son-in-law, to be leader, or *Imam,* of the community. Ali was eventually chosen as the fourth in a succession of caliphs, but his Shii followers suffered Ali's assassination after five years of rule (656–661) and then the subsequent massacre of Ali's son, the brave and charismatic Hussein, as he and his army battled to try to regain power and reinstate the true values of Islam. Hussein and his forces were defeated by the army of the caliph Yazid in 680 C.E. The death or martyrdom of Hussein in the Battle of Karbala became a defining symbol for Shii Muslims of the profound injustice of the world. It inspired and motivated Shii jihads against what they considered the un-Islamic

Umayyad and Abbasid dynasties, whose caliphs they regarded as
illegitimate.

During this time the Shii community itself split into two major
branches, Twelvers and Seveners, over the issue of leadership. The
numerical designation of each branch stems from the death or
disappearance of their Imam and thus the disruption of succession. Shii theology resolved the problem of the Imam's absence
with the doctrine of the "hidden Imam" who will return as a messianic figure, the Mahdi, at the end of the world to usher in a
perfect Islamic society in which truth and justice will prevail.

Shii history and religious symbolism has been used in every age
to bring about reform. In the twentieth century modern Shii religious leaders reinterpreted the memory of Hussein's martyrdom
to mobilize support for revolutionary movements. Portraying the
Shah of Iran as the new Yazid, the Umayyad general responsible
for the massacre at Karbala, the Ayatollah Khomeini called for a
revolution to overthrow their un-Islamic leader. Khomeini also
appealed to Shii in Sunni-dominated Iraq, Saudi Arabia, Bahrain,
and Kuwait to rise up against oppressive regimes and claim their
rightful inheritance. With Iranian backing, Lebanon's Shii
Hizbollah (Party of God), which had come into being in response
to the Israeli invasion of Lebanon, declared jihad against Israel
and its American "patron."

Sunni and Shii Conceptions of Jihad

Despite their historic differences and their ongoing conflicts today, Sunni and Shii both have the same overall conception of jihad
as a struggle in the path of God, and both distinguish between the
greater jihad, the personal, spiritual struggle, and the lesser, warfare form of jihad. They see jihad as a religious duty incumbent on
individuals and the Islamic community to defend life, land, or
faith and to prevent invasion or guarantee the freedom to spread
the faith. However, they differ with regard to who can declare a
jihad. For Sunnis, the caliph, with the support of the ulama (reli-

gious scholars), had the religious and political authority to declare a jihad. Shii view this power as having been unjustly taken from the true successors to Muhammad, the Imams. However, in the absence of their Imam, only a defensive jihad was considered permissible. This problem was resolved as some ulama claimed that all legitimate forms of jihad were defensive and therefore able to be waged in the Imam's absence. This rationale led Iran's Ayatollah Khomeini as well as Lebanon's Hizbollah to declare jihad.

Jihad in the Creation of a Worldwide *Ummah*

Sunni and Shii share a common faith rooted in the Quran and Muhammad and belong to the same global Islamic community. Like a family, the members of the *ummah*, or worldwide community of believers, may be very different. They may have bitter family feuds but nevertheless are bound together by a bond that continues to survive in Muslim faith and religious imagination. Like tribal or ethnic communities and nation states, they often pull together when faced by a common external threat but then fall back into intrareligious conflict. Thus, many Sunni Muslims identified with, celebrated, and were inspired by Iran's Islamic revolution, which Khomeini was careful to proclaim an Islamic (not simply a Shii) revolution. However, this bond dissolved when Khomeini attempted to rally the Shii of southern Iraq in the Iran-Iraq war. In this instance, the effects of nationalism and centuries-old Persian–Arab rivalries prevailed, and Iraqi Shii fought for their country.

The concept of the ummah developed as the first Muslim community at Medina quickly expanded and established its hegemony over central Arabia under Muhammad's guidance. Through military action and astute diplomatic initiatives, the tribes of Arabia were united in an Arab commonwealth with a common faith, ideology, centralized authority, and law. For the first time, an effective means had been found to end tribal vendettas, to inspire, unite, and replace tribal allegiance with a common religious bond. As the Quran commanded, Muslims were a community of believers,

Transnational (margin annotation)

in a special covenant with God that transcended all other allegiances. They were to realize their obligation to strive (jihad), to submit (*islam*) to God, and to spread their faith both as individuals and as a community.

Islam's transnational dimension was expressed through the existence of empires and sultanates from the seventh to the eighteenth century as Islam became the global power and civilization of its day. The breakup of Muslim empires, the fragmentation of the Muslim world by European colonialism, and the creation of modern nation states in the twentieth century reduced the concept of the ummah to a more distant ideal. In the twentieth century, the resurgence of Islam and the spread of international communications have reinforced and reinvigorated Muslim awareness and identification with the worldwide Islamic community. The influential activist and ideologue Sayyid Qutb describes an ummah that reflects an international perception today:

> In this great Islamic society Arabs, Persians, Syrians, Egyptians, Moroccans, Turks, Chinese, Indians, Romans, Greeks, Indonesians, Africans were gathered together—in short, peoples of all nations and all races. Their various characteristics were united, and with mutual cooperation, harmony and unity they took part in the construction of the Islamic community and Islamic culture. This marvellous civilisation was not an "Arabic civilisation," even for a single day; it was purely an "Islamic civilisation." It was never a "nationality" but always a "community of belief."[2]

Consciousness of the ummah has been reinforced in the past few decades by world events, greatly assisted by media coverage. Muslim sentiment, support, and engagement were triggered by the jihad against the Soviet occupation of Afghanistan, in which thousands of Muslims from the Arab world and beyond came to fight. The Iranian revolution had a similar impact. The creation of international Arab and Muslim newspapers and media, such as al-Jazeera

the television station al-Jazeera, with daily coverage from embattled Muslim frontiers, as well as CNN, the BBC, and the Internet have brought the many struggles, or jihads, of Muslim communities in Palestine and Afghanistan, Bosnia, Iraq, Chechnya, and Kashmir into the living rooms and everyday consciousness of Muslims around the world.

The creation and proliferation of Muslim organizations world-wide that sought to change the circumstances in which they lived intensified the language of jihad to fire up the determination needed in their struggle for reform. However, as we shall see, who can declare a jihad and what constitutes a legitimate defensive jihad as opposed to an aggressive unholy war of aggression would, like beauty, be determined by the eye of the beholder/believer. Jihad would remain a powerful defining concept for ideologues seeking, in times of crisis, to use their tradition to return power, peace, and social justice to their communities. How did Islam and jihad get redefined for use in the twentieth century? Who was responsible for the creation and spread of these ideas? To begin to answer these questions we must again visit a distant past.

Historical Sources of Revolutionary Jihad

TERROR AND JIHAD IN THE NAME OF GOD

The world of early Islam, like many Muslim societies today, experienced the terror of religious extremist movements. The Kharijites and the Assassins represent early examples of the way in which dissent could turn to unholy war in the name of Islam. As we shall see in the next chapter, traces of the Kharijites' militant piety and fundamentalist worldview are found in Saudi Arabia's Wahhabi movement and in radical twentieth-century movements like Egypt's Islamic Jihad and bin Laden's al-Qaeda. Kharijites

The Kharijites (from *kharaja*, to go out or exit) were followers of Ali, who broke away because they believed Ali guilty of compromising God's will by agreeing to arbitration to settle a long, drawn-out war. After breaking with Ali (whom they eventually assassinated), the Kharijites established their own separate community, based on their vision of a true charismatic society strictly following the Quran and the Sunnah. They adopted the prophetic model of hijra and a radical, militant form of jihad. First they withdrew to live in their own community and then from their encampments waged war against their enemies in the name of God.

The Kharijites believed that the Quranic mandate to "command the good and forbid evil" must be applied literally, rigorously, and without qualification or exception. Their world was divided neatly between belief and unbelief, Muslims (followers of God) and non-Muslims (enemies of God), peace and warfare. Any action that did not conform rigorously to the letter of the law constituted a grave or mortal sin. Sinners were guilty of unbelief and thus excommunicated (*takfir*, exclusion for unbelief). Grave sinners were not just seen as religious backsliders but apostates, guilty of treason and meriting death unless they repented.

The Kharijites viewed other Muslims who did not accept their uncompromising viewpoint as infidels or idolaters, and thus the enemies of God. They held the egalitarian belief that the caliph should be selected by popular consent, but they insisted that a caliph could only hold office as long as he was thoroughly upright and sinless. His fall from this state constituted a grave sin. It rendered him an apostate from Islam, outside the protection of its laws, who must be deposed and killed.

Believing that they were God's army fighting a jihad against the forces of evil, they considered that the end justified the means. Violence, guerrilla warfare, and revolution were not only legitimate but also obligatory in the battle against the sinners who ignored God's will and sovereignty. This mentality has been replicated in modern times by Islamic Jihad, the assassins of Egypt's President Anwar Sadat, Osama bin Laden, and other extremists who have called for the overthrow of "un-Islamic" Muslim rulers and for jihad against the West.

Historically, the Kharijites remained on the margins or outside of Islamic orthodoxy, politically and religiously. The same fate of marginalization awaited the Assassins, as it would later radical movements.

The notorious Assassins, a Shii offshoot, were driven by a messianic vision. They lived apart in secret communities from which they would emerge to strike at unbelievers and were guided by a series of grand masters, who ruled from the mountain fortress of Alamut in northern Persia. Each grand master became known as the Old Man of the Mountain. The Assassins' jihad against the Abbasid dynasty terrorized Abbasid princes, generals, and ulama whom they murdered in the name of the hidden Imam.[3] They struck such terror in the hearts of their Muslim and Crusader enemies that their exploits in Persia and Syria earned them a name and memory in history long after they were overrun and the Mongols executed their last grand master in 1256.

IDEOLOGUES AND MOVEMENTS OF REVOLUTIONARY JIHAD

It is therefore necessary—in the way of the Islamic movement—that in the early stages of our training and education we should remove ourselves from all influences of the Jahiliyyah in which we live and from which we derive benefits. We must return to that pure source from which those people derived their guidance . . . which is free from any mixing or pollution. . . . From it we must also derive our concepts of life, our principles of government, politics, economics and all other aspects of life.[4]

This statement by Sayyid Qutb illustrates the extent to which Muslims rely heavily on the past for meaning and guidance in the present. Many non-Muslims might be prepared to understand a believer's return to the Quran and Sunnah of the Prophet Muhammad for guidance, but they would be astonished to learn the extent to which the ideas of medieval and pre-modern theologians and movements directly impact the world of Islam today. Both modern reformers and radical extremists draw (often selectively) on the teachings and examples of early Islamic revivalist thinkers and activist movements to justify their contemporary jihads, their holy and unholy wars.

Islam possesses a long tradition of religious revivalism and social reform starting with the prophet-reformer Muhammad himself and the struggle of the early Islamic community to improve their jahiliyyah world. In every age, the glaring disparities (real or perceived) between God's will and the state of the world inspired religious reformers (*mujaddids*) and movements who called Muslims to follow Islam more faithfully and to reform their society.

For pious believers, political fragmentation and economic and social decline must be evidence of a departure from the straight path of Islam. The heart and soul of renewal require a process of purification and return to the pristine teachings of Islam. Based on a tradition of the Prophet, "God will send to this ummah [community] at the beginning of each century those who will renew its faith," Sunni Islam developed the belief that revitalization would be necessary in every age.[5] The clear disjunction between public life and the Islamic ideal contributed to the popular expectation of a future messianic figure, the Mahdi (the guided one), who would come to deliver the community from oppression by the forces of evil and restore true Islam and the reign of justice on earth. As we have seen, Shii Islam developed its own messianic variant, a belief in the awaited return of the Hidden Imam as the Mahdi. This belief was expressed popularly in the twentieth century when followers of Ayatollah Khomeini took to calling him "Imam Khomeini." Although Khomeini himself never claimed the title Imam, he never publicly discouraged others from doing so. Many Shii who did not follow Khomeini were scandalized by this practice.

Throughout the ages, in times of division and decline religious scholars and movements have risen up to call the community back to its fundamental message and mission. Several prominent examples will give us an idea of the continuing power of the past in the minds of Islamic activists today. Among the most significant reformers for today are the medieval intellectual-activist Taqi al-Din Ahmad ibn Taymiyya and the leaders of the great jihad movements of the eighteenth century. Their teachings and actions are part of a revivalist legacy from which contemporary Islamic movements, both mainstream and extremist, have drawn heavily.

IBN TAYMIYYAH

Perhaps no medieval scholar-activist has had more influence on radical Islamic ideology than Ibn Taymiyya (1268–1328). A scholar of Islamic law and theology as well as a political figure, he was a major conservative voice who in the modern period is quoted by liberals, conservatives, and extremists alike. Described by some as the spiritual father of (Sunni) revolutionary Islam, others regard him as "the model for revivalists and vigilantes, for fundamentalist reformers, and other apostles of moral rearmament."[6] Though he was addressing the problems of his society in the thirteenth century, his ideas influenced and have been appropriated by Saudi Arabia's eighteenth-century Wahhabi movement, Egypt's modern activist ideologue Sayyid Qutb, Islamic Jihad's Muhammad al-Farag, and contemporary extremists like Osama bin Laden.

Ibn Taymiyya lived during one of the most disruptive periods of Islamic history, which had seen the fall of Baghdad and the conquest of the Abbasid Empire in 1258 by the Mongols. The empire's defeat represented the impossible—the apparent conquest of the caliphate and of Islam. Ibn Taymiyya's family was forced to flee to Damascus; his painful experience as a refugee colored his attitude toward the conqueror Mongols throughout his life. A professor of Hanbali law, the most conservative of the four Sunni schools of law, he balanced the life of a religious scholar with political activism. Like many mujaddids who have followed him, his writing and preaching earned him persecution and imprisonment in Egypt and Syria.[7] Combining ideas and action, his belief in the interconnectedness of religion, state, and society has exerted both conscious and unconscious influence on eighteenth-century and twentieth-century revivalism.

Ibn Taymiyya called on a rigorous, literalist interpretation of the sacred sources (the Quran and Sunnah, and the example of the early Muslim community) for the crucially needed Islamic renewal and reform of his society. These sources constituted his yardstick for orthodoxy. Like many who came after him, he regarded the community at Medina as the model for an Islamic state. His goal was the purification of Islam. A return to the pristine purity of the period of Muhammad and the First Four Righteous Caliphs, he believed, was necessary to restore the Islamic community's past power and greatness. He distinguished sharply between Islam and non-Islam (the dar al-Islam and the dar al-harb), the lands of belief and unbelief. In contrast to his vision of a close relationship between religion and the state, he made a sharp distinction between religion and culture. Although a pious Sufi (a practitioner of Islamic mysticism), he denounced as superstition the popular practices of his day such as saint worship and the veneration of Sufi shrines and tombs.

Ibn Taymiyya's ire was especially directed at the Mongols. Despite their conversion to Islam, the Mongols had been locked in a jihad with the Muslim Mamluk rulers of Egypt. Because the Mongols continued to follow the Yasa code of laws of Genghis Khan instead of the Islamic law, Shariah, for Ibn Taymiyya they were no better than the polytheists of the pre-Islamic jahiliyyah. He issued a fatwa that labeled them as unbelievers (*kafirs*) who were thus excommunicated (takfir). His fatwa regarding the Mongols established a precedent: despite their claim to be Muslims, their failure to implement Shariah rendered the Mongols apostates and hence the lawful object of jihad. Muslim citizens thus had the right, indeed duty, to revolt against them, to wage jihad.

Later generations, from the Wahhabi movement to modern Egypt's Sayyid Qutb, Islamic Jihad, the assassins of Anwar Sadat, and Osama bin Laden, would use the logic in Ibn Taymiyya's fatwa on the Mongols to call for a jihad against "un-Islamic" Muslim rulers and elites and against the West. Applying the emotive pre-Islamic term jahiliyyah to societies infiltrated by tribal or Western culture, they would draw a rigid distinction between true belief and unbelief, level the charge of unbelief, proclaim excommunication, and call for a jihad.

EIGHTEENTH-CENTURY JIHAD MOVEMENTS

The global emergence of eighteenth-century revivalist movements holds the key to understanding the mindset of reformers and extremists today. The world of Islam in the eighteenth century experienced an Islamic revivalist wave that, as is happening again today, swept across the Muslim world, from Africa to Asia. In contrast to prior periods when Islamic revivalism occurred in a specific empire or region, eighteenth-century movements extended from modern-day Sudan, Libya, and Nigeria, across the Arabian peninsula and the Indian subcontinent to Southeast Asia.

For our purposes, we will focus on the ideas of the Wahhabi movement in Arabia, a prominent example of eighteenth-century Islamic revivalism, which had a profound impact on Arabia and the development of Saudi Arabia. Perhaps most important, it continues to be a significant force in the Islamic world, informing both mainstream and extremist movements from Afghanistan and Central Asia to Europe and America.

Muhammad ibn Abd al-Wahhab (1703–1791) studied Islamic law and theology in Mecca and Medina and took Ibn Taymiyya as his exemplar. Disillusioned by the spiritual decline and moral laxity of his society, he denounced popular beliefs and practices as idolatry and jahiliyyah, rejected much of the medieval law of the ulama (religious scholars) as innovation (*bida*) or heresy, and called for a fresh interpretation of Islam that returned to its revealed sources.

Central to al-Wahhab's theology and movement was the doctrine of God's unity (*tawhid*), an absolute monotheism reflected in the Wahhabi's self-designation as "unitarians" (*muwahiddun*)—those who uphold the unity of God. Citing the tradition that Muhammad had destroyed the pantheon of gods in his Meccan shrine, the Wahhabi forces set out to destroy "idolatrous" shrines, tombstones, and sacred objects. They spared neither the sacred tombs of Muhammad and his Companions in Mecca and Medina nor the Shiite pilgrimage site at Karbala (in modern Iraq) that housed the tomb of Hussein. The destruction of this venerated site has never been forgotten by Shii Muslims and has contributed to the historic antipathy between the Wahhabi of Saudi Arabia and Shii Islam in both Saudi Arabia and Iran. Centuries later, many would point to Wahhabi-inspired iconoclasm and religious fanaticism as the source behind the Taliban's wanton destruction of Buddhist monuments in Afghanistan, an action condemned by Muslim leaders worldwide.

Muhammad ibn Abd al-Wahhab joined religious zeal with military might and allied with Muhammad ibn Saud, a local tribal chief, to form a religiopolitical movement. Ibn Saud used Wahhabism as a religious ideal to legitimate his jihad to subdue and unite the tribes of Arabia, converting them to this puritanical version of Islam. Like the Kharijites, the Wahhabi viewed all Muslims who resisted as unbelievers (who could be fought and killed). They were therefore to be subdued in the name of Islamic egalitarianism. In the early nineteenth century Muhammad Ali of Egypt defeated the Saudis, but the Wahhabi movement and the House of Saud proved resilient. In the early twentieth century, Abdulaziz ibn Saud recaptured Riyadh. With the *Ikhwan* (brotherhood), a nontribal military, he once again united the tribes of Arabia, restored the Saudi kingdom, and spread the Wahhabi movement. The kingdom melded the political and religious; it was led by a succession of kings from the House of Saud with the close support of the religious establishment, many of whom are descendants of al-Wahhab, since they had married into the royal family.

The House of Saud's appeal to Wahhabi Islam for legitimacy has also been used against it by dissidents. As discussed in the next chapter, in November 1979 militants seized the Grand Mosque in Mecca, accused the royal family of compromising their Wahhabi faith, and called for the overthrow of the House of Saud. Again in the 1990s and the aftermath of the Gulf war, the Saudi government had to move forcefully to arrest and silence independent, nongovernment ulama in Mecca, Medina, and Riyadh who were calling for greater political participation and accountability and denouncing religious deviance and corruption.

Internationally, the Saudis, both government-sponsored organizations and wealthy individuals, have exported a puritanical and at times militant version of Wahhabi Islam to other countries and communities in the Muslim world and the West. They have offered development aid, built mosques and other institutions, funded and distributed religious tracts, and commissioned imams and religious scholars. They exported their Wahhabi ideology and provided financial support to Afghanistan, Pakistan, the Central Asian republics, China, Africa, Southeast Asia, the United States, and Europe. Wealthy businessmen in Saudi Arabia, both members of the establishment and outsiders such as Osama bin Laden, have provided financial support to extremist groups who follow a militant fundamentalist brand of Islam with its jihad culture.

Trailblazers of the Islamic Revolution

Western historians have marveled at the speed with which Islam took root and grew. Muslim tradition had always viewed the remarkable spread of Islam as a miraculous proof and historic validation of the truth of the Quran and Islam's claims and as a sign of God's guidance. But European colonialism from the eighteenth to the first half of the twentieth century and the subsequent failure of many modern Muslim states posed a serious challenge to this belief. Some Muslims came to believe that Islam had lost its relevance, and many others concluded that Western dominance and Muslim dependency were the result of unfaithfulness and departure from the path of Islam. This was a powerful argument that encouraged holy warriors to struggle (jihad) to bring the ummah back to the straight path. Muslim responses to European colonialism precipitated a new debate about the meaning of jihad.

As discussed in the next chapter, Islamic modernists and movements like the Muslim Brotherhood of Egypt and Pakistan's Jamaat-i-Islami (Islamic Society) worked to combine religious reform and political mobilization. Islamic activist organizations framed their struggle in a call for a jihad against British imperialism and corrupt Muslim rulers.

3 activists

Volumes have been written on the ideologues who inspire contemporary activists and terrorists. While a comprehensive discussion is impossible here, three key intellectual-activists—Hasan al-Banna, Mawlana Mawdudi, and Sayyid Qutb—have been so influential in creating the vision of modern Islamic reform that they warrant our attention. It is almost impossible to exaggerate the direct and indirect impact and influence of these three men. Their writings have been published and distributed throughout the Muslim world. Their ideas have been disseminated in short pamphlets and audiocassettes. The leadership of most major Islamic movements, mainstream and extremist, nonviolent and violent alike, has been influenced by their ideas on Islam, Islamic revolution, jihad, and modern Western society. Their recasting of Islam as a comprehensive ideology to address the conditions of modern Muslims produced a reinterpretation of Islamic belief that has been so widely used, it has been integrated unconsciously into the religious discourse of Muslims throughout the world who would normally disassociate themselves from Islamic movements.

When Hasan al-Banna (1906–1949) established the Egyptian Muslim Brotherhood and Mawlana Mawdudi (1903–1979) created the Jamaat-i-Islami in Pakistan, few in the West or in their own societies took serious notice. Both al-Banna and Mawdudi recognized that change would be slow to come. Expecting rejection and persecution, their focus was to train future generations. They were very successful in achieving their goal.

Sayyid Qutb (1906–1966) built upon and radicalized the ideas of al-Banna and Mawdudi. Qutb created an ideological legacy that incorporated all the major historical forms of jihad, from the reforms of Muhammad to the extremes of the Kharijites and the Assassins. Within a few short decades, the ideas of al-Banna's Muslim Brotherhood and Mawdudi's Jamaat-i-Islami, often viewed through the prism of Qutb's more radicalized interpretation, became the primary models for new activist organizations across the Muslim world.

Though part of a centuries-old revivalist tradition, all three men were modern in their responses. They were neofundamentalist in the sense that they returned to the sources or fundamentals of Islam. But they reinterpreted Islamic sources in response to the challenges of the modern world. This is apparent in their teachings, organization, strategy, tactics, and use of modern science and technology. Indeed, many Islamic activists are the product of modern educations, leaders in professional associations of physicians, engineers, lawyers, journalists, university professors, and students.

HASAN AL-BANNA AND MAWLANA MAWDUDI

The Brotherhood and the Jamaat were established in 1928 and 1941 respectively, both within Muslim societies in crisis. Hasan al-Banna, a teacher, and Mawlana Mawdudi, a journalist, were pious, educated men with traditional Islamic religious backgrounds and a knowledge of Western thought. Both placed primary blame for the ills of their society and the decline of the Muslim world upon European imperialism and westernized Muslim elites. Like revivalists of old, they initially called for moral and social reform but soon also became embroiled in political activism and opposition.

For Hasan al-Banna the failure of liberal nationalism in Egypt was reflected in the creation of Israel and the consequent displacement of millions of Palestinians as well as continued British occupation, massive unemployment, poverty, and corruption. He rejected the preference for the spiritual jihad (greater jihad) over a military (lesser jihad) one. Since Muslim lands had been invaded, he said, it was incumbent on all Muslims to repel their invaders just as it was an Islamic imperative for Muslims to oppose rulers who blocked the establishment of Islamic governments.

For Mawdudi, the decline of Muslim rule in South Asia and the dismemberment of the Ottoman Empire were the products of British and French colonialism. Muslim identity and unity were threatened by the rise of Hindu secular nationalism and the imposition of modern nationalism, a foreign Western ideology whose purpose was to weaken and divide the Muslim world by replacing the universal pan-Islamic ideal of the equality and solidarity of all Muslims with an identity based upon language, tribe, or ethnicity.

Though inspired by the past, in particular the eighteenth-century revivalist movements, al-Banna and Mawdudi did not retreat to it but responded to modern society. They were just as critical of the failure of the religious establishment's conservatism as they were of secular Muslim elites' Western-oriented reformist visions. Although they were influenced by Islamic modernist reformers, who had attempted to bridge the gap between tradition and modernity, they nevertheless believed that Islamic modernism tended to westernize Islam, to recast Islam in light of Western standards and solutions to the challenge of modernity. Though antiwesternization, they were not against scientific and technological modernization. They both stressed the self-sufficiency of Islam, not the ulama's irrelevant medieval Islamic vision but a new interpretation and application of Islam's revealed sources that addressed the political, economic, and cultural challenges of modernity.

Both al-Banna and Mawdudi proclaimed Islam the clear alternative to the ills and shortcomings of Marxism and Western capitalism. As al-Banna declared, "Until recently, writers, intellectuals, scholars, and governments glorified the principles of European civilization, gave themselves a Western tint, and adopted a European style and manner; today on the contrary, the wind has changed, and reserve and distrust have taken their place. Voices are raised proclaiming the necessity for a return to the principles, teachings and ways of Islam . . . for initiating the reconciliation of modern life with these principles, as a prelude to final 'Islamization.'"[8] Despite differences, Hasan al-Banna and Mawlana Mawdudi shared a common ideological worldview which would come to inspire and inform the struggle (jihad) of later Islamic movements. The following represents the main points of the worldview that the two men shared:

1. Islam is a total, all-encompassing way of life that guides each person and his or her community and political life.
2. The Quran, God's revelation, and the Sunnah of the Prophet and the early Muslim community are the foundations of Muslim life, providing the models that guide daily actions.

main points

3. Islamic law (Shariah) provides the ideal and blueprint for a modern Muslim society not dependent on Western models.

4. Departure from Islam and reliance on the West are the causes for Muslim decline. A return to the straight path of Islam will restore the identity, pride, success, power, and wealth of the Islamic community in this life and merit eternal reward in the next.

5. Science and technology must be harnessed and used. This must be achieved within an Islamic context, not by dependence on foreign Western cultures, to avoid the westernization and secularization of society.

6. Jihad, to strive or struggle, both personally and in community, in ideas and in action to implement Islamic reform and revolution, is the means to bring about a successful Islamization of society and the world.

Both men posited a struggle (jihad) between the forces of God and Satan, good and evil, darkness or ignorance (jahiliyyah) and light. Each envisioned his organization as a vanguard, a righteous community that would serve as a dynamic nucleus for true Islamic reformation within the broader society. Though they were quick to denounce imperialism and the threat of Western culture, they nevertheless realized (as do many Islamic organizations today) that the Muslim predicament was first and foremost a Muslim problem. Rebuilding the community and redressing the balance of power between Islam and the West must begin with a call (*dawah*) to all Muslims to return and reappropriate their faith in its fullness or totality of vision.

Dawah

Dawah has two meanings: an invitation to non-Muslims to convert to Islam and the call to those who were born Muslim to be better Muslims. The Brotherhood and the Jamaat emphasized the latter, calling on Muslims to renew their faith and practice in order to bring about a social revolution, the re-Islamization of the individual and society. The Brotherhood and Jamaat disseminated their message through schools, mosques, publications, student organizations, professional associations, and social services that combined religious commitment, modern learning and technology, and social and political activism.

The jihad (struggle) that became a central concept in describing the process of self-transformation and political activism, both against European colonialism and later against corrupt, un-Islamic Muslim states, was primarily one of reform, not violent revolution. Yet, it did include the defense of the Muslim community and of Islam against colonialism and injustice. As a youth, Hasan al-Banna was impressed by an abortive revolt against British occupation: "Despite my preoccupation with Sufism and worship, I believed that duty to country is an inescapable obligation—a holy war."[9] The conclusion he drew as a thirteen-year-old regarding the relationship of religion to politics would become a foundation stone for the Muslim Brotherhood, from its domestic political opposition in Egypt to its involvement in the war in Palestine.

Despite criticism of Western models of development, al-Banna accepted, though he qualified and Islamized, notions of patriotism, nationalism, and parliamentary democracy. He accepted Egypt's constitutional government, but criticized the extent to which its laws deviated from Islamic norms regarding alcohol, gambling, prostitution, and usury.[10]

Mawdudi's early rejection of nationalism and democracy as un-Islamic was influenced more by his opposition to westernization and secularization than by religion. He would later come to accept both with qualifications, and the Jamaat would participate in elections and serve in government. Mawdudi's prolific writing on Islam, translated into many Muslim languages, has had a global impact. His writing on jihad, in both its defensive and corrective roles, would have unforeseen consequences.

Mawdudi's conception of "what jihad really is" starts with his argument that jihad has become so difficult for Muslims and non-Muslims to understand because of two major misconceptions. First of all, Islam, he said, is not a religion in the sense of "a hodge podge of some beliefs, prayers and rituals."[11] Rather, "it is a comprehensive system that tends to annihilate all tyrannical and evil systems in the world and enforce its own program . . . in the interests of mankind."[12] Secondly, Muslims are not a nation in the conventional sense of the term because Islam urges "mankind as a whole to bring about revolution and reform."[13] Therefore, Islam is "a revolutionary concept and ideology which seeks to change and revolutionise the world social order and reshape it according to its own concept and ideals."[14] And so Mawdudi sees Muslims as an international party organized to implement Islam's revolutionary program, and jihad as the term that denotes the utmost struggle to bring about an Islamic revolution.[15] Mawdudi stresses that jihad is not a war between nations for selfish or material ends, but a "struggle for the Cause of Allah," that is devoid of all selfish motives such as "gaining wealth and splendour, name and fame, or any personal glory or elevation" and "should be directed to achieve the one and the only end, i.e., the establishment of a just and equitable social order for humanity as a whole."[16] For Mawdudi, jihad is both offensive and defensive at one and the same time, offensive because the opposing principles and ideology (not the land of the opponents) must be assaulted, and defensive because Muslims must retain power in order to implement their new ideology.[17] Mawdudi's position on the nature of jihad would be elaborated on by others including the Muslim Brotherhood's Sayyid Qutb, the ideologue of Islamic revolution in the Sunni world, and the Ayatollah Khomeini in Shii Iran.

While both al-Banna and Mawdudi sought to work within the system, the growth of their organizations and condemnation of rulers and regimes brought them into conflict with governments. After World War II, the Brotherhood stepped up their opposition to the British occupation and the Egyptian government's policies. In 1948 a Brotherhood member assassinated the prime minister; in 1949 Hasan al-Banna was assassinated by members of the secret police.[18]

Mawdudi and the Jamaat found themselves at loggerheads with the government on many occasions but were nevertheless able to continue to function. Indeed, at one point, although Mawdudi had been sentenced to death, his conviction was overturned. Although Pakistan was ruled by military regimes, state repression was always far less than in Egypt and much of the Arab world and its court system more independent. Thus, the Jamaat remained an opposition able to function within the system. By contrast, the repression of the Muslim Brotherhood under Egypt's Gamal Abdel Nasser would lead to the emergence and growth of radical jihad organizations.

SAYYID QUTB: GODFATHER AND MARTYR OF ISLAMIC RADICALISM

It would be difficult to overestimate the role played by Sayyid Qutb in the reassertion of militant jihad. He was a godfather to Muslim extremist movements around the globe. In many ways, his journey from educated intellectual, government official, and admirer of the West to militant activist who condemned both the Egyptian and American governments and defended the legitimacy of militant jihad has influenced and inspired many militants, from the assassins of Anwar Sadat to the followers of Osama bin Laden and al-Qaeda.

Just as the interpretations of Hasan al-Banna and Mawlana Mawdudi were conditioned responses to the political and social realities of their times, so too Sayyid Qutb's Islam grew out of the militant confrontation between the repressive Egyptian state and the Brotherhood in the late 1950s and 1960s. Increasingly radicalized by Gamal Abdel Nasser's suppression of the Brotherhood, Qutb transformed the ideology of al-Banna and Mawdudi into a rejectionist revolutionary call to arms. Like al-Banna, he would be remembered as a martyr of the Islamic revival.

Qutb, like al-Banna, had a modern education. He studied at Dar al-Ulum, a college set up by reformers to train teachers in a modern curriculum. He became a great admirer of the West and Western literature. After graduation, he became an official in the Ministry of Public Instruction, as well as a poet and literary critic.

A devout Muslim who had memorized the Quran as a child, he began to write on Islam and the Egyptian state. In 1948, he published *Islam and Social Justice*, in which he argued that Islam possessed its own social teachings and that Islamic socialism avoided both the pitfalls of Christianity's separation of religion and society and those of Communism's atheism.

In the late 1940s Qutb visited the United States. This proved to be a turning point in his life, transforming an admirer into a severe critic of the West. His experiences in America produced a culture shock that made him more religious and convinced him of the moral decadence of the West. He was appalled by its materialism, sexual permissiveness and promiscuity, free use and abuse of alcohol, and its racism, which he directly experienced because of his dark skin. His views on America are summarized in his influential tract, *Milestones*:

> Look at this capitalism with its monopolies, its usury . . . at this individual freedom, devoid of human sympathy and responsibility for relatives except under force of law; at this materialistic attitude which deadens the spirit; at this behaviour, like animals, which you call "free mixing of the sexes"; at this vulgarity which you call "emancipation of women"; at this evil and fanatic racial discrimination.[19]

Qutb's stay in America coincided with the establishment of Israel as a state guaranteed by the United States and the beginning of the Cold War between the U.S. and USSR, during which Egypt, under Nasser, aligned itself with Russia and secular nationalism, moving even farther away from the prospect of establishing an Islamic state. In addition, Qutb felt betrayed in America when he saw what he considered to be anti-Arab and pro-Jewish coverage in the newspapers and movies that fostered contempt for Arabs and Muslims. As a final blow, during these years in America, Hasan al-Banna was assassinated and the Muslim Brotherhood was significantly weakened. Shortly after his return to Egypt, Qutb joined the Muslim Brotherhood.

Qutb quickly emerged as a major voice in the Brotherhood and as its most influential ideologue amidst the growing confrontation with a repressive Egyptian regime. Imprisoned and tortured for alleged involvement in a failed attempt to assassinate Nasser, he became increasingly militant and radicalized. While in prison, Qutb witnessed a massacre in which twenty-five members of the Muslim Brotherhood were killed and close to fifty were injured, an experience that strengthened his conviction that the Egyptian government was un-Islamic and jahiliyyah and must be overthrown.

Qutb was an incredibly prolific author, publishing over forty books, many translated into Persian and English and still widely distributed. "Qutb's fiery style provoked great emotions of dignity, solidarity, unity, universality and . . . could uplift the reader to the greatness of Islam. His style was also capable of stimulating through his criticism, profound anger and revulsion."[20] During ten years of imprisonment in the equivalent of a concentration camp, Qutb developed a revolutionary vision captured in *Milestones*, which was used as evidence against him and led to his being sentenced to death. The power of his writings was recognized in the fact that anyone in Egypt who owned a copy of *Milestones* could be arrested and charged with sedition. Qutb took many of the core concepts of al-Banna and Mawdudi, reshaped and sharpened them to exhort Muslims to radical action. His ideas reverberate loudly today in the radical rhetoric of revolutionaries from Khomeini to bin Laden.

Qutb developed prescriptions for belief and action that would help Islamic movements in the Muslim world to function within repressive, anti-Islamic governments and societies. As he explains:

> It is necessary to revive that Muslim community . . . which is crushed under the weight of those false laws and customs which are not even remotely related to the Islamic teachings, and which in spite of all this, calls itself the "world of Islam."[21]

Like Ibn Taymiyya before him, he sharply divides Muslim societies into two diametrically opposed camps, the forces of good and of evil, those committed to the rule of God and those opposed, the party of God and the party of Satan. There was no middle ground:

no middle ground

> . . . the callers to Islam should not have any superficial doubts in their hearts concerning the nature of Jahiliyyah and the nature of Islam and the characteristics of Dar-ul-Harb and of Dar-ul-Islam for through these doubts many are led to confusion. Indeed, there is no Islam in a land where Islam is not dominant and where its Shariah is not established; and that place is not Dar-ul-Islam where Islam's way of life and its laws are not practised.[22]

Strongly influenced by Mawdudi, Qutb emphasized the need to develop a special group of true Muslims within this corrupt and faithless society:

> How is it possible to start the task of reviving Islam? . . . there should be a vanguard which sets out with this determination and then keeps walking on the path, marching through the vast ocean of Jahiliyyah which has encompassed the entire world . . . and I have written Milestones for this vanguard which I consider to be a waiting reality about to be materialized.[23]

The Islamic movement (*haraka*), the true Muslims, would create a righteous minority adrift in a sea of ignorance and unbelief, akin to the un-Islamic society in which Muhammad was born. Their models for training would be what Qutb considered to be the first unique generation of Muslims whose instruction came solely from one pure source, the Quran. "From it we must also derive our concepts of life, our principles of government, politics, economics and all other aspects of life"[24] because "our foremost objective is to change the practices of this society . . . to change the jahili system at its very roots—this system which is fundamentally at variance with Islam and which, with the help of force and oppression is keeping us from living the sort of life which is demanded by our Creator."[25] Qutb used the classical designation for pre-Islamic Arabian society, jahiliyyah—a period of ignorance—to paint and condemn all modern societies as un-Islamic and anti-Islamic:

> We must free ourselves from the clutches of jahili society, jahili concepts, jahili traditions and jahili leadership. Our mission is not to compromise . . . nor can we be loyal to it . . . we will not change our own values and concepts . . . to make a bargain with this jahili society. Never! We and it are on different roads, and if we take even one step in its company, we will lose our goal entirely and lose our way as well.[26]

Sayyid Qutb's teachings recast the world into black and white polarities. There were no shades of gray. Since the creation of an Islamic government was a divine commandment, he argued, it was not an alternative to be worked toward. Rather, it was an imperative that Muslims must strive to implement or impose immediately:

> There is only one place on earth which can be called the home of Islam (Dar-ul-Islam), and it is that place where the Islamic state is established and the Shariah is the authority and God's limits are observed and where all the Muslims administer the affairs of the state with mutual consultation. The rest of the world is the home of hostility (Dar-ul-Harb).[27]

Given the authoritarian and repressive nature of the Egyptian government and many other governments in the Muslim world, Qutb concluded that change from within the system was futile and that Islam was on the brink of disaster. Jihad was the only way to implement the new Islamic order.

For Qutb, jihad, as armed struggle in the defense of Islam against the injustice and oppression of anti-Islamic governments and the neocolonialism of the West and the East (Soviet Union), was incumbent upon all Muslims. There could be no middle ground. Mirroring the Kharijites, Qutb taught that those Muslims who refused to participate were to be counted among the enemies of God, apostates who were excommunicated (takfir) and who should be fought and killed along with the other enemies of God. Many radical extremist groups formed decades after Qutb's death have kept his vision alive in their ideologies and tactics.

Like Hasan al-Banna and Mawlana Mawdudi, Qutb regarded the West as the historic enemy of Islam and Muslims as demonstrated by the Crusades, European colonialism, and the Cold War. The Western threat was political, economic, and religiocultural. Equally insidious were the elites of the Muslim world who rule and govern according to foreign Western secular principles and values that threaten the faith, identity, and values of their own Islamic societies. Going beyond al-Banna and Mawdudi, Qutb denounced governments and Western secular-oriented elites as atheists against whom all true believers must wage holy war.

Qutb's revolutionary antiestablishment rhetoric can be heard distinctly in this call to jihad by Iran's Ayatollah Khomeini:

> Give the people Islam, then, for Islam is the school of jihad, the religion of struggle; let them amend themselves and transform themselves into a powerful force, so that they may overthrow the tyrannical regime imperialism has imposed on us and set up an Islamic government. . . . If certain heads of state of Muslim countries . . . permit foreigners to expand their influence . . . they automatically forfeit their posts. . . . Furthermore, it is a duty of the Muslims to punish them by any means possible.[28]

The two options for an Islamic revolution, evolution, a process of revolutionary change from below, and violent revolution, the use of violence and terrorism to overthrow established ("un-Islamic") governments, have remained the twin paths of contemporary Islamic movements. Both types of movement began to spring up and spread like wildfire across the Muslim world in the 1970s. The quiet that seemed assured after Gamal Abdel Nasser's apparent neutralization of the Muslim Brotherhood in the late 1960s was shattered by the proliferation of radical groups during the rule of his successor, Anwar Sadat.

Armies of God: the Vengeance of Militant Jihad

Sayyid Qutb's revolutionary ideology bore fruit across the Middle East amidst the worsening living conditions experienced by the majority of Arabs following the failures of the 1967 Arab-Israeli war. Numerous radical organizations in Egypt, Lebanon, and Palestine waged jihad against incumbent governments and the West. By the mid-1970s, the stability and security of Egyptian government and society were threatened by a number of secret Islamic revolutionary organizations; among them, Muhammad's Youth (sometimes referred to as the Islamic Liberation Organization), Jamaat al-Muslimin (Society of Muslims), more popularly known as Takfir wal Hijra (Excommunication and Flight), Salvation from Hell, Gamaa Islamiyya (Islamic Group), and Jamaat al-Jihad or Islamic Jihad. In contrast to mainstream groups like the Egyptian Brotherhood, which rejected Qutb-inspired extremism and pursued a nonviolent path of social and political activism, these clandestine groups espoused violence and terrorism to disrupt and destabilize society politically and economically and sought to overthrow the government.

Their common goal was the creation of a true Islamic society under a restored caliphate. A clear and at times chilling articulation of the new jihadist culture and its indebtedness to the past can be found in the writing of Muhammad al-Farag, a member of the radical organization Islamic Jihad, who articulated its ideology in *The Neglected Duty*. Farag drew heavily from al-Banna, Mawdudi, and especially Ibn Taymiyya and Sayyid Qutb. He takes the ideas of Ibn Taymiyya and Qutb with respect to jihad and pushes their application to its radical conclusion regarding the condition of the Muslim world and Egypt in particular.

Farag believed that the decline of Muslim societies was made possible by those who had lulled the community into believing that jihad was nonviolent; the restoration of the Muslim world to the straight path of Islam hinged on reclaiming the true meaning of jihad, the forgotten or neglected requirement of Islam. Farag maintained that jihad was the sixth pillar of Islam, forgotten or obscured by the majority of ulama and Muslims:

Jihad . . . for God's cause [in the way of Allah], in spite of its importance for the future of religion, has been neglected by the ulama . . . of this age. . . . There is no doubt that the idols of this world can only disappear through the power of the sword.[29]

As in the time of Muhammad, Farag maintained, this was the task of a minority, a vanguard who must be prepared to fight against unbelief and apostasy, prepared to suffer and die for their faith. Looking at the state of the ummah, and especially Muslim governments, he concluded unbelief and apostasy were endemic diseases:

The Rulers of this age are in apostasy from Islam. They were raised at the tables of imperialism, be it Crusaderism, or Communism, or Zionism. They carry nothing from Islam but their names, even though they pray and fast and claim to be Muslim.[30]

The punishment for their apostasy is loss of all rights, including their right to life. Given the authoritarian and corrupt nature of regimes and their societies, a true Islamic state could not be established through nonviolence but only through radical surgery, militant jihad, and the overthrow of apostate rulers.

We have to establish the Rule of God's Religion in our own country first, and to make the Word of God supreme. . . . There is no doubt that the first battlefield for jihad is the extermination of these infidel leaders and to replace them by a complete Islamic Order.[31]

Islamic Jihad and Farag saw the bulk of Egyptian society as basically good Muslims who were caught between the land of Islam or peace and the land of war, living in un-Islamic states, governed by un-Islamic laws and nominal Muslims. Holy war against Egypt's "atheist" state and ruler was both necessary and justified, an obligation for all true believers. The creation of an Islamic state required the eradication of Western law and implementation of Islamic law and the toppling of regimes through armed revolution:

This state is ruled by heathen laws despite the fact that the majority of its people are Muslims. These laws were formulated by
infidels who compelled Muslims to abide by them. And because
they deserted jihad, Muslims today live in subjugation, humiliation, division and fragmentation. . . . the aim of our group is to
rise up to establish an Islamic state and restore Islam to this
nation. . . . The means to this end is to fight against heretical
rulers and to eradicate the despots who are no more than human beings who have not yet found those who are able to sup-
press them with the order of God Almighty.[32]

Muhammad Farag's *Neglected Duty* and Islamic Jihad's ideological worldview were but another stage in the spread of Islamic
radicalism's jihad across the Muslim world, promulgating the rationale for extremist movements and the growth of networks that
would later, as a result of the jihad in Afghanistan, become a global jihad. Their narrow, extremist interpretation of Islam and jihad
was one side in the struggle within Islam between extremist and
moderate Muslims, and it demonstrated yet again the ability of
religious scriptures and tradition to be interpreted, reinterpreted,
and misinterpreted.

The Struggle for the Meaning of Jihad

As this review of the development of jihad in response to challenges through the ages amply illustrates, there is no single doctrine of jihad that has always and everywhere existed or been
universally accepted. Muslim understanding of what is required
by the Quran and the practice of the Prophet regarding jihad has
changed over time. The doctrine of jihad is not the product of a
single authoritative individual or organization's interpretation. It
is rather the product of diverse individuals and authorities inter-
preting and applying the principles of sacred texts in specific historical and political contexts.

JIHAD IN WARFARE

Jihad is often simply translated as and equated with aggressive holy war. For many in the West, it has come to symbolize Islam as a religion of violence and fanaticism. Religious extremists and terrorists reinforce this belief as they freely declare jihad to justify attacks against and murders of all who disagree with them. In fact, as we have seen, Muslims throughout the ages have discussed and debated and disagreed about the meaning of jihad, its defensive and expansionist, legitimate and illegitimate forms. Terrorists can attempt to hijack Islam and the doctrine of jihad, but that is no more legitimate than Christian and Jewish extremists committing their acts of terrorism in their own unholy wars in the name of Christianity or Judaism. Therefore, looking at what Islamic history, law, and tradition have to say about jihad and warfare becomes critical both in trying to understand the mind of a bin Laden and in forging future relations between Islam and the West.

Quranic passages referring to jihad as armed struggle fall into two broad categories: defensive, those that emphasize fighting against aggression, and offensive or expansionist, a more general command to fight against all unbelievers and spread the message and public order or Pax Islamica of Islam.

Muslims are urged to fight with great commitment so that victory will come and battle will end: "If you meet them in battle, inflict on them such a defeat as would be a lesson for those who come after them, and that they may be warned" (8:57). However, as is noted in the following passage, if they propose peace, then the fighting must end: "But if they are inclined to peace, make peace with them, and have trust in God for he hears all and knows everything" (8:61).

Many modern reformers, defending Islam against charges that it is a violent religion and sensitive to Western criticisms that violence is endemic to Islam, have emphasized that jihad is only justified for defense and have rejected earlier attempts to abrogate Quranic verses that emphasize defensive jihad by the "sword verses." Prominent modern Shii scholars such as Ayatollahs Mahmoud Taleqani and Murtaza Mutahhari argue that jihad is the defense of one's life, faith, property, and the integrity of the Muslim ummah. However, Mutahhari and others have interpreted defense broadly to include resistance to oppression not only in one's society but also against oppression anywhere, defense of the oppressed of the earth. In commenting on the Quranic dictum, "There is no compulsion in religion" (2:256), and that therefore wars aimed solely at the spread of Islam by force are not allowed, they also maintain that religious oppression must be resisted whether it is in a Muslim or non-Muslim society.[33]

As with other religious traditions whose controversies must also be understood within their historical contexts, Muslim disagreement over the use of jihad through the ages has been deeply influenced by social and political contexts. The right or obligation to wage jihad against religious, political, or social oppression has gained widespread usage in recent decades in order to justify holy and unholy wars. Khomeini used it to call on Muslims throughout the world, especially in the Gulf, to rise up against un-Islamic rulers. It was a means of legitimating Iran's export of revolution to Lebanon and elsewhere. The Shii of Lebanon experienced both violent and nonviolent expressions of jihad. Imam Musa Sadr was a tall, striking, charismatic Iranian-born religious leader, educated in Qom, the religious center associated with the Ayatollah Khomeini and sometimes referred to as "the Vatican." Musa Sadr moved to Lebanon and in the 1970s led a major social movement, the Movement for the Dispossessed, to protest and demand Muslim equity within Lebanon's Maronite Christian–dominated society. The radical organization Hizbollah emerged in the early 1980s as a resistance movement, inspired by Khomeini and supported by Iran, in reaction to the Israeli invasion and occupation of Lebanon.

Sunni Muslims have been equally drawn to this use of jihad. Hamas in Palestine defines itself, and justifies its jihad, as a resistance movement to Israeli occupation and oppression. Terrorist groups from Egypt to the southern Philippines have also used political and religious oppression as an excuse for their violent jihads.

While the Chinese and Indian governments repress the Uighurs and Kashmiris respectively, Islamic opposition groups press what they regard to be a jihad against oppressive states that have threatened their autonomy and independence. Chechens have harnessed their Islamic identity and called for jihad to resist Russia's reoccupation, and Islamic movements in several Central Asian republics have waged jihad against authoritarian rulers. Even Osama bin Laden has found it useful to claim that his jihad is to overthrow the oppressive and corrupt Saudi regime and prevent the infidel U.S. force from occupying Saudi Arabia, the land of Muhammad.

If some feel a need to justify all jihads as defensive, others do not. Thus, Muslims who insist that the defense of Islam is the only justification for jihad, and that all of the wars in the early days of Islam were defensive, have been criticized by others who believe that the restriction of jihad to defensive wars alone is a product of European colonialism and an unwarranted accommodation to the West.

JIHAD FOR CONVERSION

The common Western image is that Islam is a religion of the sword, that Muslims are required to use every means, including force and warfare, to spread and impose their faith. This issue like others is subject to a spectrum of opinions. While most Muslim scholars have agreed that it is never justified to wage jihad against non-Muslims simply because of their faith or to convert them, some bluntly state, as Ibn Khaldun, an acclaimed medieval Muslim historian, did: "In the Muslim community, holy war is a religious duty, because of the universalism of the Muslim mission and (the obligation to) convert everybody to Islam either by persuasion or by force."[34] Other medieval authors, like their Christian counterparts, went even further, teaching that the purpose of jihad is to rid the earth of unbelievers.

Because of the Islamic vision of the inseparability of religion and politics, oppression and injustice came to be equated with unbelief. However, although jurists and commentators on the Quran often failed to distinguish disbelief from political injustice, they did not sanction jihad merely on grounds of difference in belief. Many modern Muslim thinkers have distinguished disbelief from persecution or injustice and hold that unbelief alone is not a sufficient condition for waging war. The famous twentieth-century Egyptian jurist Mahmud Shaltut, former rector of Egypt's al-Azhar University, an internationally recognized seat of Islamic authority, argued that the Quranic verses that command fighting against the unbelievers are not referring to a jihad against all unbelievers as such but rather to unbelievers who had assailed the Muslim mission.

Even Sayyid Qutb rejected forced conversions, believing instead that a successful jihad included the possibility of conversion as a likely result once people were free to choose:

> It is not the intention of Islam to force its beliefs on people, but Islam is not merely "belief." . . . Islam is a declaration of the freedom of man from servitude to other men. Thus it strives . . . to abolish all those systems and governments which are based on the rule of man over men and the servitude of one human being to another. When Islam releases people from this political pressure and presents to them its spiritual message, appealing to their reason, it gives them complete freedom to accept or not to accept its beliefs. However, this freedom does not mean that they can make their desires their gods or that they can choose to remain in the servitude of other human beings, making some men lords over others.[35]

Contemporary scholars utilize Quranic passages to demonstrate Islam's acceptance of a diversity of religious beliefs and laws.[36] For example, "Surely the believers, the Jews, the Sabians and the Christians—whoever believes in God and the Last Day and does good deeds—They shall receive their reward from their Lord. They shall have nothing to fear and they shall not grieve" (5:69 and 2:62).

Jihad and Martyrdom:
The Ultimate Profession of Faith

> If you are killed in the cause of God or you die, the forgiveness
> and mercy of God are better than all that you amass. And if you
> die or are killed, even so it is to God that you will return (3:157–
> 158).

martyrdom !

To die for one's faith is the highest form of witness to God, according to the Quran. Like the Greek word martyr, which simply means
witness, as in witness to your faith, the Arabic Quranic word for
martyr, *shahid*, means witness. Martyrdom comes from the same
root as the Muslim profession of faith (*shahada*) or witness that
"There is no God but God and Muhammad is the Prophet of God."
When jihad is invoked to urge Muslims to take part in wars against
nonbelievers, its main motivator is the belief that someone who is
killed on the battlefield, called a shahid, will go directly to Paradise.

With the severe dislocations experienced in much of the Muslim
world from the eighteenth century to the present, a new understanding of martyrdom has been born. Martyrdom was a powerful
theme in the Iran-Iraq war where both Sunni Iraqis and Shii Irani-
ans relied on the promise of martyrdom to motivate their soldiers.
Since the late twentieth century, the term martyrdom has been used
broadly by Muslims around the world for all of those who die for
their faith or in the defense of Muslim territory in "just" causes in
Palestine, Iran, Egypt, and Lebanon as well as Azerbaijan, Bosnia,
Chechnya, Kashmir, and the southern Philippines.

Shii Islam has a particularly powerful martyrdom tradition and
legacy, starting with the martyrdom of the Prophet's grandson
Hussein, which became the paradigm for Shii theology and spirituality. This tragic event is ritually reenacted annually in Shii communities. It has expressed itself in the special place given to visiting
the graves of the martyrs, and mourning and emulating the suffering of Hussein and his companions with prayer, weeping, and
self-flagellation—a ritual analogous to the commemoration of the

passion and death of Jesus Christ. In postrevolutionary Iran, the tradition is reflected in the creation of martyr cemeteries for those who died in the Iran-Iraq war and for the revolution's clergy and supporters who were murdered or assassinated by opposition forces.

In some ways, we have come full circle since 1979–1980. However little Westerners knew about Islam, many were then able to distinguish between two major jihads, Khomeini's Islamic revolution with its threat to the West and the mujahidin's jihad to liberate Afghanistan. The United States government judged the jihad, whether it was a holy or unholy war, and its warriors, whether they were extremists or liberators, by their goals and conduct—by whether they were fighting America's Cold War adversary or an ally, the Shah of Iran. But things were never that simple. Understanding the dynamics of Muslim politics today and the dangers and threats that now exist requires a fuller understanding both of jihad itself and of how the United States got to the point where it is now number one on the hit list of Muslim terrorists.

Wherever one turns, the image and words of Osama bin Laden seem to embody jihad. He stands before us with a Quran in one hand and a Kalashnikov in the other, surrounded by his band of religious zealots. However, bin Laden is symptomatic of a broader phenomenon. His disappearance from the scene will not eliminate the danger of global Islamic terrorism.

We have seen the power that the legacy of the past, faith and tradition, holds for Muslims and the key figures or ideologues whose ideas and examples still live today in the minds and faith of many believers. They provide the multitude of meanings of jihad that individuals and movements draw on when they use the tradition of jihad to renew themselves and their communities today. How has this multifaceted concept of jihad been translated into action by Islamic organizations? What are their motivations, missions, strategies, and tactics? We turn now to the reality, the holy and unholy wars that represent reality for the twentieth and twenty-first centuries.

The Armies of God

November 20, 1979, was a day that Muslims around the world had awaited, the dawn of Islam's fifteenth century. At 5:30 A.M. as over forty thousand worshippers prayed the dawn prayer in the Grand Mosque in Mecca, the largest Islamic shrine in the world, their sacred space and time were shattered by the profane. Shots reverberated through the massive courtyard and a young man fell dead. A powerful force of armed militants, not only Saudis but also Egyptians, Kuwaitis, Bangladeshis, Yemenis, and Iraqis, pushed their way into the praying crowd and declared that the long-awaited Mahdi had arrived.

The more than three hundred members of this militant band and their families were led by Juhaiman al-Utaiba, the brother-in-law of the self-declared Mahdi, who had come to cleanse Islam before the end of the world. Juhaiman and his followers had been bitter critics of the Saudi government, its alliance with the West, and its disruptive modernization programs. They called for the overthrow of the sinful and unjust Saudi regime, the establishment of a true Islamic state, the eradication of Western cultural influences, and the end of oil exports to America.[1] The militants barricaded themselves in the mosque and held out against government forces for five days before being forced to retreat to the cellars and tunnels below the mosque where they remained for another nine days.

The Saudi government debated long and hard about how to best respond to this very delicate situation. The use of arms or fighting in the mosque is strictly forbidden. It had been unthinkable that Muslims would violate the sanctuary. Juhaiman's choice of the Grand Mosque was a fatal strategic error. Whatever its symbolic value, the group's action shocked and offended many, who were horrified by the shedding of blood in the shrine holding the *Kaaba*, the stone marking the center of Islam, the direction to which Muslims worldwide turn to pray. However legitimate their grievances, their actions were *haram*, forbidden and thus illegitimate. After initially hesitating, the king finally obtained a *fatwa* from Shaykh Abdul-Aziz Bin Baz, head of the government's Council of Ulama and the most powerful religious leader in the kingdom. Bin Baz approved the use of force within the Grand Mosque. The siege was finally ended after two weeks. Its leaders, whom the government had ridiculed as *Khawarj* (like the Kharijites, the first significant Islamic extremist movement, they had seceded and turned on their ruler), were either killed in the battle that ensued or captured and later executed.

The charismatic Juhaiman al-Utaiba had studied at Medina University, which was founded by members of the Egyptian Muslim Brotherhood who had fled Nasser's Egypt. He had also attended lectures by Bin Baz, who was known as a very learned but extremely conservative scholar. Juhaiman had left the university with a group of followers in 1974 and began to preach fiery sermons and build his new organization. In 1978, he and a large group of his followers were arrested for distributing his pamphlets calling for opposition to the House of Saud and condemning their corruption and un-Islamic lifestyles. Few in the West took note of the fact that the militants who invaded the Grand Mosque to protest against the Saudi regime and Western influences were not only Saudis but also members of Islamic activist groups in Egypt, Kuwait, the Indian subcontinent, Yemen, and Iraq.

To Western observers, this affair was baffling. An Islamic group was attempting to overthrow the government of Saudi Arabia, an Islamic state and protector of Islam's holiest sites, in the name of Islam? The House of Saud was being judged and condemned as corrupt and un-Islamic by the very Islamic yardstick that it used to legitimate itself.

This incident brought together militants from many countries. It was a precursor of changes that would become apparent in the Soviet-Afghan war, the globalization of jihad movements with holy warriors drawn from many parts of the *ummah* coming to the "defense of Islam." No one imagined then that the government of Saudi Arabia and Saudi dissidents would in the next few years become so intimately connected with the globalization of *jihad* and its tragic terrorist trajectory.

Twenty years later Osama bin Laden and al-Qaeda's declaration of war against America would bring together many elements from Muslim history (militant jihad, eighteenth-century revivalists, Wahhabi Islam, and condemnation of Western alliances with autocratic Muslim leaders) and add another dimension, the greatly enhanced power that globalization affords to terrorist groups— the ability to harness religion and modern technology to strike anywhere, anytime, and anyplace. This dark side of globalization now strengthens the threat of Islamic radicalism to our stability and security and forces us to recognize that the growing threat of terrorism in the name of Islam is part of a much bigger picture.

The terrorists responsible for the atrocities of September 11, 2001, are the radical fringe of a broad-based Islamic jihad that began in the late twentieth century. Islam's power and the idealistic concepts of jihad have been "spun" to become the primary idiom of Muslim politics, used by rulers and ruled, by reformers, political opposition, and terrorists.

Many violent radicals justify the horrors they commit by reciting a litany of deeply felt Muslim grievances against the West. Historic memories of the Crusades and European colonialism, the creation of Israel, the Cold War, and American neocolonialism— all the actions of a militant Christian West—get superimposed upon current events: the second Palestinian intifada, the presence of American troops in the Gulf, the devastating impact of sanctions on Iraqi children, jihads of resistance and liberation in Kashmir and Chechnya. These memories feed resentment, ignite new anger, and deepen anti-Americanism, not just among terrorists but also in the broader Muslim world. A climate of suspicion and animosity toward the West is reflected in the common use of words like Christian Crusaders, neocolonialism, and Zionist expansionism. And it is strikingly illustrated by the unfounded rumors that swept across the Arab and Muslim world, Europe, and America that the WTC attacks were perpetrated by Mossad and that four thousand Jews who work in the WTC did not show up for work on September 11 due to a tip from Israeli security.[2]

From the Crusades to Western Imperialism

The Crusades and European colonialism have had a universal and lasting impact on the Muslim imagination. I used to joke about an event whose significance is clearer to me now. I was at a national professional conference on the modern Muslim world. We were running late. The panel chair, to assure that there would be enough time for this nervous young professor to participate, asked his colleagues to skip the first part of their papers denouncing the Crusades and European colonialism for their long-lasting negative legacy. At the time, it seemed merely humorous. Today, some twenty-five years later, it has proven enduringly revealing.

For many in the West, the Crusades for the liberation of Jerusalem were a shining moment of religious fervor in the defense of Christianity. Western sports teams, marketing firms, and media have long used images of Crusaders as brave and powerful warriors, lofty symbols of self-sacrifice, honor, and valor. Few of us know or remember that Pope Urban called for the Crusades for political rather than his ostensible religious reasons or that, on balance, the Crusaders ultimately were the losers not the victors. The significance of the Crusades is less a case of what actually happened than what the stories taught us to believe. Each community looks back with memories of its commitment to defend its faith and to heroic tales of bravery and chivalry in struggling against "the infidel." Both Muslims and Christians saw the other as determined to conquer, convert, or eradicate the other, and thus as an enemy of God. For Westerners, Islam is a religion of the sword, of holy war or jihad. For Muslims, Christianity is the religion of the Crusades and hegemonic ambitions. The last segment of a BBC series on Islam, which covered colonialism and postcolonialism, gave support to this belief in its title, "The Final Crusade."

President George W. Bush's use of the word crusade in a speech about the war against terrorism, and the protests and apologies that followed, highlighted the distance between Muslim and Western historical memories. Muslims wondered, Would American soldiers entering Afghanistan become the first step in a broader, militant agenda? Would America repeat European colonialism and attempt to infiltrate, dominate, and ultimately redraw the map of the Middle East once again?

No one who has traveled in or studied the Muslim world can be oblivious to the tendency of many to attribute their past and current problems in large part to the second traumatic event affecting Islam and the West, the legacy of European colonialism. Again, their memories are different from ours. Many of us have forgotten what the twentieth-century map of the Muslim world reveals. The names of regions (the Middle East) and countries as well as the boundaries and rulers of countries were created by European colonial powers. Those who would understand the state and state of mind of the Muslim world today should start by examining the extent of foreign dominance and Muslim subordination to Europe in the recent past: the French in North, West, and Equatorial Africa, and the Levant (Lebanon and Syria); the British in Palestine, Transjordan (now Jordan), Iraq, the Arabian Gulf, and the Indian subcontinent; and in Southeast Asia, the British in Malaya (Malaysia, Singapore, and Brunei) and the Dutch in Indonesia.

The Ayatollah Khomeini spoke dramatically of the depth of Western penetration and extent of its threat to Muslim societies:

> The foul claws of imperialism have clutched at the heart of the
> lands of the people of the Quran, with our national wealth and
> resources being devoured by imperialism . . . with the poison-
> ous culture of imperialism penetrating to the depths our towns
> and villages throughout the Muslim world, displacing the cul-
> ture of the Quran.[3]

European colonialism reversed a pattern of Muslim rule and
expansion that had existed from the time of the Prophet. As the
balance of power and leadership shifted to Europe, much of the
once dominant Islamic civilization found itself either directly ruled
or dominated by the Christian West, threatened by crown and
cross. Many Europeans believed that modernity was evidence of
the inherent superiority of Christianity as a religion and culture.
Britain spoke of the "white man's burden" and France of its "mission to civilize" to justify European imperialism as they colonized
much of Africa, the Middle East, South and Southeast Asia.

Europe's threat to Muslim identity and autonomy raised profound religious as well as political questions for many in the Muslim world: What had gone wrong? Why had Muslims fallen
behind? Why had Muslim fortunes been so thoroughly reversed?
Was it Muslims who had failed Islam or Islam that had failed Muslims? How were Muslims to respond? More than a century later,
these same questions and issues remain. Combined with a Muslim belief that their societies must be reformed in every age, they
make a combustible mixture that readily ignites into the flame of
desire for a new world and the will to take radical action to make
this vision of reform a reality.

From Hijra and Jihad to
Modernization and Islamic Reform

Four Muslim responses to colonialism form the foundations for
much of what we see today: resistance and warfare, withdrawal
and noncooperation, secularism and Westernization, and Islamic

modernism. Resisters sought to follow the example of the Prophet: emigration (*hijra*) out of a territory no longer under Muslim rule and jihad, fighting to defend the faith and lands of Islam. Emigration for large numbers of people was impractical, however, and holy war against Europe's overwhelming military strength was doomed to defeat. For many religious leaders, the practical alternative was simply to refuse to deal with the new colonial masters, to shun their company, schools, and institutions.

Others thought their survival depended on following Europe's lead. The Egyptian modernist Taha Husayn (1889–1973) exmplified this position. A brilliant student, born blind, he attended al-Azhar University for ten years but then went on to the Egyptian University in Cairo followed by four years of study in France. He became a dominant and at times controversial figure in intellectual and academic circles. His book *The Future of Culture in Egypt* (1938) epitomized the orientation of many emerging elites who advocated a liberal secular reform program in emulation of the West. Many judged Islam as either the cause of decline or incapable of meeting the needs of modern life. They therefore advocated a modernization program that borrowed heavily from Western models of political, social, and legal change.

Taha Husayn aligned Islam with Christianity and maintained that Egypt's modern renaissance was based on Europe:

> The essence and source of Islam are the essence and source of Christianity. So far has the European ideal become our ideal that we now measure the material progress of all individuals and groups by the amount of borrowing from Europe.[4]

Muslim rulers in the Ottoman Empire, Egypt, and Iran had been quick to climb onto what they hoped would be a bullet-train to modernization. Scholars and students were sent to Europe, new universities and centers were created at home. Muslims studied languages, science, and politics, translated and published Western works. New westernized elites accepted a secular outlook that re-

stricted religion to personal life and turned to Europe to "modernize" their Muslim societies. The traditional Islamic ideology that
had for centuries given legitimacy to Muslim societies was slowly
altered as imported secular models from the West took over.

In Muslim society, this trend toward westernization created a
growing social split. Modern secular schools functioning alongside traditional religious institutions produced two classes of Muslims living side by side but developing different worldviews and
prospects for the future: a modern, westernized, elite minority and
a more traditional, Islamically oriented majority. In a very real
sense, there was a clash of cultures, one of skills and values as well
as of power and privilege. This division has remained a major cause
of the crisis of identity and resurgence of religion in many Muslim
societies.

A fourth response to the challenge of the West, Islamic modernism, tried to bridge the gap between Islamic traditionalists and
secular reformers. Islamic modernism, like much of the Muslim
response to the West today, displayed an ambivalent love-hate attitude toward the so-called Success of the West. They admired Europe for its strength, technology, and ideals of freedom, justice,
and equality but rejected its colonialist goals and policies. Modernists wanted to develop an Islamically based rationale for educational, legal, political, and social reform in order to promote a
renaissance for their community and a first step to national independence and power.

Islamic modernism was both a success and a failure: it reawakened
a sense of past power and glory, argued the compatibility of Islam
with modern reform, and distinguished between Western ideas
and technology and Western imperialism. Reformers offered an
Islamic alternative to either rejecting or uncritically assimilating
the West. Their ideas and values became part of Muslim discourse
and mainstream Muslim thought. However, the modernist intellectual movement did not produce organizations to pass on, develop and implement their ideas in a sustained manner. Some
disciples of the great modernist thinkers turned to a more secular
path. Most important, Islamic reformism was not sufficiently in-

tegrated into the curricula of religious schools (*madrasas*) and the training of religious scholars and leaders. As late as the 1970s and 1980s, Muslim and non-Muslim scholars writing about Islam and modernity or Islamic reformism would commonly point to Muhammad Abduh who died in 1905 and Muhammad Iqbal who died in 1938. While their role and legacy are important, the fact that they had been dead for decades seemed a tacit commentary on the failure of Islamic modernism to inspire new leaders and take hold within the broader community. Today the term "*salafi*," which had once been used to refer to Muhammad Abduh's Islamic modernist movement with its emphasis on Islam and rational modernism, is instead applied to some of the most extreme, anti-Western groups.

Islam and the Modern State

After World War II, the success of independence movements in overthrowing European rule and the creation of modern Muslim states brought pride and high expectations for a strong and prosperous future. Nation building in the Muslim world with its artificially drawn borders superficially uniting peoples with diverse centuries-old identities and allegiances was a fragile process that bore the seeds for later crises of identity, legitimacy, power, and authority.

When we ask today why much of the Muslim world remains politically unstable or underdeveloped, we need to remember that most modern Muslim states are only several decades old, carved out by the now-departed European powers.

The fragility of new nation-states was demonstrated time and again. In South Asia, for example, the British divided the Indian subcontinent into India and the new Islamic Republic of Pakistan. Kashmir was a state with a Muslim majority but led by an Indian maharaja who acceded to Indian rule, an arrangement that has been contested by Pakistan ever since. The majority of territory, the 54,000 square miles of Jammu Kashmir, was taken by India while Pakistan ruled a smaller parcel of 32,000 square miles, Azad Kashmir.

The creation of India and Pakistan resulted in communal warfare that left millions dead. Tens of thousands of Hindus and Muslims were forced to emigrate, Hindus to India and Muslims to Pakistan. Pakistan proved equally fragile. East Pakistan (later Bangladesh) and West Pakistan were separated by 1,000 miles of Indian territory. The difficulty of establishing a strong sense of nationalism in countries with such enormous ethnic, tribal, linguistic, and cultural diversity can be deduced from the fact that in both India and Pakistan the vast majority of the citizens in each country could not speak their national language (Hindi and Urdu respectively). The bloody results of colonial map making and nation creation were evident yet again in the brutal 1971 Pakistan civil war which led to the creation of Bangladesh, and in the bloody ethnic clashes that have threatened the stability of Pakistan to the present day. In Kashmir, the creation of a Muslim majority state within India resulted in wars between India and Pakistan in 1947 and 1965. Since 1987, Kashmiri separatists have been locked in a struggle against India's rule that has brought as many as 750,000 Indian troops to Kashmir to carry out a brutal war. To the present day, Kashmir continues to be a major incendiary issue in relations between India and Pakistan.

In the Middle East, the French created modern Lebanon by taking some portions of Syria, while Britain set the borders and rulers for Iraq and Kuwait. These arbitrary borders fed ethnic, regional, and religious conflicts that have threatened national unity or stability in numerous countries. The Lebanese Civil War (1975–1990) pitted Christian and Muslim militias against each other and also resulted in Syria's intervention and occupation. Iraq's 1990 invasion of Kuwait was justified by Saddam Hussein's claim on Kuwaiti territory. In the post–Gulf war period, Saddam Hussein's savage repression of Shii and Kurds reflected the artificiality and fragility of the Iraqi nation, a cobbled-together state led by a Sunni ruler with a long history of repressing Iraq's majority Shii population in the south and its (Sunni) Kurds in the north. Both Saddam's actions and the initial reluctance of the first (George H.) Bush administration to intervene were based on fears of Iraq's breakup or "Lebanization." Other countries, like Transjordan (Jordan), were totally new British creations. A popular story has Winston Churchill spending a lazy Sunday hunched over a map, smoking a good cigar, while drawing the boundary lines for his new "country" of Jordan.

Often the claims and legitimacy of rulers were equally artificial. The Hashimite family of Arabia provides an interesting example. The British created Transjordan and Iraq as states to be ruled by the Hashimite family. Prince Abdullah from Arabia was made emir (prince) of Transjordan. (He later upgraded to king of Jordan.) Abdullah's brother, Faisal, whose rule in Syria had been ended quickly by French intervention, was then made king of Iraq by Britain! And the most volatile example of European nation building in the Middle East remains the creation of Israel amidst competing and still-unresolved religious, nationalist, and territorial claims which resulted in the bitter legacy of the Arab-Israeli wars.

By the mid-twentieth century, most of the Muslim world had achieved political independence. Most rulers, even in those countries where Islam played an important role, had chosen the more Western-influenced secular path. Nevertheless, looking across the Muslim world, you could see three models for new states: Islamic, secular, and Muslim.

Saudi Arabia was a self-declared Islamic state. The monarchy of the House of Saud legitimated its domestic and foreign policies by claiming to govern and be governed by the Quran and Islamic law. At the other end of the spectrum, Turkey, the only remnant of the Ottoman Empire, opted for a secular state and severely restricted religion to personal life. Turkey under the leadership and direction of Mustafa Kemal (popularly known as Ataturk, Father of the Turks, d. 1938) embarked on a comprehensive process of Turkification, westernization, and secularization.

Most Muslim countries fell into a middle position. Creating modern states modeled on Western paradigms, they superficially injected Islamic provisions into constitutions requiring that the head of state be a Muslim or that Islamic law be recognized as "a" source of law even when it was not, in reality, recognized at all. These governments sought to control religion by incorporating schools, courts, and mosques into their ministries of education, law, and religious affairs. In some Muslim countries, languages for government, the courts, and universities were European. Individuals and institutions were "modern" to the degree that they were Western—in language and dress, manners and values, architecture and infrastructure.

Few questioned the accepted wisdom that modernization meant the progressive westernization and secularization of society. A modern education was the surest ticket to responsible positions in government, business, the professions, and academia. Close international ties were forged between the governments, the military, oil companies, and banks of the Muslim world and the West and set the stage for decades of educational and technical exchanges as well as political, economic, and military alliances. The United States, lacking the negative baggage of colonial powers, enjoyed a certain pride of place. It became a magnet for diplomats, bureaucrats, military, and security forces who received university and professional education there, and a haven for many who escaped poverty or persecution under authoritarian regimes. It seemed reasonable to expect that every day in every way westernization and secularization were making things better and better. How wrong that expectation turned out to be!

During the 1950s and 1960s widespread dissatisfaction with the track record of Western-inspired liberal nationalism took its toll. Monarchs and governments tumbled from power and new governments emerged in Egypt, Libya, Syria, Sudan, Iraq, and Algeria. All were based on some form of Arab nationalism/socialism with its populist appeals to Arab-Islamic roots, stress on Arab unity, criticism of the failures of liberal nationalism and the West, and promise of far-reaching social reforms. At the same time, the Muslim Brotherhood attracted tens of thousands of members in Egypt and Sudan as well as Syria, Jordan, and Palestine. Both Arab nationalism/socialism and the Brotherhood were populist movements that captured the imaginations, hopes, and aspirations of many in the Arab world and beyond. Muslim governments and societies continued to rely heavily on the West but now tilted more to the Soviet Union. Initially, Arab nationalist leaders such as Egypt's Gamal Abdel Nasser and his admirers such as Sudan's Jafar al-Numeiry and Libya's Muammar Qaddafi seemed to be in the driver's seat, controlling, marginalizing, or repressing Islamic activism. By the 1970s, however, Arab nationalism/socialism was discredited by the disastrous Arab defeat in the 1967 Arab-Israeli war, the failure of economic policies, and government corruption. In response, governments in all three countries were forced to turn to Islam to buttress their legitimacy and deal with rising Islamic reform and opposition movements.

Back to the Future: The Islamic Resurgence

Iran's Islamic revolution of 1978–1979 abruptly detoured the march toward Western modernization. Leading modernizing governments in Iran, Egypt, and Lebanon seemed to be experiencing the revenge of God. They were not alone. Islamic revivalism produced a wave of fundamentalist movements from Egypt, Sudan, and Iran to Pakistan, Afghanistan, and Malaysia.

The causes of the resurgence vary by country and region, but there are common threads: widespread feelings of failure and loss of identity in many Muslim societies, as well as failed political systems and economies. Overcrowded cities with insufficient social support systems, high unemployment rates, government corruption, a growing gap between rich and poor, and the breakdown of traditional religious and social values plagued many nations. Israel's crushing victory over the combined forces of Egypt, Jordan, and Syria in the 1967 Arab-Israeli Six-Day war symbolized the depth of Arab and Muslim impotence and the failure of modern nation-states in the Muslim world. Israel seized major pieces of territory, including the Sinai peninsula and Gaza Strip from Egypt, the Golan Heights from Syria, and the West Bank and East

Jerusalem from Jordan. The loss of Jerusalem, the third holiest city of Islam, which embraces major Muslim holy sites, the Dome of the Rock and the al-Aqsa Mosque, was particularly devastating to Muslims around the world, making Palestine and the liberation of Jerusalem an Islamic, not just an Arab or Palestinian, issue.

The year 1967 proved a turning point for many in the Muslim world who blamed Western political and economic models for their moral decline and spiritual malaise. Disillusionment with the West and in particular with the United States, its pro-Israel policy, and its support for authoritarian rulers like Iran's shah fed anti-Western feelings. Muslim religious leaders and activists believed their message had been vindicated, maintaining that the failures and troubles of Muslims were a result of turning away from God's revealed path and relying on the West. From the 1970s onward, religious revivalism and the role of Islamic movements became a major force in Muslim politics.

Building the Armies for God

Modern Islamic movements have been the driving force behind the resurgence of Islam. As discussed in the previous chapter, Muslims have a rich legacy of traditions that call upon them to reform their societies in every age. Given the vision of early Islamic power and success and then its decline for several centuries, it is not surprising to see a proliferation of Islamic movements in the twenty-first century striving to create a better world. Nonviolent revolutionary change from below and violent revolution to overthrow established un-Islamic governments have remained the twin paths of contemporary Islamic movements. Both seemed to spring up in the 1970s and spread like wildfire across the Muslim world.

The two pioneer Islamic movements described earlier, Egypt's Muslim Brotherhood and Pakistan's Jamaat-i-Islami, spread to Sudan, Jordan, and the Gulf, Bangladesh, India, and Kashmir and inspired a proliferation of similar movements across the world.

While all have been committed to a jihad to transform Muslim societies, their formation, development, strategy, and tactics have reflected the diverse political, economic, and social environments in which they arose. The direction of that jihad, whether it followed a nonviolent or violent path, has often been influenced as much by governments as by Islamic organizations. A majority of Muslim reform organizations have operated above ground, working within their societies; a radicalized militant minority has engaged in a violent jihad to seize power or attack Muslim governments, America, Europe, and Israel.

As Osama bin Laden and al-Qaeda have reminded us, what happens "over there" does in fact have an impact here in the United States and elsewhere in the West. Countries such as Afghanistan, Egypt, Israel/Palestine, and Algeria have proven fertile ground in which the seeds of violence and terrorism have thrived. No country better demonstrates the many faces of political Islam, violent and nonviolent, domestic and international, than Egypt. The birthplace of the Brotherhood, of its paths of political participation and violent revolutionary jihad, Egyptian society has produced a long list of reformers and terrorists, the progeny of Hasan al-Banna and Sayyid Qutb, extending from Muhammad Farag, the ideologue for Islamic Jihad, the assassins of Anwar Sadat to Dr. Ayman al-Zawahiri and other al-Qaeda leaders of the jihad against America.

Egypt and the Rage for God

> *"I have killed Pharaoh and I do not fear death"*
> Khalid Islambuli, the assassin of Anwar Sadat

Egypt has long been a leader in the Arab and Muslim world, a long-time ally of the United States. It is a major destination for foreign tourists who are fascinated by its pyramids, pharaohs, and mummies. Egypt's marketing image and major tourist sites that feature ancient Egyptian history, however, have long masked its deep Islamic identity, character, and culture.

The most modern and modernizing of countries, politically, culturally and religiously, Egypt has also been the most prominent site of both Islamic reform and radical extremism. Egypt's Islamic movements have spanned the spectrum from the modernists in the late-nineteenth and twentieth centuries to recent extremist groups such as Takfir wal Hijra, Islamic Jihad, and Gamaa Islamiyya who have terrorized Egyptian society, inspired Osama bin Laden, and became part of his al-Qaeda network. The Egyptian experience offers a full-blown example of political Islam from its pioneers to its mainstream and terrorist fringes today and reflects the ironic fact that some of the most developed countries in the Middle East have experienced and been victims of significant violence and terrorism. What can we learn about the nature of political Islam and the role of violence and acts of terror? What is the legacy of Egypt's movements for global terrorism in the twenty-first century? Recent history will help to answer these questions.

THE BELIEVER-PRESIDENT AND JIHAD

When Anwar Sadat succeeded Gamal Abdel Nasser as president of Egypt, he faced a formidable task. He replaced an enormously popular charismatic leader, influential not only in Egypt but also throughout the Arab world. In some Arab countries, you might see more pictures of Nasser than of the local president. At first Sadat's portrait was hung next to Nasser's to bolster his legitimacy. Later, however, to escape living in Nasser's shadow, Sadat shifted gears and made strong appeals to Islam. Sadat wished to distance himself from Nasser's party, his failed socialist ideology, policies, and allies, and to define his own path and policies.

Sadat assumed the title the Believer-President, an allusion to the Islamic caliph's title Commander of the Faithful. He began and ended his speeches with verses from the Quran. TV broadcasts frequently featured him in a mosque, cameras zeroing in on his prominent prayer mark, a callous caused by touching the forehead to the ground in prayer. Sadat encouraged the growth of Islamic student associations on campus and was able to gain enough control over the shaykh (rector) and leading religious scholars at al-Azhar University to be able to count on their support for the Egyptian-Israeli peace treaty. This treaty won him great praise in the West and a Nobel Peace Prize. However, despite generous aid from the United States following the Camp David Accords in 1978–1979, the standard of living for most Egyptians continued its steady decline, and the Palestinians, always the symbol of the success or failure of Arab leadership, remained stateless and persecuted under military occupation.

It soon became clear to Sadat that appealing to Islam was a two-edged sword. Using strict Islamic criteria, activists judged Sadat to be a hypocrite and traitor for his relations with the West, his failure to implement the Shariah as the official law of Egypt, and his liberal family-law reforms, which critics, who saw them as Western rather than Islamically inspired, sarcastically dubbed "Jihan's laws" after Sadat's half-British wife.

By the mid-1970s, the quiet achieved by Nasser's 1960s suppression of the Muslim Brotherhood was gone. New members who were attracted to emerging organizations included those who had believed in westernization and modernization, but who were now disaffected by the continuing economic decline. They included the majority of the unemployed younger generation as well as former secularists. The Muslim Brotherhood was back and so were new extremists, secret revolutionary groups like Muhammad's Youth, Takfir wal Hijra (Excommunication and Flight), and Islamic Jihad promoting their jihad of violence and terrorism. They seized buildings, kidnapped and executed government officials, and tried to assassinate Sadat and declare an Islamic republic.

In a nationwide crackdown, the government arrested 620 militants; 454 were tried by special military courts and imprisoned. The leaders of Muhammad's Youth and Takfir were executed. Many militants went underground only to reemerge as new groups, the Army of God (Jund Allah) and Islamic Jihad (Jamaat al-Jihad, or Holy War Society).

Increasingly, Sadat responded to all of his Islamic critics, mainstream and radical alike, with a heavy hand. He warned: "Those who wish to practice Islam can go to the mosque and those who wish to engage in politics may do it through legal institutions."[5] The government tried to imprison all opposition, gain control of all mosques, and ban Islamic student associations. Sadat also moved to silence others: intellectuals, journalists, lawyers, university professors, former cabinet ministers who had criticized his policies. When food riots shook Cairo in January 1977, Sadat blamed Marxists and Leftists, and continued to arrest any opposition. While he was being praised in the West as a progressive Muslim leader, for many in Egypt Sadat's new economic open-door policy just meant greater Western (especially American) economic involvement. It meant lining the pockets of multinational companies and Egyptian elites, not solving basic economic and social problems:

> How can the peasant, the hardworking Egyptian fellah, maintain his dignity when, after sweating in the hot sun all day long, he has to stand in line to receive a frozen American chicken? . . . As he sits in the evening with the family to watch the television that his son has purchased from the fruits of labor in Saudi Arabia, the intrigues of J.R. Ewing and Sue Ellen on Dallas strip him of what is left of his legitimacy as a culture bearer in his own culture. Between programs, he is told in English that he should be drinking Schweppes or in dubbed Arabic that he should use deodorant, and that all his problems are caused by having too many children—a total package of imported ideas.[6]

The September 1978 Camp David Accords were viewed by Arabs and Muslims at home and abroad as an opportunistic capitulation to Israel and its American patron. Sadat's foreign minister resigned, and protest demonstrations throughout Egypt denounced the accords as a treasonous act of an "unbeliever." Only Egypt seemed to benefit from the accords, as Israel eventually withdrew from the Sinai, and Egypt got massive aid from the United States as a reward for signing. However, Israel's occupation of Palestinian territories on the West Bank and Gaza, as well as of Syria's Golan Heights, remained in place. Al-Azhar's endorsement of the peace agreement was seen as simply reconfirmation that it had become a puppet of the government. Although the Muslim Brotherhood initially responded cautiously, by March 1979 it had called for a holy war against Israel.

In early September 1981, faced with mounting discontent and opposition, in a sensational move the government launched a massive dragnet, arresting more than 1,500 people. Secular and Islamic opposition publications were banned. Those imprisoned represented the entire political spectrum, from extreme right to extreme left, Muslim Brothers and militants, as well as Marxists, Muslims, and Copts, young and old, journalists, writers, professors, and other professionals. They included Dr. Nawal Saadawi, the prominent Egyptian author, feminist, and former cabinet minister. In a television address, Sadat maintained that he was saving Egypt from political and religious "sedition." Many believed that politically he had signed his "death warrant"; tragically, this prediction would prove to be literally true.[7] Like the shah of Iran when faced with mounting opposition, Sadat became more autocratic and increasingly identified the Egyptian state with his own personality and will. As Saad Eddin Ibrahim has noted,

> Sadatinization of Egypt was expressed in almost every song on radio and television. . . . Two processes were at work: a Sadatanization of Egypt on the one hand and a deification of Sadat on the other—the rebirth of the Egyptian pharaoh.[8]

Despite the growing tensions in Egyptian society, few expected what happened on October 6, 1981. Anwar Sadat, adorned in his gold-braided uniform sat amidst two thousand dignitaries from all over the world viewing a weapons display that commemorated the "success" of the 1973 war. As they shielded their eyes from the blazing sun, they watched fighter-plane aerobatics above and a slow-moving procession of artillery trucks below. Suddenly, four gunmen, appearing from behind the trucks, fired their automatic rifles and threw their grenades at the reviewing stand. The Believer-President, struck by at least five bullets as well as shrapnel, died almost immediately. Sadat was assassinated by members of Jamaat al-Jihad or Islamic Jihad, the organization that developed from an abortive coup staged by Muhammad's Youth. Their leader, a military officer, cried out, "I am Khalid Islambuli. I have killed Pharoah and I do not fear death!" Years later Khalid's brother, Mohammed Islambuli, would surface with Osama bin Laden in Afghanistan. Sadat's state funeral was attended by a host of celebrities, presidents, and politicians from Europe and America. However, Arab leaders were prominently missing, and the people of Egypt did not mourn for their Believer-President.

ISLAMIC JIHAD

The Egyptian Islamic Jihad has had a long track record of violence and terrorism. Its well-educated members have come from the presidential guard and military intelligence and include civil servants, radio and television workers, university students, and professors. They were recruited from religious societies and Quran study groups. Their social centers provided students with free books and tutoring and families with much-needed food, clothing, and housing.

The mission of Islamic Jihad was to create a true Islamic state and society in Egypt. This was to be the first step in achieving their long-term goal: a single Muslim government under a true Islamic caliphate. They have rationalized their holy war against Egypt's "atheist" state and rulers as required, the obligation of all true believers.

Islamic Jihad's war is waged against all nonbelievers, Muslim and non-Muslim alike. Extremist groups like Jihad reject Islam's traditional tolerance of the protected communities of Jews and Christians, People of the Book (*dhimmi*). Like Osama bin Laden, they see Jews and Christians as part of a historic battle or Crusade connected with European colonialism and Zionism, and they regard Israel as a Trojan horse of the West, a fifth column within Muslim societies.[9] Once people have been condemned as unbelievers who must be subject to the sword, they forfeit their right to life, security, and property. Shaykh Omar Abdel Rahman, spiritual adviser to Islamic Jihad and Gamaa Islamiyya, issued a fatwa sanctioning the killing and plundering of Christians in Luxor in 1997 because they were anti-Muslim. This outlook has been passed on to other groups in the Arab and Muslim world who believe that international conspiracies, Jewish Zionism, the Christian West, and atheistic communism all intend to divide the Muslim world and destroy Islam. In public protests they chant: "Holy war against lackeys—Jews, Christians, and Atheists" and "No to America! and No to Israel!"

After Sadat's assassination, Islamic Jihad regrouped and declared jihad against the new government of Hosni Mubarak. They re-emerged in the 1990s along with Gamaa Islamiyya to threaten the security of Egyptian society. Dr. Ayman al-Zawahiri returned from the Afghan jihad and brought many other Arab Afghans with him and right into the Jihad organization. Egyptians had made up a large proportion of the foreigners fighting the Soviets. They returned to Egypt with new ideas, extensive *mujahidin* credentials, and the taste of victory against overwhelming odds. They brought Egypt's Islamic Jihad and Gamaa Islamiyya a new ideological dimension, transforming the more limited nationalist agenda to create an Islamic state in Egypt into a commitment to wage global jihad.

Islamic Jihad's activities reflected their rage and their agenda. In 1990, five Jihad members were arrested for killing the speaker of the National Assembly. Jihad members who unsuccessfully attempted to assassinate the interior minister and the prime minister in 1993 were believed to be behind the 1995 assassination attempt on President Mubarak in Addis Ababa, the bombing of the Egyptian embassy in Islamabad, and the slaughter of fifty-eight tourists at Luxor in 1997—a crime for which al-Zawahiri was sentenced to death *in absentia*. Jihad's spiritual adviser, Omar Abdel Rahman, was exiled to the United States, but continued to influ-

ence Jihad as well as Gamaa Islamiyya. He was implicated in the
1993 World Trade Center bombing and imprisoned for participation in a conspiracy to commit other bombings in America. Jihad
split into two wings, one loyal to Abboud al-Zamour, one of the
original founders, and the other, Vanguards of Conquest or the
New Jihad Group led by bin Laden protégé al-Zawahiri, who would
merge his group with al-Qaeda.

The Gamaa Islamiyya (Islamic Group) began during the Sadat
era as student Islamic groups active on university campuses and has
evolved into a terrorist network. It became an umbrella organization for violent extremists' clandestine cells active in Cairo, Alexan-
dria, and Upper Egypt. It attracted younger, less-educated followers
from more desperate conditions of poverty and unemployment who
espoused a more radical ideology and engaged in more random acts
of violence to destabilize the government politically and economically. They attacked tourists, a major source of Egypt's foreign rev-
enue, bombed and burned government buildings and banks, as well
as theaters and video and book stores that popularized Western culture. The Gamaa especially targeted Christians, bombing and burn-
ing churches and homes, robbing, beating, and murdering Christian
Egyptians. The Gamaa's other targets included columnist Farag Foda,
who was killed in 1992, and Egypt's Nobel laureate writer Naguib
Mahfuz, who in 1994 was stabbed in order to silence and intimi-
date outspoken critics of fundamentalists.

A DUAL REVOLUTION:
MAINSTREAM AND MILITANT JIHAD

During the Mubarak years extremists and government security
forces and police have been locked in an all-out unholy war in
which both sides use deadly force and terrorism against their enemy. The struggle has cost more than one thousand lives and led
to charges by human rights organizations, international media,
and political experts that the effort to capture and eradicate extremists has degenerated into indiscriminate state repression. More
than twenty thousand Islamists have been imprisoned, many de-

tained without charge and subjected to torture. Extralegal military courts that exclude the right of appeal were created; laws were enacted to restrict freedom of the press, take control of mosques, and prevent elected Islamists from leading professional associations.

Like other authoritarian regimes in the Middle East, the Mubarak government seized the opportunity to use its war against terrorism to silence both extremists and mainstream legal opposition, not only those movements that have carried out violent attacks, but one, namely the Muslim Brotherhood, that had become dominant in university faculties, labor and professional associations, and many municipalities.[10]

By 2000 the Mubarak government's strategy had clearly paid off. Imprisoned leaders of Gamaa Islamiyya had declared a unilateral cease-fire; the government released thousands of detainees. Islamic Jihad in Egypt, significantly weakened, many of its leaders imprisoned or in exile, soon followed suit. But Islamic Jihad abroad, in particular Ayman al-Zawahiri and Islamic Jihad leaders in Afghanistan, rejected the ceasefire and continue their global jihad.

MAINSTREAM FUNDAMENTALISM AND THE STATE

Despite the apparent success of the Mubarak government in containing Islamic radicalism, it is not responding successfully to the declining standard of living, high unemployment, and decreased freedom and democratic rights. As a consequence, Islamic revivalism has had a significant impact on mainstream Egyptian society. Egyptian society has itself become more Islamized at the grassroots level. New Islamic trends are seen in new educated religious leaders who have mass followings from middle- and upper-class audiences. Physicians, journalists, lawyers, political scientists, men and women write and speak out on issues of Islamic reform such as pluralism, women's rights, and social justice. Islamic belief, symbols, and values inform the government, courts, professions, dress, and values of society (modern as well as traditional sectors) *countering* the expectations of secular modernization theory and the policies of the Mubarak government.

The Muslim Brotherhood exemplifies the quiet social revolution that has been taking place in Egypt's cities and towns. Islamic activism has become institutionalized. Islamic schools, clinics, hospitals, and social services, as well as Islamic banks and publishing houses, are part of mainstream society, an alternative set of social institutions and services. They present an indirect indictment of the government's failure to respond to people's needs. The performance of Islamists at the polls has been equally impressive. Prevented by law from participating as a legal political party, the Muslim Brotherhood formed coalitions and alliances and emerged as the leading opposition in those parliamentary elections in which they participated.

The story of Egypt, an ally of the United States, is one of the many examples of how political and economic conditions coupled with repression spawn militant opposition movements that misuse Islam to motivate and legitimate violence and terrorism.

The Jihad in Palestine: Hamas

If someone confiscated your land, demolished your home, built settlements to prevent you from coming back, killed your children and blocked you from going to work, wouldn't you want to fight for your country?[11]

Major Islamic movements arise in response to failures and crises in their societies and to vacuums in effective leadership. Nowhere has this been more dramatically visible than in Israel/Palestine. The late 1980s produced two militant Islamic responses to the failures of the Israeli and Palestinian leadership—Hamas and Islamic Jihad. Hamas, though always a minority, has proven the more effective, harnessing religion with political and social activism, and increasingly using acts of terrorism in the escalating violence and terror of the Palestinian-Israeli conflict.

Hamas is an offshoot of the Palestinian Muslim Brotherhood. It was created in 1987 during the Palestinian uprising (*intifada*) against Israeli occupation and rule in Gaza and the West Bank. The Brotherhood's support had dwindled, especially among the younger generation, after the Arab defeat in the 1967 Arab-Israeli war. Its apolitical path, focused on running schools, youth camps, and social welfare services, did not address the core causes of the continued disenfranchisement of the Palestinians and so fell short of the desperate mood of the times. Leaving the Brotherhood on the periphery, the majority of Palestinians turned to Yasser Arafat's Fatah and the Palestinian Liberation Organization (PLO), the coalition of Palestinian groups of which Fatah is a member.

However, when the intifada erupted in 1987, the Brotherhood moved quickly, taking advantage of Arafat's failures and the outpouring of frustration and rage against Israel to establish its relevance during the uprising. The Brotherhood created Hamas, ("fervor"), an acronym for the Islamic Resistance Movement; Hamas quickly took on a life and mission of its own, assuming a major leadership position during the intifada. Filling a vacuum, it provided a militant Islamic alternative to the secular nationalism of the PLO. Because of the Brotherhood's size, broad-based activities, and influence, Hamas became the principal alternative to the PLO.

From the beginning, Hamas's struggle to end the Israeli occupation was conducted as a jihad, a multifaceted struggle of political action, social welfare, and militant resistance, including acts of violence and terrorism. Hamas combined its religious message with social reform, which attracted the older generation, and with resistance and jihad, which spoke to the frustrations and fury of Palestinian youth. Hamas's success overshadowed the Brotherhood and challenged Yasser Arafat and the PLO's leadership in the struggle.

Hamas, like other Islamic movements, is engaged in a process of *dawah* (the call to become better Muslims) and jihad (the call to fight against oppression). The predicament of the Palestinian people, the hegemony of Israel, is attributed to loss of faith and departure from the straight path of Islam. Hamas calls all Muslims to give up their secular culture and lifestyles and return to religious observance: prayer, fasting, Islamic dress, moral and social values to re-create a proper Islamic society so that Muslim society can again become strong and wage a successful jihad to liberate Palestine from Israeli control.

As its charter states, Hamas "found itself at a time when Islam disappeared from life. Thus, rules were broken, concepts were vilified, values changed and evil people took control; oppression and darkness prevailed, cowards became tigers; homelands were invaded, people were scattered . . . when Islam is absent from the arena, everything changes."[12] From this perspective, Israel's occupation is seen as a punishment from God for deviations from Islam. Thus, independence, civil and political rights, dignity, and development will all be achieved only by a return to Islam, a re-Islamization of Palestinian Muslim society.

Hamas views the Muslim claim to the land of Palestine as religiously anchored and immutable: "The Islamic Resistance Movement believes that the land of Palestine has been an Islamic *Waqf* [religious endowment] throughout the generations and until the day of resurrection. . . . this waqf will endure as long as heaven and earth last." Islam is combined with Palestinian and Arab nationalism in Hamas's mission; Hamas's jihad is the defense of Palestine, a complementary combination of political and military activities, incumbent on all Muslims to liberate Palestine from Israeli occupation: "Nothing is loftier or deeper in nationalism than waging jihad against the enemy and confronting him when he sets foot on the land of the Muslims. . . . When our enemies usurp some lands, jihad becomes a duty on all Muslims."[13]

The PLO charter, on the other hand, identifies the enemy as Zionism, the European Jewish movement to create the state of Israel, which disregarded the rights of Palestinians whose land was needed to establish the state. The PLO goal is a secular state with equal rights for all citizens, Muslims and Christians (a significant minority of the Palestinian population). In contrast, Hamas rejects the distinction between Judaism and Zionism, seeing the Palestinian-Israeli conflict in religious terms as a confrontation between Islam and Judaism as represented by the religious state of Israel. In the words of Hamas's leader Mahmoud Zahar: "They [the Jews] made their religion their nation and state. . . . They have declared war on Islam, closed mosques and massacred defenseless worshippers at al-Aqsa and in Hebron. They are the Muslim-killers and under these circumstances we are obliged by our religion to defend ourselves."[14]

Like Takfir wal Hijra and Islamic Jihad as well as Osama bin Laden's al-Qaeda, Hamas sees the Palestinian-Israeli conflict as the most recent iteration of an age-old struggle between Islam and Judaism, dating back to the Jews' rejection of Muhammad and Islam in the seventh century.[15] Like many Muslim groups it draws on Western anti-Semitic literature, especially *The Protocols of the Learned Elders of Zion*, an apocryphal book that describes a fictitious Jewish conspiracy to destroy Christian civilization and establish Jewish hegemony, to bolster its indictment. Thus, for Hamas the Palestinian struggle is a jihad in the fullest militant sense of the term, a holy war between Muslims and Jews based on conflicting religious and territorial claims.

MEMBERSHIP AND ACTIVITIES

Hamas was founded by Shaykh Ahmad Yassin, the charismatic paraplegic leader of the Palestinian Muslim Brotherhood. Its leadership has included religious officials (*imams*), but most members are professionals and technocrats trained in medicine, engineering, science, or business. Members are recruited from a network of mosques, schools, and charitable institutions into this religious, social, political, and military movement. The combination of political and social activism with guerrilla warfare earned the financial and moral support of many Palestinians and others in the broader Arab and Muslim world. Its extensive network of community and charitable projects and programs—kindergartens, schools, scholarships, support for students studying abroad, libraries, social and sports clubs, and other social welfare services—was a primary reason for its popularity and following.

Hamas has engaged in political education, mobilization, and protest, challenging the legitimacy and platform of the PLO, claiming to offer a more authentic and equitable Islamic alternative. Political forums, pamphlets, and cassettes, as well as mass demonstrations and strikes, have been effective political instruments for them. Of course, their popularity and support, their ability to get votes from the majority depend on progress or, more correctly, lack of progress, in the peace process. When relations between Israel and the Palestinians deteriorate, the popularity of Hamas candidates in municipal, professional associations, chambers of commerce, and university student elections soars because the dominant PLO is blamed for continued failure. Hamas, in this sense, benefits from the continuing deadlock between the Palestinians and Israelis. Those two powers are blamed for the continued humiliation of the Palestinian people and frustration of their desire for political and civil rights. Hamas promises to get tough with Israel in order to achieve Palestinian rights: that is the purpose of its militant and terrorist acts.

NATIONALIST MOVEMENT OF RESISTANCE OR TERRORIST ORGANIZATION?

Whatever the accomplishments of Hamas as a social and political movement, only its violent activities are known in the West. Members of Hamas participated in the everyday confrontations with Israeli forces during the intifada. The Qassem Brigade, a specialized military wing fully operational by 1992, engaged in well-planned guerrilla warfare against Israeli military and police. Qassem's members worked in small clandestine cells. Their identity was unknown to the majority of Hamas members and they functioned with relative autonomy.

When Israel and the United States condemned Hamas as a terrorist organization, Hamas leaders responded by saying that the use of violence is both legitimate resistance and retaliation that was restricted to political and military targets in the occupied territories. Their actions were a response to Israel's occupation and its use of unrestrained violence and terror against Palestinians. This position changed dramatically after the 1993 Oslo Accords and in response to two events in Israel and the West Bank and Gaza.

On February 25, 1994, a Jewish settler named Baruch Goldstein walked into the Mosque of the Patriarch in Hebron, opened fire, and killed 29 Muslim worshippers during their Friday congregational prayer. In response, Hamas introduced a new type of warfare, the suicide bombers. Their attacks increased exponentially. Promising swift revenge for the Hebron massacre, the Qassem Brigade undertook five operations within Israel itself in Galilee, Jerusalem, and Tel Aviv. The most deadly took place on October 19, 1994, in the heart of Tel Aviv with the bombing of a bus that killed 23 and injured nearly 50 people. The Israeli assassination of Yahya Ayash, a suicide-bomb maker, resulted in another series of retaliatory suicide-bomb attacks. Peace negotiations in July 1997 were again disrupted when suicide bombers killed 13 and wounded more than 150 in a Jerusalem market.

What drives young Muslims to become suicide bombers? Many Palestinians have seen generations grow up in refugee camps or under Israeli occupation since the creation of Israel in 1948. Their sense of oppression and victimhood has been compounded as the promise of the Oslo Accords evaporated, like those of Camp David, under Yasser Arafat's Palestinian National Authority. The visit of Ariel Sharon with Israeli security forces to the Temple Mt. sparked the second (Al-Aqsa) intifada in late September 2000. Growing up oppressed and under siege, facing a future with little hope, high unemployment, and endemic poverty can produce an anger and desire for revenge against those responsible. Just as among inner city youth in the United States, some of those young people lose all hope. For others, religion holds the answer. For a small minority, suicide bombing seems a proud and powerful response.

Completely out of their league militarily when compared to Israel, these militant Palestinians boast of their new and most effective deadly weapon. As student posters at universities in the West Bank and Gaza declare: "Israel has nuclear bombs, we have human bombs."[16] Suicide is forbidden in Islam, but militant Palestinians do not see this as suicide. It is self-sacrifice for the cause of Palestinian freedom. The simplicity of the act enables an otherwise impotent individual to slip into a crowd unnoticed and then with a simple detonation wreak horrendous carnage. The use of concepts like jihad and martyrdom to justify suicide bombing provides a powerful incentive: the prospect of being a glorified hero in this life and enjoying Paradise in the next.

Suicide bombing has taken the conflict beyond the military and into the streets; Hamas has struck an unparalleled sense of vulnerability and terror into Israeli society. Because it is so effective, its use has escalated along with the Sharon government's escalation of violence, bombings, missile attacks, and assassination of Palestinian leaders. While the Palestinians are no match for Israel in numbers or weapons, Dr. Abdel Aziz Rantisi, a senior Hamas leader, believes such attacks ensure that "Israelis will have no stability and no security until the occupation ends. Suicide bombers are Israel's future."[17]

The new tactics of suicides and slaughter of civilians opened deep political cleavages within Hamas and summoned both support and condemnation on religious grounds in the broader Muslim world. Some Hamas leaders say targeting civilians is counterproductive; "The truth is that it did a lot of damage to Islam's image in the West. . . . Any time you kill civilians that happens."[18] Others countered that Hamas was responding legitimately to Israel's war against Palestinian civilians, its "illegal occupation" of the West Bank and Gaza, and its "barbaric treatment" of Palestinians.[19] Shaykh Yassin, founder of Hamas, and many other Palestinian religious leaders have argued that suicide bombing is necessary and justified. Other international Islamic leaders have been divided in opinion. Shaykh Tantawi, the grand *mufti* of Egypt, defends it, while Shaykh al-Sheikh, the grand *mufti* of Saudi Arabia, has condemned all suicide bombing as un-Islamic.

The attempt to distinguish between the political and the military wings of Hamas, especially when it comes to suicide bombings and terrorism, has been contentious. Critics reject the distinction as disingenuous. Both the Clinton and George W. Bush administrations have placed Hamas on their lists of terrorist organizations and outlawed all contributions to Hamas by Americans or American-based organizations, refusing to acknowledge any distinction between its social welfare and humanitarian work and its militia.

Unlike extremist organizations like bin Laden's al-Qaeda, the history of Hamas, like that of many other Islamic movements, demonstrated an ability to balance ideology and a pragmatic activism that responds to political and social realities. At no time has this been clearer than in the post-Oslo years, when Hamas was challenged on many fronts. Although the PLO's leadership of Palestinians had been seriously questioned since the 1980s, the Oslo Accords demonstrated that Yasser Arafat and the PLO had negotiated with Israel in the name of the Palestine people and thus had obtained official recognition as leaders of the Palestinian people. Hamas, the most viable option to the PLO, was caught off guard by the quietly and privately negotiated settlement. Its continued opposition to Arafat and the accords and its call to continue the Palestinian struggle against Israel now put it at odds not only with Israel but also with the PLO and the newly established Palestinian National Authority (PNA). Prior to the accords, the PLO and Hamas both had been dismissed as terrorist organizations. With the "rehabilitation" and legitimation of Yasser Arafat and the PLO by the international community, Arafat the "terrorist" now became Arafat the statesman. In contrast, Hamas became the common enemy of Israel and the PLO, the primary obstacle to peace, and roundly denounced as extremist and terrorist.

The post-Oslo period saw growing divisions within Hamas. Younger militants, especially in the Qassem Brigade, were convinced the Oslo Accords would fail to bring Palestinian independence, just as Sadat's Camp David Accords had. They believed they were just another ruse by Israel who would find an excuse to abandon them and blame the Palestinians. Rather than a process, they wanted the occupation ended completely and immediately. Unlike the PLO, which had accepted the legitimacy of the state of Israel within its pre-1967 boundaries in accordance with UN Security Council resolutions and international law, Hamas never accepted the legitimacy of the state of Israel. They therefore wanted to step up the armed struggle against Israeli occupation and continue the intifada. Hamas boycotted the Palestinian National Authority elections, and the main political wing grappled with the fact that nonparticipation in elections would further marginalize them. Some wanted to form a political party to assure that Hamas's voice was a presence in the PNA government and Palestinian politics. Hamas founder Shaykh Yassin, in a series of letters from prison, reflected on these choices and cautiously opted for participation.

Yassin's pragmatism was embraced by the general Hamas leadership, who accepted Arafat's election as president of the PNA and disassociated themselves from militants whose radical rejection has led to continued armed struggle. While rejecting the accords, a majority adapted to the political realities, renouncing violence and engaging in direct participation in politics. A small minority continues to espouse violence and terrorism to liberate the whole of Palestine.

Algeria: The Army vs. the Army of God

While for many in the West the 1980s were dominated by fears that "Islam" would come to power through revolutions or the violent overthrow of governments by clandestine groups, Algeria saw their Islamists succeed through the ballot box. But this initial Islamist political success gave birth to a spiral of violence and counterviolence that has threatened the very fabric of Algerian society. Following bloody antigovernment riots in October 1988, the Algerian government, long regarded as the most monolithic, single-party political system in the Arab world, felt constrained to hold multiparty elections that included the Islamic Salvation Front (FIS), North Africa's first legal Islamic political party. Islamic opposition parties had flourished when Algerian state-socialism failed to resolve its social and economic problems.

The FIS, with a national organization and an effective mosque and social welfare network, emerged as one of the strongest opposition parties. Its support included small-business owners and prosperous merchants, civil servants, university professors, physicians, lawyers, and other professionals. They constituted a new and different elite, with modern educations but a more Islamic orientation, looking for a national identity that reflected Algeria's religious and cultural heritage and a government that responded more effectively to the country's political, economic, and moral failures. Other support came from the unemployed, socially marginalized youth, called the "hittists" (those who lean against the walls), who had become fixtures on the streets and in the alleyways.

In the June 1990 municipal elections, the first multiparty election since independence from France in 1962, the FIS scored a stunning victory, capturing 54 percent of the vote, while the FLN ruling party garnered 34 percent. Even after arresting the FIS leaders and gerrymandering to redraw districts more favorably, the FLN failed to prevent an even more surprising electoral victory by the FIS in the June 1997 parliamentary elections. Amidst euphoric celebrations of Islamists within Algeria and across the Muslim world, the Algerian military intervened, forced the resignation of the President, arrested FIS leaders, imprisoned more than 10,000 in desert camps, outlawed the FIS, and seized its assets.

Threatened by the performance of the FIS, the Algerian military tightened their control on power and moved quickly to repress any significant legal opposition or political alternative through arrests and trials before special military courts, trials that were denounced by international human rights organizations. Having driven FIS leaders into exile or underground, the Algerian military had set in motion a cycle of violence and counterviolence. Originally moderate, nonviolent FIS members whose leaders had been imprisoned or exiled became an FIS militia, the AIS (Islamic Salvation Army). The result was a protracted civil war. The majority of Algerians were caught in the middle, victims of terror between a faction of hard-line military and security forces (the *éradicateurs*), who rejected dialogue and would only be justified by the eradication of Islamism, and the equally uncompromising Armed Islamic Group (GIA, Groupe Islamique Armé). The GIA, a radical extremist movement, emerged after the repression of the

FIS; its members included Arab Afghans, men who had returned from the jihad in Afghanistan, and it became one of the many currents within the FIS.[20] The military's intervention, abrogation of the FIS victory, and suppression of the FIS radicalized these battle-seasoned Afghan veterans and triggered their militant jihad. The failure of the FIS's aborted electoral victory had global implications: it was used by jihad groups against more moderate voices to argue that participation in elections is a useless strategy. They pointed to this as yet another example that even if Islamic parties prevailed in elections, authoritarian "un-Islamic" states, with support from their Western allies, would block them from coming to power peacefully.

The hard-liners prevailed in 1995 when the government refused to participate in or to recognize a summit of Algeria's major secular and Islamist leaders and political parties sponsored by the St. Egidio Catholic community in Rome. The parties' fourteen-point agreement, approved by the United States and France, a close ally of Algeria, was rejected by the military as a capitulation to the Islamists.

By the late 1990s, the number of fatalities from this protracted struggle had risen to 100,000. In 1997 and 1999, new parliamentary and presidential elections were held and a cease-fire was called between the government and the AIS, the military wing of the FIS. Parliamentary elections were marred by criticisms from UN observers and charges of massive fraud by losing parties as President (formerly General) Liamine Zeroual's National Democratic Rally won 156 of 380 seats. Although the FIS was prohibited from participating, two other Islamic parties, the Movement for Society and Peace and the Renaissance Party, won 69 and 38 seats respectively. Presidential elections in April 1999 were flawed by the last-minute withdrawal of all six opposition presidential candidates, who charged that the military had rigged the elections in favor of Abdelaziz Bouteflika, who received less than 30 percent of the votes cast by the less than 25 percent of registered voters.[21]

While the military-backed government remains in control, conditions for national reconciliation and stability remain fragile. The

military continues to dominate if not control the political process, and the GIA continues its bloody jihad. Bouteflika has maintained his refusal to lift the eight-year ban on the FIS and has
done very little to significantly strengthen civil society. Algeria
continues to be plagued by severe longstanding economic and
social problems: an official unemployment rate of 30 percent (some
put it at 50 percent), an acute housing shortage, an unresolved
national and cultural identity crisis, and a "gap between a tiny
minority of superrich and the overwhelming majority of the people
impoverished by rising prices and cuts in social benefits."[22]

The electoral performances of Islamic movements defied the
conventional wisdom that Islamists would be rejected at the polls.
Ironically, the successes of Islamic movements within the democratic process were viewed as an even more dangerous threat than
armed revolution. While many world leaders were on guard against
"other Irans," the FIS victory in Algeria raised the specter of an
Islamic movement coming to power through ballots, not bullets.
Yet, as one Algerian expert noted:

> There is now a preponderance of evidence from Algeria's last six
> years to indicate that the human suffering, environmental dev-
> astation and potential regional destabilization have been infinitely
> greater than they could have been under any imaginable scenario
> involving an Islamist regime coming to power through universal
> suffrage. It is hard to dispute that the fundamental source of con-
> flict is a denial of popular legitimacy. To portray it as cultural or
> ideological, secular or fundamentalist, is misleading and plays
> into the hands of extremists and anti-democrats alike. What is at
> stake is an increase or decrease of power and privilege.[23]

The Wahhabi Threat

Although originally associated with Saudi Arabia, Wahhabi Islam
or Wahhabism has come to be used popularly, although inaccu-
rately, as a blanket term for Islamic fundamentalism, religious

extremism, and radicalism. For this reason, some prefer the terms
Salafi or Salafiyyah movement. This has the advantage of both reflecting the activists' claim to be returning to the pristine Islam of
Muhammad and the first generation of Muslims (*salafi*, or pious
ancestors) and of indicating, more accurately, that this ultraconservative, rigid, and exclusivist worldview is common to many groups
and organizations. Saudi Arabia's Wahhabi Islam is but one strand.
Ultimately, both Wahhabi and Salafi can be misleading, as they are
used as umbrella terms that incorporate diverse ideologies and movements, medieval and modern, nonviolent and violent.

Since the late-twentieth century, the term Wahhabi has been
applied to militant movements that have taken up arms against
existing governments. This particular labeling is not all that new.
In nineteenth-century colonial India, the British labeled indig-
enous, anti-imperialist, Islamic revivalist movements, Wahhabi.
In recent years, Wahhabi Islam has been identified not only with
the Taliban and Osama bin Laden's al-Qaeda but also with Islamic
opposition movements in other areas, in particular Russia, the
Caucasus, Chechnya, Dagestan, and Central Asia.

First and foremost, Wahhabi describes Saudi Arabia's ultraconservative, puritanical brand of Islam: literalist, rigid, and exclusivist.
Presenting their version of Islam as the pristine, pure, unadulterated message, the Wahhabi seek to impose their strict beliefs and
interpretations, which are not commonly shared by other Sunni
or by Shii Muslims throughout the Muslim world.

The Wahhabi vision went international in the 1960s in response
to the threat posed by Arab nationalism and socialism. It was fueled
by petrodollars, especially the wealth from skyrocketing revenues
after the 1973 oil embargo. Saudi Arabia and other monarchies were
threatened in particular by Nasserism and in general by radical Arab
socialist governments that came to power promising a social revolution for the masses and condemning conservative Arab monarchies. Under the leadership of Prince (later King) Faisal, the Saudis
championed a pan-Islamic policy against Nasser's "secular, socialist" pan-Arabism with its ties to "atheistic communism" in the So-

viet Union and Eastern Europe. Saudi Arabia asserted its global Islamic leadership as custodian of Islam's two holiest sites and made common cause with other Muslim governments in the struggle against Nasser and his disciple, Libya's Muammar Qaddafi.

Saudi Arabia created state-financed international Islamic organizations to promote its Wahhabi-based, pan-Islamic vision and ideology. Established in 1962, the World Islamic League vigorously engaged in an energetic international dawah, preaching and propagating Wahhabi Islam to other Muslims (as well as non-Muslims), financing the building of mosques, schools, libraries, hospitals, and clinics. It trained and supported imams for mosques, distributed tens of millions of Saudi-approved translations of the Quran and religious literature. Other Gulf countries like Kuwait and the United Arab Emirates followed suit.

The Jeddah-based Organization of the Islamic Conference (OIC) was created in 1969 to promote Islamic solidarity among member states, to safeguard the holy sites of Mecca and Medina, and to support the "struggle" in Palestine and the "struggle" of all Muslim people. In the 1970s, the OIC created the Islamic Development Bank to promote the development of an Islamic banking system and finance development projects in Muslim countries. Through such organizations, the Saudi government and many wealthy Saudi businessmen have exported Wahhabi Islam to the rest of the Muslim world as well as to Europe and America.

The Saudi government also developed close ties with major Islamic movements such as the Muslim Brotherhood and the Jamaat-i-Islami. Despite significant differences, they shared a religious vision based on a return to the fundamentals of Islam and an antipathy to common enemies—Nasserism, secularism, and communism. Saudi Arabia gave asylum to Muslim Brothers such as Muhammad Qutb, the brother of Sayyid Qutb, who fled Nasser's suppression of the Brotherhood in the mid-1960s. The Saudi government and other Gulf countries provided significant funding for Islamic movements and conferences. Petrodollars became a major enabling mechanism for the movements to internationalize and spread organizationally, to translate the writings of al-Banna, Qutb, Mawdudi, and later to produce audiotapes to be distributed around the world, creating an international Islamist discourse. In addition, many Islamists from other countries, well educated and possessing needed professional and technical skills, were employed in the Gulf and could send funds back to their homelands to support mainstream and clandestine movements. Saudi funding to Islamic groups worldwide accelerated dramatically after the Iranian revolution, in order to counter the challenge from Iran's alternative revolutionary Islamic system. Iran's call and support for a global (Sunni and Shii) Islamic revolution and its funding of Shii groups in the Middle East and South Asia to counter Saudi influence threatened Saudi Arabia's Islamic leadership.

Saudi initiatives produced a rapid growth of Islamist groups and the dissemination of their worldview and fundamentalist interpretation of Islam in many countries. The Islamists' informal alliance with the Saudis and their acceptance of refuge or patronage was in fact a marriage of convenience, since many regarded the monarchy to be an un-Islamic form of government and were critical of the un-Islamic behavior and corruption of many royals.

Many of those benefiting from Saudi largesse learned that it came with a hefty price tag, the purification or eradication of local belief, practice, and culture. Particular targets for purification are Sufism and Shiism. Much as Saudi armies destroyed major Shii shrines in the nineteenth century, Saudi aid agencies have been responsible for the destruction or reconstruction of many historic mosques, libraries, Quran schools, and cemeteries in Bosnia and Kosovo because their Ottoman architecture, decorations, frescoes, and tombstones did not conform to Wahhabi iconoclastic aesthetics that regard statues, tombstones, or artwork with human representations as idolatry and polytheism. To the extent that the Taliban reflected this puritanical, militant mentality—seen in their strict ban on television and music, their insistence on the veiling and public segregation of women, their use of religious police to enforce Islamic behavior, and their destruction of Buddhist monuments—they have been labeled Wahhabi. However, Saudi and Taliban strict controls on some modern technology such as the Internet or satellite dishes have often been driven less by religious concerns than by security concerns. They certainly cannot represent a complete rejection of modern technology; Islam has not proven to be an obstacle in their use of other modern communications technology, weapons, and transport.

The influence of Wahhabi Islam on the Taliban was cultivated and reinforced through the madrasa system of Islamic schools and seminaries, many of which were set up in Pakistan after the Soviet-Afghan war. Pakistan's madrasa system has for many decades enjoyed substantial funding from Saudi Arabia and the Gulf, an important reason why the number of madrasas in Pakistan has grown from 147 in 1947 to more than 9,000 today. In the 1970s, Saudi Arabia was worried about the influence of the Left in Pakistan, epitomized by Prime Minister Zulfiqar Ali Bhutto, a Berkeley- and Oxford-trained secular socialist. However, when Bhutto needed to rebuild Pakistan after the 1971 civil war in which East Pakistan broke away to become Bangladesh, he turned to the oil-rich Arab states, appealing to their common Islamic heritage. In exchange for funding from the Gulf, Bhutto recast his socialism as Islamic socialism, introduced Islamic laws, and supported Islamic institutions and projects. The growth of madrasas increased exponentially during the rule of Bhutto's successor, General Zia ul-Haq, who seized power using the name of Islam to overthrow, try, and execute Bhutto and implement an Islamic system of government. Zia provided generous patronage to the *ulama* and embarked on an ambitious expansion of the madrasa system with generous assistance from Saudi Arabia and other Gulf states.

After the Afghan war, madrasas continued to thrive both as part of Saudi Arabia's ongoing export of its ideology and as a means to create a strong Sunni wall against Iran's export of its revolution. Governments, their religious agencies, and wealthy members of the business community pumped in large amounts of money to build and support madrasas. In Pakistan, a country of some 150

Deobandi

million with a nearly two-thirds illiteracy rate and an annual average per capita income of $450, the madrasas provided much-needed
shelter along with free education for millions of Afghans who found
refuge there as well as for Pakistanis whose state (secular) educational system had collapsed due to lack of funding.

Pakistan's Deobandi established hundreds of madrasas. The
Deobandi movement began in India in the nineteenth century as a
reformist movement that attempted to harmonize traditional or
classical Islam with modern life. Pakistan's Deobandi, however, have
increasingly espoused a more rigid and militant conservatism, forging close ideological and political ties with Saudi Arabia and with
its Wahhabi ulama. Most of Pakistan's mainstream madrasas offer a
sound classical Islamic education supplemented by a modern curriculum. Deobandi madrasas, however, are often run by religious
teachers with little knowledge of or appreciation for classical Islam
and whose chief task was promoting a militant jihadist vision and
culture. The Deobandi vision became jihadist and global in scope,
intolerant of competing or alternative Sunni beliefs, and fanatically
anti-Shii. Their madrasas trained Taliban and tens of thousands of
Pakistanis, many who went off to fight the jihad in Afghanistan.
Others became religious leaders and teachers. Some estimate that as
many as 80,000 to 100,000 Pakistanis trained in Pakistan's madrasas
and fought in Afghanistan between 1994 and 1999.[24]

The Deobandi are represented by a major religious political party
that has been active since the creation of Pakistan, the Jamiyyat-i-
Ulama-i-Islam (JUI). In 1996 the Taliban turned over training camps
for the education and training of Pakistanis and Arab militants to
JUI partisans; in July 1999, the JUI issued death threats to all Ameri-
cans in Pakistan if Pakistan extradited bin Laden to the United
States.[25] Two radical JUI offshoots, Sipah-Sahaba Pakistan (Pakistan's
Army of the Companions of the Prophet) and Lashkar-e-Jhangvi
(Jhangvi's Army), became notorious for their acts of violence and
terrorism, including the slaughter of hundreds of Shii. When
Pakistan's president Nawaz Sharif cracked down on their organi-
zations after two alleged attempts to assassinate him, their leaders

fled to asylum in Kabul. The Taliban-JUI alliance for many years benefited from significant support from Saudi Arabia and from the intelligence agency of Pakistan (the ISI).

THE WAHHABI THREAT IN
RUSSIA AND CENTRAL ASIA

While the primary use of the name Wahhabi designates Saudi Arabia's ultraconservative Islam, Wahhabi's second and more overtly political meaning is Islamic extremism, radicalism, and terrorism, with a direct connection to the Taliban and bin Laden. This usage is exploited by many governments, including those of Russia and the Central Asian republics. Governments find the label "Wahhabi" especially useful because it implies a foreign source for indigenous problems and equates their political opposition with an "Islamic threat." Local conditions and grievances (failed economies, corruption, and self-interested power holders), and local opponents (especially the younger generation who want to replace or overthrow the old, corrupt systems) are placed under the "Wahhabi Threat" umbrella and are thereby more easily dismissed or ignored.

The blanket use of Wahhabi to describe militant jihad groups obscures more than it enlightens. Organizations and movements are branded as Wahhabi because they possess common "family resemblances" such as ultraconservative, literalist, puritanical, and exclusivist religious doctrines. However, many of these movements, as well as Osama bin Laden, actually owe more to the militant ideology of Sayyid Qutb or Egyptian radical groups such as Islamic Jihad, Takfir wal Hijra, and Gamaa Islamiyya than to Saudi Arabia's Wahhabi tradition, which by and large is religiously and politically conservative rather than revolutionary. That said, Saudi policies of supporting Wahhabi-oriented schools worldwide have resulted in unintended consequences as witnessed by the Taliban–bin Laden alliance and jihadi madrasas.

Despite Soviet domination and anti-Islam policies in Central Asia, Islam remains a core component of individual and community identity and an important part of religious and cultural life.

Following the breakup of the Soviet Union, Islam has been integral to the process of nation building in post-independence Central Asia, contributing to the development of new national identities, value systems, guidelines for social and political life, and new relations with the Muslim world.

The attitude of Central Asia's post-independence ruling elite toward Islam has fluctuated since 1992. At first, governments coopted Islam and Islamic symbols as a component of national identity. However, as soon as Islam emerged as a potent political force, countries like Uzbekistan and Tajikistan moved from cooptation to repression, resulting in a devastating civil war in Tajikistan and repression and armed conflict in Uzbekistan.

Like many other parts of the Muslim world, Central Asia has in fact in recent years faced a religious revival that has affected both faith and politics. The post-independence boom in the building of mosques, schools, and libraries, the distribution of Qurans and other Islamic materials, and the activities of missionaries from other Muslim countries like Saudi Arabia, the Gulf, Pakistan, and Turkey have brought greater piety, religious divisions and conflicts, and Islamic political activism and opposition movements.

Militant groups have been especially active in Uzbekistan and Tajikistan, whose governments have been the most repressive. Most began as protest and opposition movements against governments led by former communist officials. Among the more prominent has been the Islamic Renaissance Party (IRP) in Tajikistan, the first populist Islamic movement in Central Asia, bringing together a cross-section of religious leaders, professionals, and disaffected youth to oppose communist rule. It emphasized spiritual renewal and political and economic independence. Hizb al-Tahrir al-Islami (The Islamic Liberation Party) is an import from the Middle East, with roots in Jordan and Saudi Arabia. Its global goal has been the establishment of an Islamic caliphate. Having entered Central Asia in the mid-1990s, it has worked to spread its influence first in the Farghona Valley, which borders both Tajikistan and Uzbekistan, and then throughout Central Asia.

The most feared militant group is the Islamic Movement of Uzbekistan (IMU), which has operated in Uzbekistan, Tajikistan and Kyrgyzstan. In late September 2001, the United States government declared the IMU both a foreign terrorist organization and an al-Qaeda member, reiterating the previous administration's designation of September 2000. Although the IMU grew as an opposition movement in Uzbekistan, widespread repression under President Islam Karimov's government led to violent confrontations in the 1990s. IMU leaders found refuge with and support from the Taliban and Osama bin Laden in Afghanistan. Like many other militant groups, they began as opposition within their home countries and only went to Afghanistan when in need of help and training or to set up their own training camps. Many obtained training and fought with the Taliban but then returned home to continue their domestic jihad. In 1997, after several police officers were killed in Namangan, Uzbekistan, the government arrested hundreds on charges of belonging to extremist groups.

The IMU was blamed (as were all opposition groups initially) for bombing attacks in February 1999, part of an alleged assassination attempt against President Karimov of Uzbekistan which led to a bloody crackdown. The IMU struck back with a number of highly visible attacks including kidnappings of Japanese and Americans. By the late 1990s, its ranks had been swelled with fighters from Central Asia, Chechnya, and Pakistan, reflecting the growing global jihad culture. Blocked in Uzbekistan, IMU leaders shifted their activities to Kyrgyzstan in August 1999, taking control of some areas in southern Kyrgyzstan that border Uzbekistan and Tajikstan. In November 2001, its legendary leader Juma Namangani was reported killed in heavy fighting near the northern Afghan city of Kunduz.

It is not easy to assess the presence, growth and vitality of religious extremist groups in Central Asia and the northern Caucasus. Hard data are difficult to come by because of the groups' clandestine nature but even more because of the tendencies of regimes to exaggerate terrorist groups' presence and threat.

All major conflicts or opposition movements tend to be interpreted as an Islamic threat to Russia and Central Asia via Afghanistan. The alleged Taliban-Wahhabi fundamentalist threat was the basis for a pact among Russia, Uzbekistan, and Tajikistan in 1998, designed to prevent Islam from destabilizing the region. Uzbekistan's president Islam Karimov referred to "the threat which is coming to us from the south . . . a threat of aggressive fundamentalism, aggressive extremism, and above all Wahhabism."[26] President Karimov's sweeping definition of fundamentalism as religion that interferes in politics means that mere involvement in politics, without any commitment to violence and terrorism, constitutes fundamentalism. Karimov has presented himself as the protector of Uzbekistan from Islamic fundamentalism's threat to and spread in Central Asia. Equating fundamentalism with radicalism is so pervasive that even those Russian and Central Asian observers who strive to present a balanced account tend to define any Muslim opposition to government as Islamic radicalism. Russian president Vladimir Putin provided a vivid example of the exploitation of the rhetoric of "Islamic threat" when he used the specter of Wahhabi fundamentalism and Taliban-trained mujahidin in the Caucasus to justify launching a war to reassert Russian authority over Chechnya. A veteran human rights activist who visited Grozny, the capital of Chechnya, early in the war disputed the charges, dismissing official Russian accounts as a "monstrous lie" and was equally dismissive of the claims that three hundred Afghan mujahidin fought fiercely against the Russian troops in Grozny. Visiting all the places in Grozny where the Russian government claimed there were Afghan mujahidin, he found no evidence of their presence.

Chechnya's president Aslan Maskhadov also used the threat of Wahhabism to crack down on domestic political opposition. In an October 1998 speech before the Congress of the Chechen People, President Maskhadov repudiated Wahhabism as an unwelcome import preached in Chechnya by foreigners, alien to Chechnya's traditional Islam, and responsible for acts of violence.

The actual size and threat of radical Wahhabi-inspired move-ments is hotly contested and difficult to verify. Russian and Cen-tral Asian governments charge that Wahhabis trained at bases in countries such as Afghanistan, Pakistan, and Sudan infiltrate mosques, Islamic teaching centers, and charitable organizations to indoctrinate and recruit. Wahhabi-inspired groups are accused of waging a jihad of violence and terrorism, suicide bombings, and attacks on marketplaces, schools, offices, and places of wor-ship that result in civilian casualties, and of using drug money to finance terrorist campaigns. Drug traffic is believed to have fi-nanced the developing global terrorist networks, the purchase of weapons and supplies, and the creation of social welfare organiza-tions under the guise of mainstream Islamic activism.

Religious leaders in countries that claim Wahhabi influence of-ten criticize Wahhabism for challenging their religious authority and rejecting traditional and local Islamic beliefs and practices. They say Wahhabism breaks one of the cardinal rules of warfare in Islam—that Muslims should not fight other Muslims. The Wahhabi, their critics charge, get around this by dividing the world strictly into believers and nonbelievers who must be fought.

Although governments have clearly exaggerated the threat for their own purposes, Wahhabi religious ideology has found fertile soil in societies where economic development is poor and moral and political decay are rampant. Its claim that returning to a purer, more moral way of life will restore law and order can be very at-tractive to those suffering from chronic poverty and political re-pression. The Wahhabi compare very favorably in educational levels to local religious leaders in Central Asia; Soviet policy and persecution had a devastating impact on the recruitment and train-ing of Islamic scholars. The younger generation, struggling in au-thoritarian states with a scarcity of jobs and housing, is attracted to Wahhabism as a means to reject the status quo (the Soviet-era communist elite culture) in favor of an apparently more indig-enous source of identity, nationalism, and values. Prosperous mer-chants and others are sometimes attracted by the Wahhabi emphasis on law and traditional morality against individualism, liberalism, and mass culture.

The powerful symbolism and revolutionary meaning of jihad dominates modern Muslim politics to an extent unparalleled in history. Islamic movements and organizations have become primary vehicles for its spread and implementation. If many thought that Iran's revolution was a singular event, succeeding decades have demonstrated the force and pervasiveness of an Islamic activism that has moved from the periphery to the center of Muslim societies. Islamic experiments in Egypt, Palestine, Algeria. and Central Asia have also revealed the many faces and voices of political Islam and the diverse understandings of jihad. Peaceful or violent, all share a common commitment to an Islamic revolution, a jihad or struggle to implement an Islamic order or government.

The "armies of God" have passed through several stages, becoming ever more global in outreach. Initially, most groups focused on their own countries. They were primarily Egyptian, Algerian, or Tunisian movements. The Afghan jihad against Soviet occupation marked a turning point as Muslims in record numbers traveled to Afghanistan to join in the jihad against oppression of Muslims. The experience and success of that jihad created a new, more global jihad sentiment and culture embodied in Arab Afghans—Arabs and other Muslims who had fought in Afghanistan—and in a sense of solidarity, which subsequently brought Muslims from various parts of the world to participate in jihads in Bosnia, Kosovo, Kashmir, Central Asia, and Chechnya. Some few have become mercenaries in the more radicalized efforts not just to defend Muslims against oppression, but to overthrow world powers believed responsible for their suffering, through terrorist strategies. Jihad today has thus become the evocative symbol and rallying cry for mobilization in holy and unholy wars, in wars of resistance and liberation as well as in global terrorism.

Jihads expressing a "Rage for God" have increased and have spread. From Algeria and Egypt to Afghanistan and Central Asia, governments, often authoritarian, found themselves under siege in the 1990s. Afghanistan and Pakistan became primary centers for the globalization of jihad and the culture of jihad through networks of madrasas and training camps. The Taliban and al-Qaeda provided refuge and training for militants, many of whom have had to flee their home countries, from Egypt, Algeria, Yemen, Saudi Arabia, Malaysia, Thailand, the Philippines, Uzbekistan, Tajikistan, Kyrgyzstan, Chechnya, as well as Uighurs from the Xinjiang province in China. A hitherto little-noted part of the world spawned a Taliban–al-Qaeda alliance that became the base for a network of organizations and cells from across the Muslim world that hijacked Islam, indiscriminately slaughtering non-Muslims and Muslims alike.

September 11, 2001, marked a turning point, signaling the ability of terrorists to land a devastating strike on its primary international target, the United States, at home. In the mid-1990s both Paris and New York had been attacked by terrorists. North American and European countries had been monitoring terrorists and potential terrorist groups. However, few had anticipated so massive an attack, a diabolical act that carried out bin Laden's declaration of war and marked the global expansion of al-Qaeda's unholy war of terror to the West.

Having routed the Taliban and al-Qaeda in Afghanistan, where do we go from here? September 11 has resurrected old questions, giving them a new urgency: Is there a clash of civilizations between Islam and the West? Why do they hate us? Is there a direct connection between Islam, anti-Americanism, and global terrorism? Are Islam and modernity incompatible? We now turn to these and other issues that will determine all of our futures.

4

Where Do We Go from Here?

In the aftermath of September 11, 2001, as we ask, Why did this happen?, government officials, pundits, and experts bombard us with a litany of certitudes: bin Laden and al-Qaeda are religious fanatics; this is proof positive of a clash of civilizations between Islam and the West; the terrorists hate our American way of life—our power, prosperity, and freedoms; Islam is incompatible with modernity and democracy; violence and terrorism are integral to Muslim belief and practice; we are now facing a global jihad against the West.

Making Sense of Islam and the Muslim World

Several decades ago, a Muslim ambassador to the United Nations wrote a short book, *Islam: The Misunderstood Religion*. At that time, given the invisibility of Muslims on the American landscape and in our educational curriculum, the author's choice of title seemed appropriate. Today, we know more, but much of our knowledge has been gained through headline events, from the Iranian Revolution to September 11. When the Iranian Revolution occurred in 1978, despite the fact that Islam was the second largest of the world's religions, encompassing more than fifty countries, during the hostage crisis the *Today Show* coanchor found it necessary to interrupt his reading of the news to give Americans a brief background on Islam. It was very brief: Islam is the second largest world religion; it has a scripture called the Quran and a prophet named

Muhammad. This most basic information was deemed necessary for viewers in one of the world's most advanced and educated nations! At the same time, most Americans would have expected that any educated person in the world would recognize the terms Judaism, Christianity, and Bible and the names Moses and Jesus.

Our knowledge of the Islam of the vast majority of Muslims and its connection to the Judeo-Christian tradition remains minimal or nonexistent. While Christians today have been raised to appreciate family resemblances with Judaism and to speak of a Judeo-Christian tradition, at best Islam has been presented as a foreign, non-Western religion, often grouped with Hinduism and Buddhism. The fact that Islam, like Judaism and Christianity, has its origins in the Middle East, that it represents belief in heaven, hell, and the Day of Judgment, and venerates prophets from the Old and New Testaments including Abraham, Moses, and Jesus is unknown to the vast majority of non-Muslims.

How many Jews and Christians know that they join Muslims as "Children of Abraham," that Muslims believe that they are the religious descendants of Ismail, the first-born son of Abraham and his servant Hagar? How many know that the Quran acknowledges, "We believe what you believe, your God and our God is one" (29:46)? Yet, while Yahweh is generally known to be the Hebrew name for the God of the Bible, Allah is often still regarded as the proper name of an alien God rather than the Arabic word for God, used by Arab Christians as well as Muslims when they pray.

Christians have come to know and value their Jewish neighbors because of decades of living together and the active efforts of many to establish linkages, in particular an awareness of a shared religious heritage, a Judeo-Christian tradition, and the scourge of anti-Semitism which culminated in the Holocaust. Muslims have gone from the unknown "other" or the product of oriental stereotypes of Arabian Nights—sheiks and harems and flying carpets—to masked, armed hijackers and hostage takers. While many in the United States have come to appreciate the historic persecution and victimhood of Jews and understand the creation of Israel, American textbooks

and media in past years had precious little to say about the Palestinian side of the story: the Israeli occupation of Palestine, the hundreds of thousands of refugees and generations raised in refugee
camps, strangers in their homeland. The Palestinian-Israeli conflict
is a tragedy for two peoples with mutual claims, entitlement, and
histories of suffering, violence, and terrorism.

Despite increased coverage and awareness of Islam, the necessity of responding to Osama bin Laden and al-Qaeda forced many
policymakers, commentators, the media, and the general public
to realize how little they really knew about a major religion and
strategic part of the world. As one Senate leader confessed, "I know
a lot about many things but nothing about Islam and the Muslim
world—and neither do most of my colleagues!" While many are
sincere in their desire to know more, others epitomize the saying:
"My mind's made up, don't confuse me with the facts!" At one
level, it is easy to portray September 11 as the latest phase in a
historic battle between Islam and the West, as militant Islam has
now gone global. However, this dangerous oversimplification mim-
ics the distorted, polarized worldview and message of the bin
Ladens of the world. If we start out by presuming that the other is
completely different, we can find whatever we are looking for.

As we move forward in the twenty-first century, a key reality to
keep in mind is that Islam is the second largest and fastest growing religion not only out there, but also in Europe and America.
Improving our understanding of the faith of our fellow citizens
and neighbors will require that we look at Muslims with new eyes
and judge Islam by the totality and teachings of the faith, not just
the beliefs and actions of a radical few.

An important first step is to guard against judging Islam by a
double standard. When we approach Judaism or Christianity or
understand our own faith, we operate differently. We interpret the
violent, bloody texts in the Bible in their historical contexts. We
explain the history of violence, slaughter, and imperialism in the
name of Judaism or Christianity in terms of the times and context, or we condemn such acts as aberrations or extremist. The

Christianity that inspired Archbishop Desmond Tutu and many others in the struggle against apartheid in South Africa has also been claimed as the religion of Afrikaaners, the faith of American slave owners and their pastors on the one hand and Martin Luther King, Jr., on the other. The Judaism of members of the Jewish Defense League or of the young assassin of Yitzak Rabin is the transcendent, transforming faith of the prophets of Israel and countless pious Jews through the ages. Most people readily recognize distinctions between those who are true examples of faith and those who hijack the faith, as well as between the mainstream and extremists on the fringe.

Looking to the future, as we become more familiar with Islam as a major world religion and the soon-to-be second largest faith in America, the idea of a Judeo-Christian-Islamic religious tradition will become more internalized. We will recognize that each faith represents shared beliefs and values as well as distinctive differences. Points of conflict are one part of the story but so are religious and cultural cooperation and co-existence, past and present. Theological similarities and competing interests put Christianity and Islam, the West and the Muslim world on an early collision course. Both of these major world religions had a universal message and mission, the belief that their covenant with God was the final and complete fulfillment of God's earlier revelation to a previous community that had gone astray. We don't often remember that while Christendom experienced Islam's expansion as a threat to its hegemony, Islam proved more tolerant and provided greater religious freedom for Jews and indigenous Christians, and it eliminated the persecution of heretics for which imperial Christianity was noted:

> By an exquisite irony, Islam reduced the status of Christians to that which the Christians had earlier thrust upon the Jews, with one difference. The reduction in Christian status was merely juridical; it was unaccompanied by either systematic persecution or a bloodlust; and generally, though not everywhere and at all times, unmarred by vexatious behavior.[1]

As it becomes more commonplace to work with Muslim colleagues and live with Muslim neighbors, it will be even more important to know about events in our history that have been overlooked. Many do not know that the development of imperial Islam and Jewish-Christian-Islamic coexistence produced a rich Islamic civilization and a religious and cultural synthesis and exchange. With significant assistance from Christian and Jewish subjects, Muslims collected the great books of science, medicine, and philosophy from the West and the East and translated them into Arabic from Greek, Latin, Persian, Coptic, Syriac, and Sanskrit. The age of translation was followed by a period of great creativity as a new generation of Muslim thinkers and scientists made their own contributions to learning: in philosophy, medicine, chemistry, astronomy, algebra, optics, art, and architecture. Then the cultural traffic pattern was again reversed when Europeans, emerging from the Dark Ages, turned to Muslim centers of learning to regain their lost heritage and to learn from Muslim advances. These historical dynamics should be kept in mind when we are tempted to view Islam and Muslims as aliens with whom we have nothing in common.

Muslims are now in a position similar to other ethnic and religious groups in their relationship to modernity. In the not too distant past, many non-WASP (White Anglo-Saxon Protestant) immigrants to America (Irish, Italian, Polish, etc.) were viewed as the other and not accepted as equals. My friends and I grew up very conscious that Catholic ethnics were seen as laborers but hardly material for Ivy League schools and corporate leadership. Years later, after I had endured a dinner party of Italian jokes and speculation that one of our prosperous neighbors must be mafia, a friend said to me, "Remember John, to them, you're not Italian, you have a Ph.D."

Those who believe that Arab or Muslim culture is inherently incompatible with modernization need to reflect on Western attitudes toward non-Western societies in the recent past. Only a few decades ago, if you received a gift that was stamped "made in Japan" you knew you had an inferior product, a cheap imitation of goods from Paris, London, or New York. Westerners all knew that the Japanese as well as other Asian civilizations or cultures were somehow Third World, that they lacked Western knowledge, creativity, or work ethic. History now tells a different story. Today, Lexus competes head to head with Mercedes and Jaguar, and Toyota and Honda outsell American brand-name cars.

Religions like societies change and develop. Similarly, civilizations are not monolithic and static. New ideas began in one civilization—Chinese, European, or Islamic—and then spread, were appropriated, and further developed by others. Science, technology, philosophy, and morality ultimately have no fixed boundaries. They are not the preserve of any single people, civilization, or religion. Today, in a reverse process, we see the transfer of science and technology and the spread of modern notions of democratization and pluralism from the West to the Muslim world and beyond. Globalization has also resulted in collaborative efforts in modern science. Increasing numbers of Muslims are trained in the sciences, many in the best universities of America and Europe, and work in the West or in the Muslim world with multinational corporations.

To ask whether Islam is compatible with Western civilization is to ignore past and present exchanges and cross-fertilizations. It also privileges Western civilization as the universal norm and implies that civilizations are mutually exclusive and diametrically opposed. In fact civilizations and cultures overlap; they have similarities and differences. What are the essentials of Western civilization—reason, individualism, science, democracy, human rights, pluralism, secularism, capitalism? However different and diverse, most Muslims, like most people on this planet, rely on reason, science, and technology, desire greater political participation and freedom, and seek economic advancement and prosperity. At the same time, like conservative Christians and Jews, many Muslims believe that religion is under siege from secular liberalism first and foremost within their own societies.

Historically, over many decades, Christianity and Judaism made their own accommodations with modernity. The process produced further divisions and differences among them: liberal, fundamentalist, and evangelical Protestantism; orthodox, conservative, reform, and reconstructionist Judaism; orthodox or traditionalist and liberal Catholics. Catholicism was for some time a distant third to Protestantism and Judaism in dealing with modernity. Until the second Vatican Council in the 1960s, pontiffs had condemned much of modernity—including modern biblical criticism, democracy, pluralism, and women's rights. Despite change, all of the children of Abraham continue to struggle with modernity. The global resurgence of religion is driven by a desire of many well-educated believers of different faiths to rethink and reevaluate the relationship of religion to modernity. Many question the excesses of modernity, trying to reassert a faith and values that limit the unbridled use of science and technology, the sexual freedoms that weaken family life, the emphasis on individual rights rather than on responsibilities, or the accumulation and maldistribution of wealth.

Muslims struggle with many of the same questions and issues of modernity faced by the West but with distinctive differences. They have not had the luxury of time, the centuries the West had had to develop and accommodate modernity. Despite the violence we see today, however, the Muslim encounter with modernity has occurred without anywhere near the West's high cost of bloody wars (for example, the French and American revolutions, the American Civil War, and the wars of the Reformation). Furthermore, many Muslim countries face serious political and economic handicaps. The Muslim world's dominance by the West and marginalization as a world power, which has challenged Islam's relevance to modern life, and its lack of control over the forces of development have been daunting barriers to progress. When in power, Muslim empires were open and pluralistic in engaging foreign cultures and civilizations. When in charge of the process, there was little fear of loss of identity, faith, and pride. In defeat, Muslims faced questions of identity as well as faith: Does being modern mean our only option is to talk, dress, think, live and act like them? How would Americans or Europeans respond if modernization and globalization meant domination by Japan, politically, economically, militarily, linguistically, and culturally? The closest example we have in the West is perhaps the wrenching adjustment former European empires like England and France have had to make to American international ascendance .

Religion, Modernization, and Development

Modernization or development theory in the mid twentieth century could be summarized by the adage: "Every day in every way, things are and will continue to get more and more modern and secular," which meant better and better. It was taken for granted that modernizing meant the progressive westernization and secularization of a society: politically, economically, legally, and educationally.[2] The choice faced by developing countries such as those in the Muslim world seemed to be between the polar dichotomies of tradition and modernity, Mecca and mechanization. Christianity encountered the same secularizing trends. Theologians spoke of demythologizing the scriptures, of a secular gospel for the modern age, of the triumph of the secular city (as opposed to Augustine's City of God), and of a "death of God theology."[3] Religious faith was at best supposed to be a private matter. In academia, the degree of one's intellectual sophistication and objectivity was judged according to a secular liberalism and relativism that seemed antithetical to religion. In politics, while church or synagogue membership was recognized as useful, most candidates avoided discussing their faith or religious issues in public.

The global resurgence of religion in the late twentieth century has led presidents, corporate leaders, and athletes to do a wide turnaround, freely discussing their faith and morality in the media. Congressional prayer breakfasts and prayer groups of athletes, lawyers, and physicians are commonplace. A few decades ago, it was important for a president to have a church to attend on major holidays but not to profess his faith in public. Now presidents from Jimmy Carter to George Walker Bush publicly profess that they are "born again," and presidential and congressional candidates make no secret of their religious beliefs or the fact that some are clergy. In the 2000 presidential campaign, George W. Bush comfortably cited Jesus as his hero, and Senator Joseph Lieberman, an orthodox Jew, frequently appealed to God in his speeches.

Moreover, the global religious resurgence has been especially evident in international politics. Religion, nationalism, and ethnicity have proven to be enduring sources of identity and conflict from Somalia and Rwanda to Lebanon, Bosnia, Kosovo, Kashmir, India, and Sri Lanka.

These changes in the public profile of religion have challenged and discredited the secular expectations of modernization models. The prominent sociologist of religion Peter L. Berger, a key figure in articulating secularization theory, has also changed his mind, declaring that "a whole body of literature by historians and social scientists loosely labeled 'secularization theory' is essentially mistaken."[4] Indeed, much is now made of a "desecularization of society" as religion is recognized as an increasingly key factor in domestic, transnational, and international relations.

An Inevitable Clash of Civilizations?

In a controversial 1993 article, "The Clash of Civilizations?," Samuel P. Huntington warned that a "clash of civilizations will dominate global politics"[5] and precipitated a heated worldwide debate among scholars, political leaders, commentators, and the media. Many in the Muslim world saw this important American academic and opinion maker, who had also held a prominent position in government, as articulating what they always thought was the West's attitude toward Islam. If some academics and government officials were quick to distance themselves from Huntington's position, the sales of his subsequent book, its translation into many languages, and the sheer number of international conferences and publications that addressed the question demonstrated that there was "a market for clash." The attacks of September 11 and the global threat of Osama bin Laden and al-Qaeda have resurrected a knee-jerk response of "the clash of civilizations" for an easy answer to the question, Why do they hate us?

Huntington, like many others today, played into old stereotypes by characterizing Islam and the West as age-old enemies—"Conflict along the fault line between Western and Islamic civilizations has been going on for 1300 years"[6]—and by citing Islam's resistance to secular Western models as necessarily hostile to human rights and progress—"Western ideas of individualism, liberalism, constitutionalism, human rights, equality, liberty, the rule of law, democracy, free markets, the separation of church and state, often have little resonance in Islamic [and other] . . . cultures." [7]

In his 1997 follow-up book, Huntington concluded that "Islam's borders are bloody and so are its innards."[8] His blanket condemnation went beyond Islamic fundamentalism to Islam itself: "The underlying problem for the West is not Islamic fundamentalism. It is Islam, a different civilization whose people are convinced of the superiority of their culture, and are obsessed with the inferiority of their power."[9] Though Huntington has now significantly refined his position, September 11 unleashed new, updated versions as many found it more expedient to fall back on convenient stereotypes of a monolithic Islam and historic clash of civilizations rather than to examine the complex causes of terrorism.

Ironically, the clash of cultures appears as evident with reference to our allies in the Muslim world as with our enemies. Whatever the common economic and political interests, primarily centered on oil, the contrasts between Saudi Arabia and the United States are stark. The religious and cultural traditions of America's long-time ally—religiously puritanical and exclusivist worldview, sexually segregated society, lack of political parties and elections, punishment of theft by amputation, prohibition of building churches or practicing Christianity—as well as the fact that bin Laden and so many of the hijackers of September 11 were Saudi, indicate that we live in two different worlds. Similarly, the declared war of religious extremists and terrorists against entrenched

Muslim governments and the West—all in the name of Islam—
seems to underscore the incompatibility of Islam and democracy.
However, while the actions of extremist groups and of authoritarian governments, religious and nonreligious, reinforce this perception of a cultural clash, the facts on the ground present a more
complex picture.

Neither the Muslim world nor the West is monolithic. Common sources of identity (language, faith, history, culture) yield
when national or regional interests are at stake. While some Muslims have achieved a transient unity in the face of a common enemy, as in the Iranian Revolution, their solidarity quickly dissipates
once danger subsides and competing interests again prevail. The
evidence that there is no monolithic Islam is abundant. The inability of Arab nationalism/socialism, Saudi Arabia's pan-Islam, or
Iran's Islamic Republic revolution to unite and mobilize the Arab
and Muslim worlds, the competition and conflict between countries like Egypt, Libya, Sudan, and Saudi Arabia, the disintegration
of the Arab (Iraq and the Gulf states) coalition against Iran after
the Iran-Iraq war, and the subsequent Iraqi invasion of Kuwait
and divisions in the Muslim world evident in the 1991 Gulf war
are but a few examples. As James Piscatori observed, "The problem
with assuming a unified response is that it conceals the reality of
. . . entrenched national differences and national interests among
Muslims."[10] The failure of Osama bin Laden , like Saddam Hussein
and Khomeini before him, to effectively mobilize the Islamic world
in his unholy war, despite his global terrorist network, is a reminder
that Muslims, like every global religious community, are indeed
diverse. Moreover, as Islamic history makes abundantly clear, mainstream Islam, in law and theology as well as in practice, in the end
has always rejected or marginalized extremists and terrorists from
the Kharijites and Assassins to contemporary radical movements
such as al-Qaeda.

In responding to the attacks of September 11, some charged that
the clash of civilizations revolved around conflict with our modern
Western way of life, with, for example, democracy, women's rights,

and capitalism. In fact, capitalism exists in the Muslim world both in home-grown forms as well as Western-inspired versions. The issue for many in the Muslim world is not capitalism but the dangers of Western economic hegemony and its side effects. In fact, Islam does not have any problem with many of the essentials of Western capitalism. It is important to recall that Muhammad's early followers included prosperous merchants. He himself engaged in financial and commercial transactions to make a living. The Quran, *hadith* (traditions about what the Prophet said and did), and Muslim historical experience affirm the right to private property and trade and commerce. As Maxime Rodinson, a French scholar and Marxist, wrote in his *Islam and Capitalism*: "Economic activity, the search for profit, trade, and consequently, production for the market, are looked upon with no less favor by Muslim tradition than by the Koran itself."[11] Mosques throughout the world, such as the Umayyad mosque in Damascus and the magnificent mosques of old Cairo and Teheran, are often adjoined by magnificent bazaars. Traders and businessmen were among the most successful sectors in society and were responsible for the spread of their faith.

Perhaps the best response to those who ask whether Islam and capitalism are compatible is to look at the lives of the millions of Muslims who live and work in our midst in America and Europe. Many have come here to enjoy freedom and the opportunities offered by our economic and political systems. Like other religious and ethnic minorities before them, they too struggle with issues of identity and assimilation but not with their desire to enjoy the best that we represent.

Another frequently cited issue, used to demonstrate a civilizational clash, is Islam's treatment of women. If there is one image used to depict Islam and Muslims, it is that of oppressed, gender-segregated women, covered by the veil. Rather than considering that women's status might be caused by the continued strength of patriarchy, Islam is presumed to be particularly misogynist. Gender in Islam remains a highly charged issue today at the popular level and among scholars and religious leaders. If some blame Islam for the oppression of women, others see it as a beacon of light and reform. Still others insist that the status and role of women in Muslim societies should be attributed primarily to socioeconomic forces rather than to religious belief. The explanations are as diverse as the Muslim world itself.[12] Thus, charting the progress or regression of women, whether under secular or religious governments, is a tricky task. Often we compare our "ideal" to selected "realities" in other religions and cultures, overlooking the diversity that exists within them.

For several decades women in Muslim societies have been part of the dialectics of change, an erratic, vacillating, and contradictory process that creates many anomalies. In Egypt, long regarded as one of the most modernizing of Muslim states, women cannot serve as judges, and yet in Morocco more than 20 percent of judges are women. Women in Egypt and Malaysia have access to the best education and hold responsible professional positions in virtually every sector. Yet, like women in most Muslim societies, they need a male family member's permission to travel. Women in Saudi Arabia own much of the real estate in Riyadh and Jeddah, can own businesses but cannot drive a car, are sexually segregated, and restricted to "appropriate" professions. In nearby Kuwait, women function in society, hold responsible positions in many areas, but have not been able to get the vote. In Iran, where they must wear the chador in public, women constitute the majority in universities, hold professional positions, serve in Parliament, and there is a female vice president in the Islamic republic. Though Pakistani women can vote, serve as ambassadors and as prime minister, they, particularly the poor and powerless, also suffer under Islamic laws enacted by General Zia ul-Haq and still in force. In Afghanistan, the Taliban in the name of Islam forced professional women to give up their jobs and prohibited girls from attending school.

Critics charge that fundamentalists, religious extremists, want to drive modern Muslim societies back to a medieval past. Feminist organizations from Algeria to Malaysia warn that Islamist power-sharing would reverse the educational and social gains of the post-independence period, remove women from public life, and again restrict their roles solely to that of wife and mother.

For those who wish to implement a more Islamic order, reforms affecting women and the family provide a quick fix, legitimated in religious tradition and easy to apply. Affirming the centrality of the family in Islam is both an act of piety and of political expediency. The Muslim family has long been regarded as the nucleus of the Islamic community, its identity, piety, and strength. Women as wives and mothers have played a pivotal role in the upbringing, education, and training of their families. If westernized reforms seemed to threaten the identity and values of family life, reestablishing its Islamic roots through the Islamization of the family can become the panacea. Formulating and implementing an Islamic state or returning to the use of Islamic law (*Shariah*) in politics, business, and economics has proved difficult, and so many activists have found it easier to focus on women and the family.

Viewed as culture bearers, women have been put at the center of the wars of religious and cultural identity being fought in many Muslim countries today. Sometimes they are agents of change but often they are the victims. Throughout the twentieth century, regimes have used women's bodies to prove their modern orientation and identity. Reza Shah Pahlavi in Iran, Attaturk in Turkey, and Bourghiba in Tunisia banned or discouraged veiling and encouraged Western dress as a sign of modernity. The abolition of the veil in 1936 by Reza Shah Pahlavi has often been celebrated as a major step toward women's emancipation. However, this reform chiefly benefited upper-class elite women. For many middle- and lower-class Iranian women, the forcible removal of the veil was traumatic. In addition, despite the shah's modernizing symbols, the regime did not substantially change patriarchal values and attitudes (its own or those of the religious establishment): "I felt no matter what class they belonged to, women were considered as dolls and objects by their male colleagues."[13]

If many associate the veil with the oppression of women, others regard veiling as an authentic practice that preserves the dignity, freedom, and modesty of women, enabling them to act and to be treated in terms of who they are and not how they look. Since the 1970s, a significant number of modern women from Cairo to Jakarta have turned or returned to wearing Islamic dress. Often this is a voluntary movement led by young, urban, middle-class women, who are well educated and work in every sector of society. In many cases, the process is distinctly modern, with new fashions and styles encompassing new understandings of the status and role of women. Such women are not passive victims of male-imposed mores but active agents for change. Some who wear Islamic dress believe that they are better able to function as active, self-directed, independent subjects, commanding respect, acknowledged and treated as persons rather than (sex) objects. Islamic dress is also used as a sign of protest and liberation. It has developed political overtones, becoming a source of national pride as well as resistance to Western (cultural as well as political) dominance and to authoritarian regimes.

A new source of women's empowerment today has become active participation in the mosque and use of Islam's tradition to reclaim their rights in Islam. Reformers today emphasize that just as women during the time of the Prophet prayed in the mosque, so too today they actively exercise that right. In the centuries after the death of Muhammad, women played a small but significant role as transmitters of hadith (prophetic traditions) and in the development of Sufism (Islamic mysticism). Gradually, however, women's religious role and practice, particularly their access to education and the mosque, were severely restricted. Male religious scholars cited a variety of reasons, from moral degeneration in society to women's bringing temptation and social discord, to restrict both their presence in public life and their access to education and the mosque.[14]

Today, in many Muslim countries and communities, particularly those that have been regarded as among the more modernized, such as Egypt, Jordan, Malaysia, and in the United States, women lead and participate in Quran study and recitation groups as well as in mosque-based educational and social services. In countries such as Iran, women serve as prayer leaders (imams) for congregational prayers; however, they are only permitted to lead groups of women. Female reformers look to early Islam for examples of women noted for their learning, leadership, and piety to strengthen the rationales for women's contemporary role in public activities. Strong, public female figures during the Prophet's time include Khadija, Muhammad's first wife of twenty-five years, who owned her own business, in which Muhammad had been employed, and played a formative and significant role in the birth of the Muslim community. After Khadija's death, Muhammad's wife Aisha was very prominent as a major source of religious knowledge, an authority in history, medicine, and rhetoric.[15]

Though patriarchy, legitimated in the past by religion, remains very much alive as an ideology and value system, in many Muslim countries it is progressively challenged by women in the name of religion as well as for economic realities. Rather than breaking with tradition, female reformers argue that their religious activism today reclaims an ideal forgotten by later generations. As a result of this new approach, increasing numbers of women have an alternative model that enables them to broaden their expectations both inside and outside the home.

Voices of Reform and Dialogue

Because acts of violence and terrorism grab the headlines, we seem to know a lot more about Islamic advocates of a "clash," the militant jihadists, than about those who are working toward a peaceful revolution and civilizational dialogue. Today, Islam's encounter with the West and the need for Islamic reform are being addressed by intellectuals, religious leaders, and activists alike. Like the Islamic modernist movements in the late nineteenth and early twentieth centuries and later the Islamic (fundamentalist) movements of the Muslim Brotherhood and the Jamaat-i-Islami, today's Islamically oriented intellectuals and activists continue the process of Islamic modernization and reform. However, today's reformers represent a creative new stage in that they not only reformulate Islam conceptually but also implement their ideas through their positions in government and the public arena.

Three remarkable examples reflect the diverse voices of Islamic reform and civilizational dialogue that can be heard from the Middle East to Asia.[16] Active as intellectuals and politicians, Anwar Ibrahim, former deputy prime minister of Malaysia, Mohammad Khatami, president of the Islamic Republic of Iran, and Abdurrahman Wahid, former president of Indonesia, have played important roles in defining the terms for an intercivilizational dialogue, rather than a clash of civilizations. At the same time, each takes a position that is uniquely different from the West's, reflective of his own culture and political environment. Though all three object to concepts of development that presume the desirability of Western secularization for Muslim societies, they recognize the strengths and weaknesses of Western-style modernity. Thus, they advocate an active two-way dialogue among civilizations, especially between Islam and the West.

ANWAR IBRAHIM: GLOBAL *CONVIVENCIA*

When Anwar Ibrahim, sometimes called "Malaysia's own Islamic zealot," joined the government of Prime Minister Mahathir Mohammed in 1980, he stunned friends and foes alike.[17] Nevertheless, he showed that he could succeed in both worlds, rapidly evolving from a charismatic opposition leader to deputy prime minister and finance minister. Ibrahim worked effectively with diverse political forces and navigated Malaysia's complex multireligious (Muslim, Christian, Hindu, Buddhist) and multiethnic (Malay, Chinese, Indian) society. He had impressed many at home and abroad with his ability to bridge religions and cultures and to work effectively to achieve common goals. He had earned the reputation of "an unabashed globalist well suited to the modern world of markets and media"[18] and a "liberal."[19] Eighteen years later, he would be tried and convicted on politically inspired charges, an action condemned internationally by many political and religious leaders and human rights organizations. He remains, although in prison, a significant voice on issues of sociopolitical and economic development, advocating pluralism in multireligious societies and intercivilizational dialogue as the only alternative to a deadly clash of civilizations.

A pragmatic man of politics as well as of faith, Ibrahim argued that both Marxist and Western models of secular materialism had failed. "Marxism . . . severs man from his moorings in faith. . . . There was no place for ethics, morality or spirituality,"[20] and the West also rejects "any reference to moral and ethical considerations. Cultural preservation is regarded as retrogressive in the march for development."[21]

In contrast to more conservative Islamist groups that called for a return Islamic law, Ibrahim said,

> [Southeast Asian Muslims] would rather strive to improve the welfare of the women and children in their midst than spend their days elaborately defining the nature and institutions of the ideal Islamic state. They do not believe it makes one less a Muslim to promote economic growth, to master the information revolution and to demand justice for women.[22]

Anwar Ibrahim's Islam is a dynamic, developing tradition that responds to diverse times and places. He rejected the conservative imitation (*taqlid*) of the past in favor of independent analysis and reinterpretation (*ijtihad*), believing that Islam is "a pragmatic religion whose real strength and dynamism was in its ongoing revitalization. . . ."[23] A strong proponent of East-West dialogue, he believes Islam is also inclusive, and as in the past, so too today Islam should be open to all cultures.

Pluralism and tolerance based upon mutual respect and understanding are cornerstones of Anwar Ibrahim's vision of a civilizational dialogue or *convivencia*, that has deep roots in medieval Islamic history. *Convivencia* (living together) alludes to the spirit of Roger II's twelfth-century Sicily and Muslim rule in the Iberian Peninsula in centers like Toledo, Cordoba, and Granada. In Iberia, Christians, Muslims, and Jews lived together in a context of social intercourse and cultural exchange. It was a time of prosperity and achievement; the arts, literature, poetry, astronomy, and medicine flourished. Many Christians became known as Mozarabs because of the extent to which they adopted elements of Arab dress, culture, and language, including Arabic names. Some Christian scholars wrote in Arabic instead of Latin.

Ibrahim finds the roots of *convivencia* supported both in Islamic history and in the Quran, as illustrated by the verse, "Oh mankind! Verily we have created you all from a male and a female, and have made you into nations and tribes that you may come to know one another" (49:13).[24]

Convivencia, for Ibrahim, is an Islamic form of pluralism, a vision quite different from the typical Islamist programs that make a place for non-Muslims in a traditionally conceived Islamic society. It is based on the primacy of social and economic justice and equality, recognized as fundamental to other religions as well as Islam. This pluralist vision is the foundation for his call for civilizational dialogue:

> For us, the divine imperative as expressed in the Qur'an is unambiguous. Humanity has been created to form tribes, races and nations, whose differences in physical characteristics, languages and modes of thought are but the means for the purpose of *lita'arafu*—"getting to know one another."[25]

Ibrahim appreciated the urgency of diffusing global confrontations, stressing that *convivencia* is a necessity for progress. However, it must be an encounter among equals.[26] Old Western imperialist attitudes of their "civilizing mission" as well as fundamentalist rejections of the enemy West threaten human survival.

MOHAMMAD KHATAMI:
DIALOGUE OF CIVILIZATIONS

For more than twenty years America and Iran were locked in a cycle of "mutual satanization." Memories of the Iranian revolution, American diplomats held hostage, Iran's ambitious attempts to export its revolution, and Ayatollah Khomeini's *fatwa* condemning to death British author Salman Rushdie for his book *The Satanic Verses* made Iran the epitome of an Islamic global threat.

In August 1997, eighteen years after the Iranian revolution had stunned the world, the newly elected president of the Islamic Republic surprised the international community in his inaugural address. Mohammad Khatami called for a dialogue of civilizations, "in our world, dialogue among civilizations is an absolute imperative."[27] The president of a country that America labeled terrorist became one of the major advocates for a new policy debate within Iran and within the global community about the clash of civilizations.

The new climate was dramatically conveyed to the world in a televised CNN interview with Christiane Amanpour in which Khatami surprised many by stating that Western civilization and the United States were worthy of respect, citing in particular the experience of the Pilgrims at Plymouth as an important event in affirming religious freedom, and the importance of the example of Abraham Lincoln.[28]

Khatami articulated a distinctive alternative approach to relations between Islam and the West. The old-fashioned jihad–clash-of-civilizations perspective offered stark alternatives of victory or defeat. Khatami's vision combined a nonmilitant jihadist defense of Islamic identity and values with a call for civilizational dialogue by which all societies could benefit through the exchange of information and ideas.[29]

Khatami's model for dialogue does not preclude strong criticism of Western policies, especially those of the United States. Speaking of a flawed U.S. policy of domination, Khatami denounced America's use of sanctions against Iran and others. America, he said, attempts to "impose their own domestic law on the world . . . [but the] world will not tolerate a master any more—not only will we not tolerate a master, neither will the world."[30] Thus, Khatami combines strong affirmation of Iran's principles and critique of U.S. policy with an emphatic advocacy of the dialogue of civilizations and of improved Iranian-U.S. relations in particular.

Mohammad Khatami's dialogue of civilizations is an alternative both to the old militant jihadist rhetoric and to uncritical dependence on the West (what some have termed "westoxication"). In contrast to the hard-line position of Ayatollah Ali Khamenei, Khomeini's successor as Supreme Guide of the Islamic republic, Khatami boldly asserts that Islamic reform, open to a dynamic interaction with Western civilization, must build a bridge between tradition and modernity:

> We must concede that the incompatibility of modern civilization with our tradition-bound civilization is one of the most important causes of the crisis in our society. What is to be done? Should we insist on remaining immersed in our tradition, or should we melt fully into Western civilization? Or is there another way of removing this contradiction?[31]

Khatami's vision of the history and development of civilizations is dynamic; civilizations constantly change and evolve. The West is the latest,

> but not the ultimate human civilization, which like all other human artifacts, is tentative and susceptible to decay. . . . Civilizations change and there is no such thing as an ultimate and eternal civilization.[32]

Khatami believes that at the beginning of the twenty-first century the need is for the creation of a new civilization. However, his call for dialogue must be seen within the context of his particular worldview, which differs from that of many in America and Europe. Many in the West assume that dialogue with the West means that eventually non-Western peoples will see the advantages of Western civilization and become more westernized. This would be a complete misunderstanding of Khatami's vision of dialogue, which is not a passive policy of accommodation but a competitive strategy for strengthening and transforming Islamic civilization. It transcends a militant vision of jihad and offers a way to avoid destructive conflict. Dialogue with the West is an important way of strengthening Islam. Khatami's vision holds out the hope that, as the West evolves and possibly declines, Islam will regain its position as the leading progressive world civilization.

In the continued encounter of Islam and the West in the twenty-first century, Khatami's dialogue of civilizations reflects a significant perspective very different from that of both Western analysts such as Samuel Huntington and old-style Islamic advocates of militant jihad such as Sayyid Qutb and, more recently, Osama bin Laden.

ABDURRAHMAN WAHID:
COSMOPOLITAN ISLAM AND GLOBAL DIVERSITY

In October 1999, Abdurrahman Wahid, leader of the Nahdatul Ulama, (Renaissance of Religious Scholars), the biggest (35 million members) Islamic organization in the world's largest Muslim country, became the first elected president in Indonesia's history.[33] Nahdatul Ulama (NU) is a predominantly conservative, rural-based sociocultural organization founded in 1926 to defend the interests of traditional Islam and counter the threat of modernism. Wahid, however, is best described as a modern, urban, liberal Muslim intellectual. As a religious leader and social and political reformer, he has staunchly opposed those who would reassert Islam's role in politics and has warned of the dangers of Islamic fundamentalism.

Bridging the worlds of traditional Islam and modern thought, Wahid espouses a reformist intellectual synthesis and social agenda that distinguishes between unchanging religious doctrines or laws and those that can be altered to accommodate social change. Wahid is among a generation of reformers who advocate a progressive Islam, one that is inclusive, democratic, pluralistic, and tolerant. Wahid advocates a cosmopolitan Islam, the product of creative reinterpretation or reformulation, responsive to the demands of modern life and reflecting Indonesian Islam's diverse religious and ethnic history and communities.

Wahid believes that contemporary Muslims are at a critical crossroad. Two choices or paths confront them: to pursue a traditional, static legal-formalistic Islam or to reclaim and refashion a more dynamic cosmopolitan, universal, pluralistic worldview.[34] In contrast to many "fundamentalists" today, he rejects the notion that Islam should form the basis for the nation-state's political or legal system,[35] a notion he characterizes as a Middle Eastern tradition, alien to Indonesia.[36] Indonesian Muslims should apply a moderate, tolerant brand of Islam to their daily lives in a society where "a Muslim and a non-Muslim are the same," a state in which religion and politics are separate.[37] Rejecting legal-formalism or fundamentalism as an aberration and a major obstacle to Islamic reform and to Islam's response to global change,[38] Wahid has spent his life promoting the development of a multifaceted Muslim identity and a dynamic Islamic tradition capable of responding to the realities of modern life. Its cornerstones are free will and the right of all Muslims, both laity and religious scholars (*ulama*) to "perpetual reinterpretation" *(ijtihad)* of the Quran and tradition of the Prophet in light of "everchanging human situations."[39]

Wahid's cosmopolitan Islam is pluralistic and global, affirming the diversity of peoples and civilizations. The challenge for contemporary Muslims is to articulate and preserve an authentic identity informed by their Islamic heritage but open to the cosmopolitan realities of a global environment. It is based on a recognition of universal basic rights, respect for other faiths, ideologies, and cultures, and open to the best that modern science and technology have to offer.[40]

A political realist who recognized the needs to create national unity in the face of communalism, to establish the rule of law, and to develop viable economic frameworks for the equitable distribution of wealth, Wahid also put his finger on a major cause of violence and terrorism in Muslim countries. Most governments in the Muslim world rely on sociopolitical engineering, authoritarianism, political suppression, and violence to impose their vision. Wahid maintains that governments close their eyes to a fundamental issue of development when they reduce national problems solely to political and socioeconomic and technical factors. The failure to address the relationship of faith to national identity and to institution building contributes to instability and risks "massive social explosions."[41] Governments that rely on social control rather than consultation, that employ violence and repression, create a climate that contributes to radicalization and violence against the state. Wahid has astutely identified the heart of the struggle in Islam today. Movements are faced with two options, "the choice of following either a radical approach or a gradual response in their struggle for social justice, equal treatment before the law and freedom of expression."[42]

Anwar Ibrahim, Mohammad Khatami, and Abdurrahman Wahid are but three of many voices for Islamic reform. They demonstrate that there is no essentialist or monolithic Islam or Muslim society. All may share a common faith, at times articulate an Islamically inspired worldview, and use Islam as a source of legitimacy and mobilization. Still, their visions, goals, and strategies are shaped as much by diverse political and cultural contexts as by faith. They challenge those who see the world of the early twenty-first century in polarities, either confrontation and conflict or dialogue and cooperation, to appreciate the limitations and failures of old paradigms and to develop new paradigms for governance and policy that are sensitive to the importance of religion and culture.

Finally, in an increasingly global society, defining Islam and the Muslim world monolithically becomes more difficult as clear boundaries between Islam and the West evaporate. Not only are Muslim countries, societies, and institutions deeply involved with non-Muslim societies and communities but, more important, Islam is so present in America and Europe that Muslims have become part of the fabric of Western societies, as citizens, professionals, and neighbors. Many Muslims are third- and fourth-generation citizens in Western societies, no more and no less American or European than Jews, Christians, and Hindus. And yet, one of the questions we constantly hear is, Can they be democratic?

Islam and Democracy

The most glaring difference between the Muslim world and the West today is the contrast between authoritarian and democratically elected governments. Authoritarianism has been the norm not the exception in Muslim politics, cutting across the political and ideological spectrum. The track record of governments both non-Islamist (Algeria, Tunisia, and Egypt) and Islamist (Afghanistan, Sudan, and Iran) reveals a culture of authoritarianism that is incapable of tolerating any significant opposition.

Those already convinced about how different "they" are—that Islam is incompatible with modernization and that the mixing of religion and politics is an explosive formula for violent extremism and terrorism and an inevitable clash of civilizations—have solid examples to buttress their arguments. In theory, Islam and democratic or parliamentary forms of government are not incompatible. In actual practice, the results have been mixed, with strikingly contradictory experiences. Khomeini's Iran, Afghanistan's Taliban, Sudan's Islamic government have provided damning examples of political oppression, sexual discrimination, domestic and international violence and terrorism.

The case of Iran, the longest-lasting experiment in creating a modern Islamic system, demonstrates the changing dynamic relationship between religion and sociopolitical realities. During its first decade, the Islamic republic remained authoritarian, with strict and narrow limitations on political participation. However, the political system has experienced a push from both above and below along the democratization path. President Khatami's emphasis on the importance of civil society, democratization, and the rule of law has been a response to societal pressure, especially from women and the younger generation who make up a significant number of Iranian voters. However, given the ongoing struggle between reformers and a more hard-line conservative political and religious establishment led by Ayatollah Ali Khamenei, the outcome remains uncertain.

Why the glaring absence of democratic governments? As we have seen, the Muslim world is dealing with a legacy that created a powerful culture of authoritarianism still deeply entrenched in many countries. It is perpetuated today by rulers who inherited or seized power: from the unelected kings and emirs of Saudi Arabia, Jordan, Morocco, and Kuwait to the military and ex-military presidents of Sudan, Pakistan, Egypt, Libya, and Iraq. So too, political authoritarianism, whether religious or secular, has often been the norm, not only in the Islamic governments of Iran, Sudan, Pakistan, Afghanistan, and Saudi Arabia but also in the more secular governments of Tunisia, Egypt, Syria, Algeria, and Indonesia, where the situation has changed with the fall of Suharto and democratic elections but remains precarious.

Most Muslim countries remain security (*mukhabarat*) states whose rulers are focused on retaining their power and privilege at any cost through strong military and security forces. Many rulers have been "reelected" in government-controlled elections in which they garner 95 to 99.91 percent of the vote. Political parties and trade unions are nonexistent or severely restricted, elections are often rigged, and the culture and institutions of civil society are weak. Democratic elections have occurred in a number of countries (Turkey, Pakistan, Malaysia, Bangladesh, Jordan, Morocco, and Egypt) but most remain limited or guided democracies at best. Turkey and Pakistan have experienced military intervention and rule. Jordan and Morocco are monarchies. The recent succession of Syria's Bashir Assad after the death of his father, Hafez al-Assad, and the apparent grooming of Saddam Hussein's son in Iraq portend a new nondemocratic paradigm. The modern Muslim experience supports the impression that Islam and democracy are incompatible.[43]

Many say that Islam and democracy do not mix because traditional Islamic institutions such as the caliphate preclude significant popular political participation and democratic institutions. Yet, the history of religions demonstrates that religious traditions, like political ideologies such as democracy and communism, are capable of multiple interpretations and relations to the state. Modern reforms transformed European monarchies and principalities, whose rule had been religiously justified by divine right, into modern Western democratic states. Moreover, democracy itself has meant different things to different peoples at different times, from ancient Greece to modern Europe, from direct to indirect democracy, from majority rule to majority vote.[44] Judaism and Christianity, once supportive of political absolutism and divine right monarchies, have been reinterpreted to accommodate the democratic ideal. As a result, many Jews and Christians now believe that modern democracy is rooted in the Judeo-Christian tradition or at least not in conflict with their religion.

Islam throughout history has proven dynamic and diverse. It adapted to support the movement from the city-state of Medina to empires and sultanates, was able to encompass diverse schools of theology, law, and philosophy as well as different Sunni and Shii branches, and has been used to support both extremism and conservative orthodoxy. Islam continues today to lend itself to multiple interpretations of government; it is used to support limited democracy and dictatorship, republicanism, and monarchy. Like other religions, Islam possesses intellectual and ideological resources that can provide the justification for a wide range of governing models from absolute monarchy to democracy. In recent years, the democracy debate has intensified.

Experts and policymakers who worry that Islamic movements will use electoral politics to "hijack democracy" often fail to show equal concern that few current rulers in the region have been democratically elected and that many who speak of democracy only believe in "risk-free democracy." They permit political participation and liberalization as long there is no risk of a strong opposition (secular or religious) or a potential loss of power. Failure to appreciate that the issue of the hijacking of democracy is a two-way street was reflected in the responses (awkward silence or support) of many western governments and experts for the Algerian military's intervention and their abrogation of the results of the democratic electoral process, the Turkish military's suppression of the Islamic Refah party, and the growing authoritarianism of the Mubarak government in Egypt.

Democrats and Dissidents

A diversity of voices, some harmonious and others strident, discuss and debate political participation. Secularists argue for the separation of religion and the state. Rejectionists (both moderate and militant Muslims) maintain that Islam's forms of governance do not conform to democracy. King Fahd of Saudi Arabia, a long-time ally of the West, says that "the democratic system prevalent in the world is not appropriate in this region. . . . The election system has no place in the Islamic creed, which calls for a government of advice and consultation and for the shepherd's openness to his flock, and holds the ruler fully responsible before his people."[45] Extremists agree, condemning any form of democracy as *haram* (forbidden), an idolatrous threat to God's rule and divine sovereignty. Their unholy wars to topple governments aim to impose an authoritarian Islamic rule. Conservatives often argue that popular sovereignty contradicts the sovereignty of God, with the result that the alternative has often been some form of monarchy.

Reformers reinterpret key traditional Islamic concepts and institutions: consultation (*shura*) of rulers with those ruled, consensus (*ijma*) of the community, reinterpretation (*ijtihad*), and legal principles such as the public welfare (*maslaha*) of society to develop Islamic forms of parliamentary governance, representative elections, and religious reform. Just as it was appropriate in the past for Muhammad's senior Companions to constitute a consultative assembly (*majlis al-shura*) and to select or elect his successor (*caliph*) through a process of consultation, Muslims now reinterpret and extend this notion to the creation of modern forms of political participation, parliamentary government, and the direct or indirect election of heads of state.

Some advocates of Islamic democracy argue that the doctrine of the oneness of God (*tawhid*) or monotheism requires some form of democratic system. "No Muslim questions the sovereignty of

God or the rule of Shariah, Islamic Law. However, most Muslims do (and did) have misgivings about any claims by one person that he is sovereign. The sovereignty of one man contradicts the sovereignty of God, for all men are equal in front of God. . . . Blind obedience to one-man rule is contrary to Islam."[46]

The Tunisian Islamist leader of the Renaissance Party and political exile Rashid Ghannoushi provided an early example of a growing democratic trend: "If by democracy is meant the liberal model of government prevailing in the West, a system under which the people freely choose their representatives and leaders, in which there is an alternation of power, as well as all freedoms and human rights for the public, then Muslims will find nothing in their religion to oppose democracy, and it is not in their interests to do so."[47]

However, reformist efforts toward political liberalization, electoral politics, and democratization in the Muslim world do not imply uncritical acceptance of Western democratic forms. Most accommodationists would agree that it is important for Muslims not to uncritically copy what the West has done, emphasizing that there are different forms that legitimate democracy can take. Iran's president Mohammad Khatami, in a television interview in June 2001 before his country's presidential elections, noted that "the existing democracies do not necessarily follow one formula or aspect. It is possible that a democracy may lead to a liberal system. It is possible that democracy may lead to a socialist system. Or it may be a democracy with the inclusion of religious norms in the government. We have accepted the third option." Khatami presents a view common among the advocates of Islamic democracy that "today world democracies are suffering from a major vacuum which is the vacuum of spirituality,"[48] and that Islam can provide the framework for combining democracy with spirituality and religious government.

Grass-Roots Democratization

The most pervasive and vibrant example of the push from below for greater democratization and power sharing is the growing pres-

ence and implementation of Islam in civil society, in nongovernmental institutions and associations (NGOs). The development of
a strong civil society is a critical ingredient for building democratic institutions. It incorporates and inculcates the principles and
values of power sharing: greater political participation, represen-
tation, self-determination, government accountability, the rule of
law, and social justice.

Although for much of the 1980s revolutionary Iran and extremist
movements provided the dominant note, the late 1980s and 1990s
revealed the many faces of Islamic social and political activism.
Islamic movements and associations became part and parcel of
mainstream institutional forces in civil society. Islamic activist
organizations and NGOs created networks of mosques, hospitals,
clinics, day-care centers, youth clubs, legal aid societies, foreign
language schools, banks, drug rehabilitation programs, insurance
companies, and publishing houses. They fill a void and thus serve,
in some countries, as an implicit indictment of the government's
ability to provide adequate services, in particular for the nonelite
sectors of society. Their services provide an alternative to expensive private institutions and overcrowded public facilities. At the
same time, they reinforce a sense of community identity as well as
spiritual and moral renewal.

Though many Islamic associations and NGOs are nonpolitical
and nonviolent, others like Lebanon's Hizbollah and Hamas in
Palestine have combined extensive and effective educational and
social services with political action and militant jihad. Their violent confrontations with Israel and acts of terrorism have led two
successive American presidential administrations to designate
Hamas and Hizbollah as terrorist organizations and to shut down
several American Muslim organizations charged with channeling
funds to them. At the same time, Hizbollah provides an instruc-
tive example of the extent to which Islamic movements are shaped
not simply by a religious impulse but by political contexts. Hizbollah was primarily a militant Shii response to Israel's invasion
and occupation of Lebanon and the Lebanese Civil War. With the
end of the civil war, Hizbollah put down its arms in the north,

became a political party, and won seats in Parliament. However, it kept up its militant resistance to Israeli occupation of Southern Lebanon, fighting Israeli forces until Israel's withdrawal from Lebanon. Though Hizbollah remains on some countries' list of terrorist states (including the lists of the United States and Israel), it functions today within mainstream Lebanese society, combining politics with a vast network of educational and social services.

Many Islamic movements in recent years have eschewed violence and terrorism. Alongside the terrorist trail of unholy wars, there exists a democratic track record of Islamically oriented candidates who have been elected president of Indonesia, prime minister of Turkey, deputy prime minister of Malaysia, speakers of parliaments in Indonesia, Iran, Jordan, and Sudan, cabinet ministers and parliamentarians in Egypt, Algeria, Sudan, Kuwait, Pakistan, Jordan, Yemen, Malaysia, Indonesia, Turkey, and Lebanon. The performance of Islamist groups in national and municipal elections defied the predictions of those who had insisted that Islamic movements were unrepresentative and would not attract voters.

An Islamic Democratic Threat?

The wide participation of religiously motivated Muslims (political and apolitical) in Islamic professional associations and other private voluntary organizations has led to the gradual Islamization of society from below, increasingly evident throughout much of the Muslim world. Ironically, the nonviolent participation and apparent strength of Islamists in mainstream society has led to more stringent limits on political liberalization and democratization in the 1990s.

Authoritarian governments and secular elites who fear any significant opposition as a potential challenge to their power and privilege have raised the specter of fanatic fundamentalism and terrorism, charging that radical Islamists were out to hijack democracy, to come to power through ballots as well as bullets. The Algerian military seized power, imprisoned Islamists, and denied them their electoral victory. Tunisia and Egypt backed away from their commitment to open elections and instead crushed (Tunisia) or curtailed (Egypt) mainstream, nonviolent Islamist participation, making little distinction between treatment of moderates, who operated aboveground and within the system, and violent revolutionary extremists. Yielding to pressures from its powerful military, Turkey's government forced Prime Minister Ecmettin Erbakan to resign and subsequently outlawed his Welfare Party. A new, more broad-based Islamic party, Virtue, was created only to have Turkey's Parliament refuse to seat a woman parliamentarian who insisted on wearing a headscarf; finally the party itself was banned.

At best the attitude of many rulers may be characterized, in the words of one Western diplomat, as an openness to "risk-free democracy" or, as another put it, "democracy without dissent." Openness to government-controlled and -dominated change—yes; openness to a change of government that would bring to power Islamic activists (or for that matter *to any opposition party*)—no. Recent years have shown that, at best, opposition parties and groups, whether secular or religious, are tolerated only as long as they remain relatively weak or under government control and do not threaten the regime or ruling party at the ballot box. However, questions remain. Can the ills of societies be reduced to a single cause or blamed on "fundamentalist fanatics"? Are the activities of a radical minority a convenient excuse for the failure of many governments to build strong and equitable modern states? Does this perceived threat support authoritarian, military or security governments, whose nonelected rulers' primary wish is to perpetuate their own power?

The issue of democratization, like that of authoritarianism, in Muslim societies is not primarily one of religion but of history and political and economic development. Centuries of European colonial rule followed by decades of authoritarian governments have created and perpetuated conditions that are not conducive to democratization. One-man or one-party governments, limited political participation, restricted freedom of speech and of the press, government control of politics, economic, social, educational development, and of the media produce authoritarian political cultures and values. The absence or weakness of civil society (nongovernmental institutions and associations) contributes to the inevitability that many governments in the Muslim world will follow one of two paths, religious or secular authoritarianism. Despite the odds, however, democratization has increasingly become an issue in Muslim politics.

The political and economic realities of many states continue to foster alienation, opposition, and radicalism or extremism. Despite the growing desire for greater political participation and government accountability, authoritarian governments with limited political participation and freedoms remain the norm in many countries. Regarding the future role of Islam in Muslim politics, the comment of one expert on Egypt is equally relevant to other states: "Egypt's rulers can expect to see an Islam that faithfully reflects the skill or folly of their own statecraft."[49]

Democracy is an integral part of modern Islamic political thought and practice, accepted in many Muslim countries as a litmus test by which both the openness of government and the relevance of Islamic groups or other political parties are certified. However, questions about what particular forms democratization might take in diverse Muslim political cultures remain difficult to answer. Muslim political traditions and institutions, like social conditions and class structures, continue to evolve and are critical to the future of democracy in the Muslim world.

Western governments are challenged to balance longstanding relationships with regimes against the principles and values of self-determination, democratization, and human rights that they claim to stand for and support. Governments in the Muslim world are challenged to promote and strengthen the development of civil society—those institutions, values, and culture that are the foundation for true participatory government. They must be willing to allow alternative political voices to function freely in society and express their opinions and dissent through the formation of political parties, private associations, newspapers, and the media. Islamic activists and movements are challenged to move beyond slogans to programs. They must become more self-critical in speaking out not only against local government abuses but also against those of Islamic regimes in Sudan, Afghanistan, and until recently Iran, as well as acts of terrorism committed in the name of Islam by extremists. They are challenged to provide an Islamic rationale and policy that would extend to their opposition and to minorities the very principles of pluralism and political participation that they demand for themselves.

All are challenged to recognize that democratization and the building of strong civil societies in the Muslim world are part of a process of experimentation, necessarily accompanied by failure as well as success. The transformation of the West from feudal monarchies to democratic nation-states took time, trial and error. It was accompanied by political and intellectual revolutions that rocked both state and church in a long, drawn-out process, among contending voices and factions with competing visions and interests.

Global Terrorism and Islam

Terrorism has been a worldwide threat, affecting countries as dissimilar as Italy, Germany, Peru, Japan, and Greece, Israel/Palestine, Egypt, Yemen, Iran, Turkey, and Iraq. Terrorists have targeted local populations often in the name of nationalist groups or governments. In recent years, radical groups have combined nationalism, ethnicity, or tribalism with religion and used violence and terrorism to achieve their goals: Serbs in Bosnia, Hindu nationalists in India, Tamil and Sinhalese in Sri Lanka, Jewish fundamentalists in Israel, Christian extremists in the United States. However, the most widespread examples of religious terrorism have occurred in the Muslim world. Al-Qaeda (modern in terms of educational profiles, knowledge and use of modern technology from computers, faxes, the Internet, and cell phones to weapons) represents a new form of terrorism, born of transnationalism and globalization. It is transnational in its identity and recruitment and global in its ideology, strategy, targets, network of organizations, and economic transactions.

Though global terrorism has no single location or source, for the time being it has become associated with Islam and jihad. While

President George W. Bush and other national and religious leaders
have distinguished between Islam and terrorism, and many average Americans have proven remarkably supportive of Arab and
Muslim colleagues and neighbors, others have not. Although the
U.S. administration has remained consistent in its statements, the
actions of the attorney general and proposed congressional antiterrorism legislation, as well as the detention of individuals for
indefinite periods without trial or access to evidence, raise deep
concerns about the erosion of civil liberties and human rights for
Arabs and Muslims, and others as well. The issue goes to the core
of what the United States is and stands for, who we are now, and
what we might become.

Like all the world's major religious traditions, Islam has its extremist fringe. However, Osama bin Laden's steady dose of procla-
mations and threats has assured that Islam, not just extremism or
terrorism, receives special treatment. The climate today is one in
which questions can be asked and statements can be made about
Islam, not simply about the beliefs and actions of extremists, that
would not be tolerated if directed at Judaism or Christianity. The
danger of this approach is to overlook the fact that militant jihad
movements and terrorism are not just the products of warped individuals or religious doctrine, whether mainstream or extremist
interpretations, but of political and economic conditions.

Reacting to Terrorism:
American Foreign Policy in the Muslim World

After September 11, the depth of hatred expressed by bin Laden
and his al-Qaeda followers along with scenes of some Arabs cel-
ebrating in the streets revolted many but also led some to ask,
Why do they hate us? The temptation for some government officials and political commentators was to condemn and dismiss, to
explain away anti-Americanism as irrationality, ingratitude, jealousy
of our success, or hatred for "our way of life." Slogans to the effect
that we are in a war between the civilized world and terrorists; a war
between fundamentalists who hate Western democracy, capitalism,

and freedom; or a war against evil and merchants of death may reflect the rhetoric of some extremists and be emotionally satisfying, but they fail to get at deeper realities and long-term issues. Similarly, belief that overwhelming force has brought a quick victory and proven an effective answer and message to other terrorists or potential terrorists also overlooks real and future threats. Other bin Ladens exist as do the political and economic conditions that they can exploit to recruit new soldiers for their unholy wars.

Osama bin Laden, like the secular Saddam Hussein and the cleric Ayatollah Khomeini before him, cleverly identified specific grievances against Muslim regimes and the United States that are shared across a broad spectrum of Muslims, most of whom are not extremists. He then used religious texts and doctrines to justify his jihad of violence and terrorism. Anti-Americanism is driven not only by the blind hatred of the terrorists but also by a broader-based anger and frustration with American foreign policy among many in Arab and Muslim societies: government officials, diplomats, the military, businessmen, professionals, intellectuals, and journalists. Many enjoy close friendships with their Western counterparts. They have graduated from and send their children to Western schools, vacation and own property in America and Europe, admire many of the principles and values (political participation, accountability, the basic freedoms of speech, thought, and the press). But they also believe that these principles are applied selectively or not at all when it comes to the Muslim world.

Lost in our litany of slogans and easy answers is the recognition that they see more than we see. In recent years, the United States has become less international-minded and more preoccupied with domestic issues. Many members of Congress see no reason to travel abroad; a prominent congressional leader freely quipped that he had been to Europe once and saw no reason to return. Major media networks and newspapers have cut back on the number of foreign bureaus and correspondents; domestic news coverage has expanded at the expense of public awareness of international affairs. By contrast, and unlike in the past, many in the Muslim world are no longer dependent on CNN and the BBC for news of the world.

International Arab and Muslim publications and media provide daily
coverage of foreign affairs. Families sit glued to their television sets,
watching daily coverage on al-Jazeera, and see in vivid color live
news from Palestine/Israel, Iraq, Chechnya, and Kashmir.

Many see the United States' espousal of self-determination, democratization, and human rights as disingenuous in light of its foreign policies. While average Americans might see the latest explosive
headline event such as a spectacular terrorist attack in Israel, they
are not bombarded daily with images of acts of Israeli violence and
brutality, the disproportionate firepower, the number of Palestinian deaths and casualties, the use of American weapons including
F-16s and Apache helicopters provided to Israel and used against
Palestinians, including civilians, in the occupied territories. America's
relationship with Israel has proved to be a lightning rod. While
some in the West downplay or deny the significance of the Palestinian issue, surveys continue to verify its importance to Muslims
globally. A survey in spring 2001 of five Arab states (Egypt, Saudi
Arabia, the United Arab Emirates, Kuwait, and Lebanon) demonstrated that the "majority in all five countries said that the Palestinian issue was the single most important issue to them personally."[50]
In a Zogby International poll of American Muslims taken in November and December 2001, 84 percent believed that the United
States should support a Palestinian state, 70 percent believed that it
should reduce financial support to Israel.[51]

The American government's tough stand (often fully justified)
with Yasser Arafat but kid-glove treatment of Israeli Prime Minister Ariel Sharon's aggressive and brutal policies in the West Bank
and Gaza, and America's long record of relatively uncritical support of Israel—expressed in its levels of military and economic aid
to Israel, its voting record in the United Nations, official statements by American administrations and government officials, and
votes by Congress (often opposed by administrations in the past)
to move the American embassy from Tel Aviv to Jerusalem in direct contravention of longstanding UN resolutions—are seen by
many in the Muslim world as proof of American hypocrisy.

Other critical foreign policy issues include the impact of sanctions on more than a half-million innocent Iraqi children (with little direct effect on Saddam Hussein), and sanctions against Pakistan while failing to hold India and Israel to similar standards for their nuclear programs. The moral will so evident in Kosovo is seen as totally absent in U.S. policy in the Chechnya and Kashmiri conflicts. A native-born American convert to Islam, Ivy League–educated and formerly a government consultant, spoke with a frustration shared by many Muslims: "Every informed Muslim would point to America's bizarre complicity in the genocidal destruction of Chechnya, its tacit support of India's incredibly brutal occupation of Kashmir, its passivity in the ethnic cleansing of Bosnia, and even America's insistence on zero casualties in stopping the ethnic cleansing of Kosovo. These are hot spots in the so-called 'ring of fire' around the edge of the Muslim world, where Muslims are throwing off the shackles of old empires."[52]

To understand the love-hate relationship, the attraction-repulsion toward America that exists in many parts of the world and is widespread in the Muslim world, we must not only know who we think we are and how we view others but try to understand how others might see us. As Paul Kennedy has observed, few of us ask:

[H]ow do we appear to *them*, and what would it be like were our places in the world reversed. . . . Suppose that there existed today a powerful, unified Arab-Muslim state that stretched from Algeria to Turkey and Arabia—as there was 400 years ago, the Ottoman Empire. Suppose this unified Arab-Muslim state had the biggest economy in the world, and the most effective military. Suppose by contrast this United States of ours had split into 12 or 15 countries, with different regimes, some conservative and corrupt. Suppose that the great Arab-Muslim power had its aircraft carriers cruising off our shores, its aircraft flying over our lands, its satellites watching us every day. Suppose that its multinational corporations had reached into North America to extract oil, and paid the corrupt, conservative governments big royalties for that. Suppose that it dominated all international institutions like the Security Council and the IMF. Suppose that there was a special state set up in North America fifty years ago, of a different religion and language to ours, and the giant Arab-Muslim power always gave it support. Suppose the Colossus state was bombarding us with cultural messages, about the status of women, about sexuality, that we found offensive. Suppose it was always urging us to change, to modernize, to go global, to follow its example. Hmm . . . in those conditions, would not many Americans steadily grow to loath that Colossus, wish it harm? And perhaps try to harm it? I think so.[53]

The war against global terrorism should neither become a green light for authoritarian regimes in the Muslim world to further limit the rule of law and civil society or to repress nonviolent opposition, nor justify a gradual erosion of important principles and values at home and abroad. Many governments use the danger of "Islamic fundamentalism" as an excuse for authoritarian responses and policies, labeling all Islamic movements, extremist as well as moderate (whom they characterize as wolves in sheep's clothing), as a threat. Many Muslim and Western governments oppose any Islamic candidates' participation in elections, fearing that they will hijack elections. These fears often obscure the fact that many governments themselves have proven nondemocratic or authoritarian track records.

American, as well as European, responses must remain proportionate, from military strikes and foreign policy to domestic security measures and antiterrorism legislation. A reexamination and, where necessary, reformulation of U.S. foreign policy will be necessary to effectively limit and contain global terrorism. Short-term policies that are necessitated by national interest must be balanced by long-term policies and incentives that pressure our allies to promote a gradual and progressive process of broader political participation and power sharing. Failure to do so will simply perpetuate the culture and values of authoritarianism, secular as well as religious, and feed anti-Americanism. If foreign policy issues are not addressed effectively, they will continue to provide a breed-

ing ground for hatred and radicalism, the rise of extremist movements, and recruits for the bin Ladens of the world.

Globalization of the Jihad

What is distinctive about global jihad today? The Soviet-Afghan
war marked a new turning point as jihad went global to a degree
never seen in the past. The *mujahidin* holy war drew Muslims from
many parts of the world and support from Muslim and non-Muslim countries and sources. In its aftermath, the new global jihad
spread as jihad became the common symbol and rallying cry for
holy and unholy wars. Most major Muslim struggles were declared
a jihad. Afghan Arabs moved on to fight other jihads in their home
countries and in Bosnia, Kosovo, and Central Asia. Others stayed
on or were trained and recruited in the new jihadi *madrasas* and
training camps.

Today, the term jihad has become comprehensive; resistance
and liberation struggles and militant jihads, holy and unholy wars,
are all declared to be jihads. Jihad is waged at home not only against
unjust rulers in the Muslim world but also against a broad spectrum of civilians. Jihad's scope abroad became chillingly clear in
the September 11 attacks against both the World Trade Center and
the Pentagon, targeting not only governments but also civilians.

Terrorists such as bin Laden and others go beyond classical
Islam's criteria for a just jihad and recognize no limits but their
own, employing any weapons or means. They reject Islamic law's
regulations regarding the goals and means of a valid jihad (that
violence must be proportional and that only the necessary amount
of force should be used to repel the enemy), that innocent civilians should not be targeted, and that jihad must be declared by
the ruler or head of state. Today, individuals and groups, religious
and lay, seize the right to declare and legitimate unholy wars in
the name of Islam.

On the other hand, Islamic scholars and religious leaders across
the Muslim world such as those at the Islamic Research Council at

al-Azhar University, regarded by many as the highest moral authority in Islam, have made strong, authoritative declarations against bin Laden's initiatives: "Islam provides clear rules and ethical norms that forbid the killing of non-combatants, as well as women, children, and the elderly, and also forbids the pursuit of the enemy in defeat, the execution of those who surrender, the infliction of harm on prisoners of war, and the destruction of property that is not being used in the hostilities."[54]

Globalization of communications, technology, and travel has heightened a new consciousness of the transnational identity and interconnectedness of the Islamic community (*ummah*) that follows events across the Muslim world on a daily, even hourly basis. They reinforce a sense of solidarity and identification. Regardless of national and cultural identities, most Muslims are not secular; they do self-consciously identify themselves as Muslim. They celebrate or bemoan successes and failures of Muslim struggles for self-determination, freedom from oppression, and economic development across the world, as well as of militant jihads, holy and unholy wars. The dark side of globalization and interconnectedness is that communications and technology support the existence of global terrorist networks in the twenty-first century.

If Western powers need to rethink, reassess foreign policies and their support for authoritarian regimes, mainstream Muslims worldwide will need to more aggressively address the threat to Islam from religious extremists. Their jihad or struggle will be religious, intellectual, spiritual, and moral. But it must be a more rapid and widespread program of Islamic renewal that builds on past reformers but that follows the lead of enlightened religious leaders and intellectuals today more forcefully, and that more effectively engages in a wide-ranging process of reinterpretation *(ijtihad)* and reform. There are formidable obstacles to be overcome—the conservatism of many (though not all) ulama, reform in the training of religious scholars and leaders, the countering of more puritanical exclusivist Wahhabi or Salafi brands of Islam, and the discrediting of militant jihadist ideas and ideologies.

whose Islam?

Like the process of modern reform in Judaism and Christianity, questions of leadership and the authority of the past and tradition are critical. Whose Islam? Who leads and decides? Is it rulers, the vast majority of whom are unelected kings, military, and former military? Or elected prime ministers and parliaments? Is it the ulama or clergy, who continue to see themselves as the primary interpreters of Islam, although many are ill prepared to respond creatively to modern realities? Or is it modern educated, Islamically oriented intellectuals and activists? Lacking an effective leadership, will other Osama bin Ladens fill the vacuum?

The second major question is, What Islam? Is Islamic reform simply returning to the past and restoring past doctrines and laws, or is it a reformation or reformulation of Islam to meet the demands of modern life? Some call for an Islamic state based on the reimplementation of classical formulations of Islamic laws. Others argue the need to reinterpret and reformulate law in light of the new realities of contemporary society.

Religious traditions are a combination of text and context— revelation and human interpretation within a specific sociohistorical context. This has gone on for many centuries. All religious traditions demonstrate dynamism and diversity and that is why there are conservative elements as well as modernist or progressive elements in all religions. Judaism and Christianity, the Hebrew Bible and the New Testament have been used to legitimize monarchies and feudalism in the past, and democracy and capitalism, as well as socialism in the present. The Gospels and Christianity have been used to legitimize the accumulation of wealth and market capitalism as well as religiosocial movements such as those of Francis of Assisi and, in the twentieth century, Dorothy Day's Catholic Worker Movement, and liberation theology in Latin and Central America. The process continues today regarding issues of gender relations, birth control, abortion, homosexuality, and social justice, yielding multiple and diverse positions. While using the same text and referring to a common history, people come out with different interpretations. Islam too is an ideal that has taken many forms historically and has been capable of multiple interpretations, conditioned by reason and social contexts. For example, much of the debate over the relationship of Islam to women's rights must be seen in terms not only of religion but also, as in other religions, of patriarchy. The status and role of Muslim women in law and society was defined in a patriarchal past and by the male religious elites who were the interpreters of religion.

This is a time to remember the events of September 11 and to respond: a time to remember the victims, those who died and their families. It is also a time for the international community, governments, religious leaders, opinion makers, intellectuals, academics, and citizens to respond. The United States–led coalition has brought an end to Taliban rule, the first major step in the war against global terrorism. Whether Osama bin Laden is captured and however successful are attempts to contain al-Qaeda, religious terrorism in the Muslim world and beyond will continue to be a threat to nations and to the international community.

As President George W. Bush and other political leaders have recognized, we will not defeat global terrorism solely by military or economic means. Public diplomacy must be a critical component. There can be no excuse for terrorism in the name of Islam. Suicide attacks, bombings, assassinations in the name of any cause, whether justified in the name of God, justice, or state security, are still terrorism. Quick and easy responses, such as moves to quiet the Arab street through overwhelming force, may be emotionally satisfying but will in the long run prove ineffective and contribute to greater radicalization and anti-Americanism. While some forms of terrorism, like some forms of cancer, respond to radical surgery, this deadly disease can only be effectively countered first by understanding how it originates, grows stronger, and spreads and then by taking action. The cancer of global terrorism will continue to afflict the international body until we address its political and economic causes, causes that will otherwise continue to provide a breeding ground for hatred and radicalism, the rise of extremist movements, and recruits for the bin Ladens of the world.

Notes

Chapter 1

1. Indira A.R. Lakshmanan, *Boston Globe*, September 26, 2001.
2. About the bin Laden Family, PBS Online and WGBH/*Frontline*: http://www.pbs.org/wgbh/pages/frontline/shows/binladen/who/family.html
3. Ibid.
4. A Biography of Osama bin Laden, PBS Online and WGBH/*Frontline*: http://www.pbs.org/wgbh/pages/frontline/shows/binladen/who/bio.html
5. Ibid.
6. Ibid.
7. Yossef Bodansky, *Bin Laden: The Man Who Declared War on America* (New York: Prima, 2001), p. 5.
8. John K. Cooley, *Unholy War: Afghanistan, America and International Terrorism* (London: Pluto Press, 2000), p. 87.
9. As quoted in Peter L. Bergen, *Holy War Inc.: Inside the Secret World of Osama bin Laden* (New York: Free Press, 2002), p. 53.
10. Ibid.
11. Robert Fisk, "Anti-Soviet warrior puts his army on the road to peace," *The Independent,* December 6, 1993.
12. M. Nazif Shahrani, "Afghanistan," in *The Oxford Encyclopedia of the Modern Islamic World*, ed. John L. Esposito (New York: Oxford University Press, 1995), vol. 1, pp. 27–32.
13. Ahmed Rashid, *Taliban: Militant Islam, Oil and Fundamentalism in Central Asia,* (New Haven, Conn.: Yale University Press, 2000), p. 136.
14. Vernon Loeb Washington, "Terrorism Entrepreneur Unifies Groups Financially, Politically, *Washington Post*, August 23, 1998.
15. Ibid.
16. *Jane's Intelligence Review*, October 1, 1998.

17. Washington, *Washington Post*, August 23, 1998.

18. As quoted in Bergen, *Holy War Inc*, p. 88.

19. Richard Lacayo, "Public Enemy No. 2," Time.com, November 12, 2001, vol. 158.

20. Scott Baldauf, "The 'cave man' and Al Qaeda," *Christian Science Monitor*, October 31, 2001: http://www.csmonitor.com20001/1031/p6s1-wosc.html

21. *Reuters*, February 28, 1997.

22. "Bin Laden's Warning: Full Text," *BBC News*, Sunday, October 7, 2001: http://www.news.bbc.co.uk/hi/English/world/spout_asia/newsid_1585000/1585636.stm

23. Ibid.

24. Hamid Mir, "Osama claims he has nukes: If U.S. uses N-arms it will get same response," *Dawn: The Internet Edition*, November 10, 2001.

25. Interview with Osama bin Laden (May 1998), "Hunting the Enemy, " *Frontline*: http://www.pbs.org/wgbh/pages/frontline/shows/binladen/who/family.html

26. Ibid.

27. Ibid.

28. Ibid.

29. Ibid.

30. Ibid.

31. Ibid.

Chapter 2

1. Sayyid Qutb, *Milestones* (Stuttgart: Ernst Klett Printers, 1978), p. 21.

2. Ibid., pp. 88–89.

3. Bernard Lewis, *The Arabs in History* (New York: Harper & Row, 1966), p. 149; Daniel C. Peterson, "Ismailiyah," in *The Oxford Encyclopedia of the Modern Islamic World*, ed. John L. Esposito (New York: Oxford University Press, 1995), vol. 2, pp. 341–42.

4. Qutb, *Milestones,* pp. 32–33.

5. See John O. Voll, "Renewal and Reform in Islamic History: Tajdid and Islah," in *Voices of Resurgent Islam* (New York: Oxford University Press, 1983), ch. 2.

6. Emmanuel Sivan, *Radical Islam: Medieval Theology and Modern Politics* (New Haven, Conn.: Yale University Press, 1985), p. 96.

7. Ronald Nettler, "Ibn Taymiyya," in *The Oxford Encyclopedia of the Modern Islamic World*, ed. John L. Esposito (New York: Oxford University Press, 1995), vol. 2, p. 165.

8. Hasan al-Banna, "The New Renaissance," in *Islam in Transition*, ed. John L. Esposito and John J. Donohue (New York: Oxford University Press, 1992), p. 78.

9. As quoted in Christina Phelps Harris, *Nationalism and Revolution in Egypt* (The Hague: Mouton, 1964), p. 144.

10. David Cummins, "Hasan al-Banna (1906–49), in *Pioneers of Islamic Revival*, ed. Ali Rahnema (London: Zed Books, 1994), p. 136.

11. S. Abul A'la Mawdudi, *Jihad in Islam* (Pakistan: Islamic Publications, (Pvt.) Limited, 1998), p. 3.

12. Ibid., p. 15.

13. Ibid.

14. Ibid., pp. 4–5.

15. Ibid.

16. Ibid., p. 8.

17. Ibid., pp. 23–24.

18. Richard Mitchell, *The Society of Muslim Brothers* (New York: Oxford University Press, 1969), pp. 35–71.

19. Qutb, *Milestones,* p. 261.

20. Ashad S. Moussalli, *Radical Islamic Fundamentalism: The Ideology and Political Discourse of Sayyid Qutb* (Beirut: American University of Beirut, 1992), p. 42.

21. Qutb, *Milestones,* p. 12.

22. Ibid., p. 239.

23. Ibid., pp. 17–18.

24. Ibid., pp. 32–33.

25. Ibid., p. 34.

26. Ibid.

27. Ibid., p. 221.

28. Ruhollah Khomeini, *Islam and Revolution: Writings and Declarations of Imam Khomeini*, trans Hamid Algar (Berkeley: Mizan Press, 1983), pp. 75–76.

29. Johannes J. G. Jansen, *The Neglected Duty* (New York: Macmillan, 1986), p. 161.

30. Ibid.

31. Ibid., p. 193.

32. As quoted in Saad Eddin Ibraham, *Egypt, Islam and Democracy* (Cairo: The American University of Cairo, 1966), p. 63.

33. *Jihad and Shahadat: Struggle and Martyrdom in Islam*, ed. Mehdi Abedi and Gary Tegenhausen (Houston, Tex.: Institute for Research and Islamic Studies, 1986), p. vi.

34. Ibn Khaldun, *The Muqqadimah: An Introduction*, trans. Franz Rosenthal (Princeton, N.J.: Princeton University Press, 1967), p. 183.

35. Ibid., pp. 109–10.

36. See Khaled Abou El Fadl, "The Place of Tolerance in Islam," *Boston Review*, December 2001/January 2002, 36.

Chapter 3

1. Joseph A. Kechichian, "Islamic Revivalism and Change in Saudi Arabia," *Muslim World* 80 (January 1990): 8–12.

2. "The hate that will not die," *Guardian*, December 17, 2001.

3. Ruhollah Khomeini, "Message to the Pilgrims," in *Islam and Revolution: Writings and Declarations of Imam Khomeini*, trans. Hamid Algar (Berkeley: Mizan Press, 1983), p. 195.

4. Taha Husayn, "The Future of Culture in Egypt," in *Islam in Transition: Muslim Perspectives*, ed. John J. Donohue and John L. Esposito (New York: Oxford University Press, 1982), p. 74–75.

5. *Egyptian Gazette*, February 1, 1979.

6. Fedwa El-Guindi, "The Killing of Sadat and After: A Current Assessment of Egypt's Islamic Movement," *Middle East Insight* 2 (January-February 1982): 21.

7. Saad Eddin Ibrahim, *Egypt, Islam and Democracy* (Cairo: The American University in Cairo Press, 1996), p. 212.

8. Ibid., p. 23.

9. Walid Mahmoud Abdelnasser, *The Islamic Movement in Egypt: Perceptions of International Relations, 1967–81* (London: Kegan Paul, 1994), pp. 239–43.

10. Chris Hedges, "Egypt Begins Crackdown on Strongest Opposition Group," *New York Times*, June 12, 1994.

11. Jack Kelley, "Devotion, desire drive youths to 'martyrdom'," *USA Today*, July 5, 2001.

12. *The Covenant of the Islamic Resistance Movement* (Jerusalem 1988), Article 1.

13. Ibid.

14. Interview with Hamas leader Mahmoud Zahar, quoted in Beverley Milton-Edwards, *Islamic Politics in Palestine* (London: Tauris Academic Studies, 1996), p. 186.

15. Hisham H. Ahmad, *Hamas: From Religious Salvation to Political Transformation* (Jerusalem: Palestinian Academic Society for the Study of International Affairs, 1994), p. 114.

16. Kelley, "Devotion, desire drive youths."

17. Anthony Shadid, *Legacy of the Prophet: Despots, Democrats and the New Politics of Islam* (Boulder, Colo.: Westview Press, 2001), p. 124.

18. Sayyid Abu Musameh, as quoted in Shadid, *Legacy of the Prophet: Despots, Democrats and the New Politics of Islam*, p. 124.

19. Kelley, "Devotion, desire drive youths."

20. For background and analysis see Dirk Vandewalle, "Islam in Algeria: Religion, Culture and Opposition in a Rentier State," in *Political Islam: Revolution, Radicalism, or Reform?*, ed. John L. Esposito (Boulder, Colo.: Lynne Rienner Publishers, 1997); I. Williams, "Algeria: A Deaf Ear to Amnesty," *Middle East International* 21 (November 1997): 15.

21. J. P. Entelis, "Bouteflika's Algeria: Prospects for a Democratic Peace," *Middle East Insight* 14 (November-December 1999): 7.

22. R. Tiemcani, "From Bullets to Ballots," *Middle East Insight* 14 (November-December 1999): 12.

23. H. Amirouche, "Algeria's Islamist Revolution: The People Versus Democracy?," *Middle East Policy* 5 (January 1998): 100.

24. Ahmed Rashid, "The Taliban: Exporting Extremism," *Foreign Affairs* 78 (November-December 1999): 22–35.

25. Ibid.

26. Ibid., p. 6.

Chapter 4

1. Francis E. Peters, "The Early Muslim Empires: Ummayads, Abbasids, Fatimids," in *Islam: The Religious and Political Life of a World Community* (New York: Praeger, 1984), p. 79.

2. See, for example, Daniel Lerner, *The Passing of Traditional Society: Modernizing the Middle East* (New York: Free Press, 1958); Manfield Halpren, *The Politics of Social Change in the Middle East and North Africa* (Princeton, N.J.: Princeton University Press, 1963). For an analysis and critique of the factors that influenced the development of modernization theory, see Fred R. von der Mehden, *Religion and Modernization in Southeast Asia* (Syracuse, N.Y.: Syracuse University Press, 1988).

3. See, for example, Harvey Cox, *The Secular City: Urbanization and Secularization in Theological Perspective* (New York: Macmillan, 1965), and *Religion in the Secular City: Toward a Post Modern Theology* (New York: Simon & Schuster, 1984); Dietrich Bonhoeffer, *Letters and Papers from Prison*, rev. ed. (New York: Macmillan, 1967); William Hamilton and Thomas Altizer, *Radical Theology and the Death of God* (Indianapolis: Bobbs Merrill, 1966).

4. Peter L. Berger, "The Desecularization of the World: A Global Overview," in *The Desecularization of the World: Resurgent Religion and World Politics*, ed. Peter L. Berger (Washington, D.C.: Ethics and Public Policy Center, 1999), p. 2.

5. Samuel P. Huntington, "The Clash of Civilizations?," *Foreign Affairs* (Summer 1993): 22, 39.

6. Ibid., p. 31.

7. Ibid., p. 40.

8. Samuel P. Huntington, *The Clash of Civilizations and the Remaking of World Order* (New York: Simon & Schuster, 1997), p. 258.

9. Ibid., p. 217.

10. For a discussion of this point, see James Piscatori, *Islam in a World of Nation States* (Cambridge: Cambridge University Press, 1986), p. 149.

11. Maxime Rodinson, *Islam and Capitalism* (Austin: University of Texas Press, 1978), p. 76.

12. See Nikki Keddie's comments in "Introduction: Deciphering Middle Eastern Women's History," *Women in Middle Eastern History*, ed. Nikki R. Keddie and Beth Baron (New Haven: Yale University Press, 1991), pp. 1–2.

13. As quoted in Haleh Esfandiari, *Reconstructed Lives: Women and Iran's Islamic Revolution* (Baltimore: Johns Hopkins University Press, 1997), p. 85.

14. Valerie J. Hoffman-Ladd, "Women's Religious Observances," *The Oxford Encyclopedia of the Modern Islamic World*, ed. John L. Esposito (New York: Oxford University Press, 1995), vol. 4, p. 327.

15. Ibid., pp. 327–28.

16. This section is based on John L. Esposito and John Voll, "Islam and the West: Muslim Voices of Dialogue," *Millennium* (January 2001). See also our longer study *Makers of Contemporary Islam* (New York: Oxford University Press, 2001).

17. See, for example, Judith Nagata, "Religious Ideology and Social Change: The Islamic Revival in Malaysia," *Pacific Affairs* 53, no. 3 (1980): 425, and Fred R. von der Mehden, "Malaysia in 1980: Signals to Watch," *Asian Survey* 21, no. 2 (1981): 246.

18. Ian Johnson, "How Malaysia's Rulers Devoured Each Other and Much They Built," *Wall Street Journal*, October 30, 1998.

19. See, for example, the editorial "Malaysia on Trial," *New York Times*, November 4, 1998.

20. Ibid.

21. Anwar Ibrahim, "Development, Values, and Changing Political Ideas," *Sojourn: Social Issues in Southeast Asia* 1 (February 1986): 2.

22. Anwar Ibrahim, "The Ardent Moderates," *Time*, September 23, 1996, 24.

23. Address by Anwar Ibrahim at the Ismail Faruqi Award Presentation Ceremony, International Islamic University Malaysia, February 28, 1996.

24. Surah 49:13. The translation is as it was presented in the text of Ibrahim's "Islam and Confucianism."

25. Anwar Ibrahim, "The Need for Civilizational Dialogue," Occasion Papers Series, Center for Muslim-Christian Understanding, Georgetown University, 1995, p. 5.

26. Anwar Ibrahim, *The Asian Renaissance* (Singapore: Times Books International, 1996), p. 45.

27. Mohammad Khatami, *Islam, Liberty, and Development* (Binghamton, N.Y.: Institute of Global Cultural Studies, Binghamton University, 1987), p. 150.

28. The interview received extensive coverage in the news media. See Elaine Sciolino, "Seeking to Open a Door to U.S., Iranian Proposes Cultural Ties," *New York Times*, January 8, 1998; Barton Gellman, "Iranian Leader Urges Exchanges with U.S.," *Washington Post*, January 8, 1998; and "A whisper in the Wolf's Ear," *The Economist*, January 10, 1998.

29. An interesting contemporary analysis of the significance of the new approach is Saul Bakhash, "From Iran, an Understated Overture," *Washington Post*, December 18, 1997.

30. Elaine Sciolino, "At Khomeini's Tomb, Iran's President Switches Tune on U.S.," *New York Times*, January 20, 1998.

31. Khatami, *Islam, Liberty, and Development*, p. 24.

32. Ibid., pp. 28, 30.

33. Eighty-seven per cent of Indonesia's population of 220 million are Muslim.

34. Mujiburrahman, "Island and Politics in Indonesia: The Political Thought of Abdurrahman Wahid," *Journal of Islam and Christian-Muslim Relations* 10, no. 3 (1992): 342.

35. "Where To: Interview with Abdurrahman Wahid," *Inside Indonesia*, October 8, 1986, p. 3.

36. "An Islamic Awakening," *Economist*, April 17, 1993.

37. "Yes, I have enemies. But it is important that I do the right things," *Business Times* (Singapore), March 24, 1999.

38. Abdurrahman Wahid, "Reflections on the Need for a Concept of Man in Islam," Memorandum to the rector of the U.N. University, May 1, 1983, n.p., n.d, p. 3.

39. Ibid.

40. Ibid., p. 4.

41. Abdurrahman Wahid, "Religion, Ideology, and Development," n.p., n.d., p. 4.

42. Abdurrahman Wahid, "Islam, Nonviolence, and National Transformation," n.p., n.d., p. 3.

43. For an analysis of this issue, see John L. Esposito and John O. Voll, *Islam and Democracy* (New York: Oxford University Press, 1997); John L. Esposito and James P. Piscatori, "Democratization and Islam," *Middle East Journal* 45 (Summer 1991): 427–40; John O. Voll and John L. Esposito, "Islam and Democracy in a Violent World," *Humanities* (Fall 2002, forthcoming); Mahmoud Monshipouri and Christopher G. Kukla, "Islam and Democracy and Human Rights," *Middle East Policy* 3 (1994): 22–39; Robin Wright, "Islam, Democracy and the West," *Foreign Affairs* (Summer 1992): 131–45.

44. John O. Voll and John L. Esposito, "Islam's Democratic Essence," *Middle East Quarterly* (September 1994): 3–11, with ripostes, 12–19: Voll and Esposito reply, *Middle East Quarterly* (December 1994): 71–72.

45. *Mideast Mirror*, March 30, 1992, p. 12.

46. Abdelwahab El-Affendi, *Islam* 21 (October 2000).

47. John L. Esposito and John D. Voll, "Islam and Democracy," *Humanities* (November-December 2001): 24.

48. Ibid.

49. R. Bianchi, "Islam and Democracy in Egypt," *Current History*, February 1989: 104.

50. Shibley Telhami, "Defeating Terror: Confront Supply and Demand," *Middle East Insight* 16 (November-December 2001): 7.

51. "American Muslim Poll" (Washington, D.C.: Project MAPS, Georgetown University, 2001), p. 7.

52. Robert Crane, "Re-thinking America's Mission: The Role of Islam," *American Journal of Islamic Social Sciences* 19, no. 2 (Spring 2002), forthcoming.

53. Paul Kennedy, "As Others See Us," *Wall Street Journal*, October 5, 2001.

54. *Al-Hayat*, Islamic Research Council of al-Aẑhar University, November 5, 2001.

Glossary

ayatollah (ayatullah) "Sign of God," title of a high-ranking Shii religious leader.

bida innovation, deviation from Islamic tradition.

caliph for Sunni Muslims, successor of Muhammad as leader of the Islamic community.

chador traditional garment, worn in public, covering a woman from head to foot.

dar al-harb "abode of war," non-Islamic territory.

dar al-Islam "abode of peace," Islamic territory, i.e., where Islamic law is in force.

dawah "call to Islam," propagation of the faith; more broadly, social welfare and missionary activities.

dhimmi "protected" or covenanted people; non-Muslim citizen who is subject to poll tax (jizya).

faqih (fuqaha) legal expert; jurisprudent.

fatwa formal legal opinion or decision of a mufti on a matter of Islamic law.

hadith narrative report of the Prophet Muhammad's sayings and actions.

hajj annual pilgrimage to Mecca required of all Muslims at least once in their lifetime.

halal permitted, lawful activities.

haraka   "movement."

haram   prohibited, unlawful activities.

hijab   veil or head covering worn by Muslim women in public.

hijra   emigration of Muhammad from Mecca to Medina in A.D. 622, where he established rule of the Muslim community-state.

hizbollah   party of God.

ijma   consensus, or agreement of the community, a source of Islamic law.

ijtihad   independent analysis or interpretation of Islamic law.

ikhwan   brotherhood.

imam   "Leader," prayer leader. In Shii Islam, refers to successor of Prophet Muhammad, descendant of Ali, who governs as divinely inspired religiopolitical leader of Islamic community.

iman   "faith," religious belief or conviction in the fundamental doctrines of Islam.

intifada   Palestinian "uprising" against Israeli occupation.

islah   reform or revitalization of the Muslim community through return to the Quran and example of the Prophet.

islam   submission or surrender to the will of God.

Islamist   Islamic political or social activist; often commonly referred to as a fundamentalist.

jahiliyyah   period of ignorance, i.e., pre-Islamic Arabia; used by contemporary revivalists to refer to un-Islamic behavior in society.

jihad   "strive, effort, struggle" to follow Islam; can include defense of faith, armed struggle, holy war.

jizya   poll-tax on dhimmi (non-Muslims) that entitled them to protection and to practice their faith.

kaba   cube-shaped shrine located in the center of the Grand Mosque in Mecca, the focal point for daily prayer and the pilgrimage.

kafir (var., kufir)   "unbeliever" or infidel, one who is "ungrateful" and rejects the message of Islam.

kalam "speech," theology.

madrasa religious college or university, seminary.

Mahdi divinely guided leader who is to come in the future to establish God's rule on earth and a socially just society.

majlis al-shura consultative council.

maslaha "public interest" or "human welfare."

mihrab "niche" in the wall of a mosque, indicating the direction of Mecca, which Muslims face when performing their daily prayers (salat).

mufti specialist on Islamic law competent to deliver a fatwa or legal interpretation or brief

mujaddid "renewer," one who brings about the renewal (tajdid) of Islam; a widely held Muslim belief based on Prophetic tradition teaches that God sends a mujaddid at the beginning of each century to restore or strengthen Islam.

mujahid (pl., mujahidin) soldier of God.

mujtahid one who practices ijtihad or interprets Islamic law.

mullah a local religious leader.

Muslim one who submits (islam) to God's will.

qadi judge who administers shariah law.

salafi "ancestors," the first generations of the Muslim community; because of their proximity to the Prophet Muhammad, their beliefs and practice are considered authoritative.

salat official prayer or worship observed five times daily.

shahadah the confession or profession of faith: "there is no god but Allah and Muhammad is His Prophet."

shahid martyr, witness to faith.

shariah "path," Islamic law.

shaykh head of a tribe or Sufi order; term applied to a ruler, religious teacher, or tribal leader.

Shii "party or faction" of Ali; those Muslims who believe that

Muhammad designated Ali and his rightful descendants to be the true leaders of the Muslim community.

shura   consultation.

Sufi   follower of Sufism, Islamic mysticism.

sultan   ruler, military commander in medieval Islamic states.

Sunnah   normative practice or exemplary behavior of Muhammad.

Sunni   Muslims, the majority community, who believe that they represent the authority of the Sunnah or example of the Prophet Muhammad and the early Muslin community.

tajdid   revival or renewal of Islam through return to its sources, the Quran, and the example of the prophet.

takfir   excommunication, the proclaiming of a fellow believer as an infidel.

taqlid   unquestioned imitation or following of tradition, past legal or doctrinal precedents; the opposite of ijtihad.

tawhid   unity of God (absolute monotheism); Allah's absolute sovereignty over the universe.

ulama   religious scholars or clergy.

ummah   Islamic community; refers to the worldwide Muslim community.

waqf   endowment of property for religious purposes such as building mosques, schools, hospitals.

zakat   annual alms tax or tithe of 2 + percent levied on wealth and distributed to the poor.

Index

Connect-the-Dots Silly Surprise

Junie B. can think of a jillion other ways that she could get to school. Like maybe she could get fired out of a cannon! Or else maybe she could parachute out of an airplane! Start at 1 and connect the dots to see another silly way Junie B. would like to ride to school.

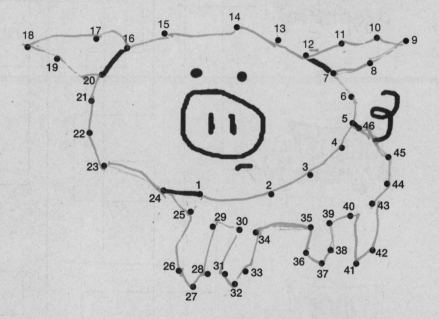

School Bus Tangle

Oh no! Mother is making Junie B. ride the stupid smelly bus to school! But only one of the buses below will take Junie B. to kindergarten. Help Junie B. find the right bus. Remember, stay on one path—don't be fooled by intersections!

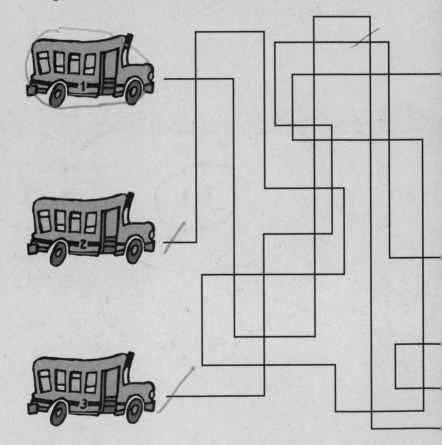

A	Z
B	Y
C	X
D	W
E	V
F	U
G	T
H	S
I	R
J	Q
K	P
L	O
M	N
N	M
O	L
P	K
Q	J
R	I
S	H
T	G
U	F
V	E
W	D
X	C
Y	B
Z	A

Stupid Smelly Code Breaker!

Junie B. doesn't like the school bus. It has a special door that folds in half. The door makes a *whishy* sound when it closes. If it closed on you by accident, you would make a *squishy* sound. Also, it *smells* on Junie B.'s bus. It smells like an

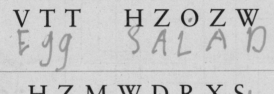

V T T   H Z O Z W

Egg Salad

.

H Z M W D R X S

Sandwich

Use the reverse alphabet code (A = Z, B = Y, C = X, and so on) to find out what Junie B.'s bus smells like.

10   *Answer key begins on page 220.*

Pat-and-Leather Matching!

Junie B. has new shoes to wear to school. Their names are Pat and Leather. (They are extra shiny because before Junie B. puts them on, she licks them!) But not all the shoes below match. Can you help Junie B. find the matching pair? Draw a line to connect them.

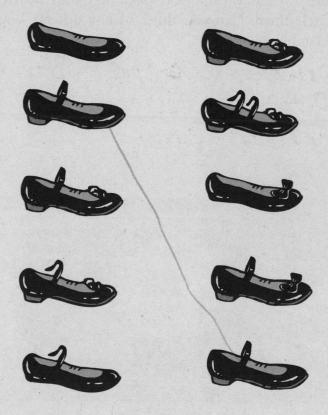

O Is for . . .

Junie B. hides in her classroom so she won't have to ride the stupid smelly bus home. After everyone else leaves, Junie B. draws pictures on the chalkboard. She draws a bean, and a carrot, and some curly hair. Also, she writes some O's. (O's are Junie B.'s bestest letter!) How many things can you find on the next page that start with O? Circle them. Can you think of any others? Write them below.

Orange	octopus	Ostrig
Outside	olives	oval
Octogon	oyster	

PAINT BOXES

Which of These Things Don't Belong?

Junie B. also hides in the nurse's office. Can you circle the items that DON'T belong in the nurse's office?

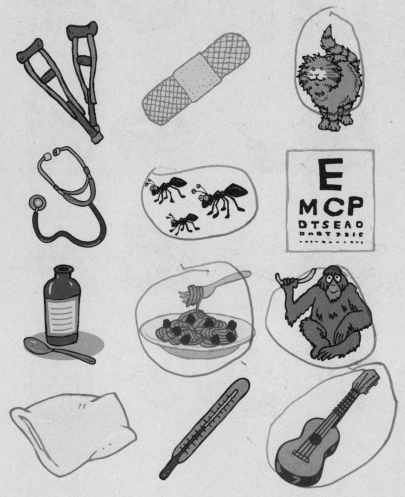

Answer key begins on page 220.

A "'Mergency" Connect-the-Dots!

911! 911! Junie B. has a "'mergency"! Start at 1 and connect the dots to see what Junie B. needs.

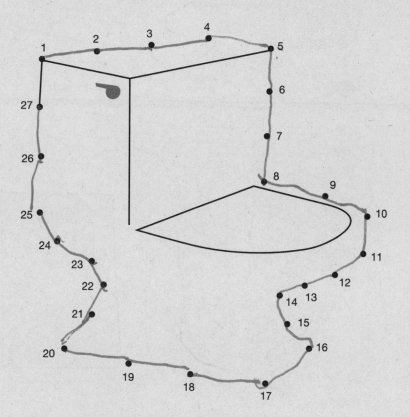

A-maze-ing!

Oh dear! Junie B.'s in big trouble!
Help her find the bathroom so she
won't have a "terrible accident"!

START

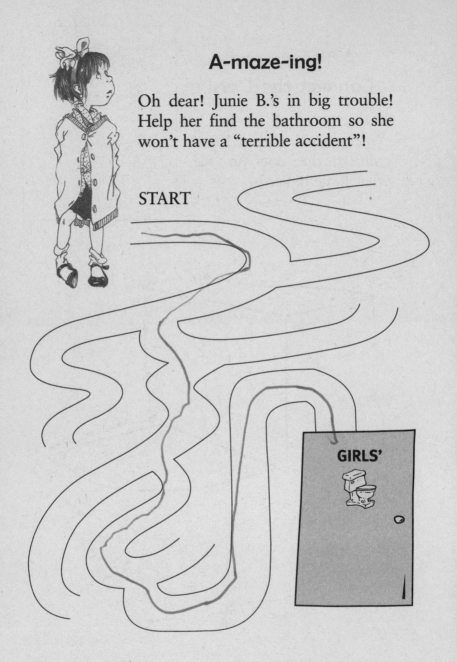

GIRLS'

Answer key begins on page 220.

"Stupid Smelly Bus" Words

How many different words can you make from the letters in STUPID SMELLY BUS? Try to make at least ten. Write them on the lines below. Junie B. wrote down two to get you started!

STUPID SMELLY BUS

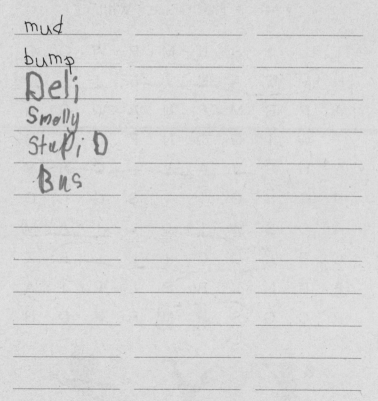

mud

bump

Deli

Smelly

StuPiD

Bus

"Find the Friends" Word Search

Junie B. meets lots of new friends at school. (Also, she meets people she doesn't actually care for.) Can you find and circle their names? Names can go horizontally, vertically, or backward.

Gus Vallony • Lucille • Meanie Jim • Mr. Woo • Mrs. • That Grace • William

```
T  L  I  S  E  M  R  W  O  O
H  M  E  A  N  I  E  J  I  M
A  R  R  M  F  U  A  W  S  L
T  W  I  S  O  N  F  C  U  B
G  U  S  V  A  L  L  O  N  Y
R  G  S  G  I  I  S  G  L  O
A  B  S  W  I  L  L  I  A  M
C  P  L  U  C  I  L  L  E  Z
E  B  N  K  B  B  L  E  I  A
P  C  G  S  R  M  R  A  D  H
```

Answer key begins on page 220.

Tic-Tac-Bow!

Junie B. thinks that friends are the happiest part of school . . . usually. Challenge a friend to a tic-tac-bow duel. Choose whether you want to be bows ▷◁ or glasses O‑O . Take turns and mark your symbol in one of the nine tic-tac-toe squares. If you get three of your marks in a row horizontally, vertically, or diagonally, you win!

More Fun for Friends!

Now challenge a friend to a bow battle. Take turns drawing lines connecting the bows, one line at a time, to make a square. Lines can go horizontally or vertically, but not diagonally. The player who completes a square gets to put his or her initials inside it and take another turn. The player with more squares wins. (Junie B. has made the first move here!)

"A Very Wonderful Thing"
Connect-the-Dots!

Yesterday, a very wonderful thing happened. It's called *Junie B.'s mother had a baby!* And it's not just a regular, boring, dumb baby, either! Start at 1 and connect the dots to see what kind of baby Junie B. thinks her new brother is.

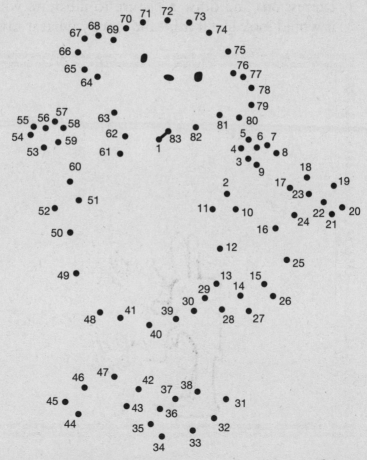

Monkey Business!

Sometimes people don't mean exactly what they say. For instance, Crybaby William *eats like a bird*. And Junie B. gets confused because Grandma Miller calls baby Ollie *a little monkey*. People also use expressions like *lucky duck* or *busy bee* or *dumb bunny*. Pick one of these expressions and draw a picture to illustrate what it would look like if it meant exactly what it says.

Couch Connect-the-Dots!

Now start at 1 and connect the dots to see what Lucille's nanna calls Lucille's daddy.

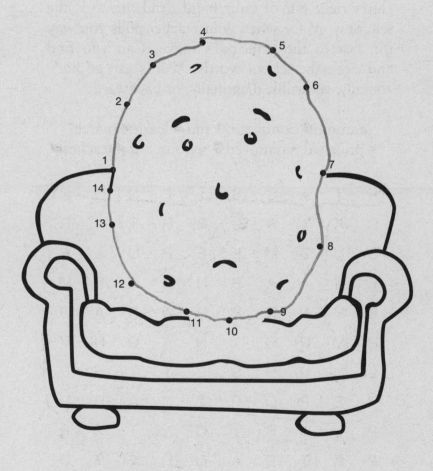

A couch _____ ____ _____ ____ ____ ____ .

School Words Word Search!

Junie B. learns lots of new words at school. *Autumn* is the school word for fall. *Confiscate* is the school word for when the teacher yanks the glitter right out of your hand. And *march* is the school word for when your teacher pulls you way too fast to the principal's office. Can you find and circle the school words? Words can go horizontally, vertically, diagonally, or backward.

autumn • confiscate • fun • learn • march
• principal • removed • report card • teacher

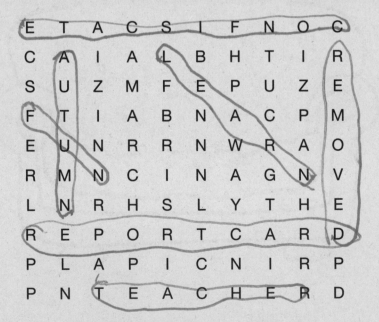

E T A C S I F N O C
C A I A L B H T I R
S U Z M F E P U Z E
F T I A B N A C P M
E U N R R N W R A O
R M N C I N A G N V
L N R H S L Y T H E
R E P O R T C A R D
P L A P I C N I R P
P N T E A C H E R D

Answer key begins on page 220.

Job Day Scramble!

It's Job Day in Room Nine! Lucille is a princess. Crybaby William is a superhero. And Meanie Jim is a kung fu karate guy. Unscramble the words below to find

other jobs. Then look at the letters in the circles to see what Junie B. wants to be.

jdgue Ⓙ U D G Ⓔ

aritst Ⓐ R T I S T

frimane F I R E M A Ⓝ

ipolt P Ⓘ L O T

tcehaer Ⓣ E A C H E R

dtocor Ⓓ Ⓞ C T O R

wiaetr W A I T O Ⓡ

Junie B. wants to be a

Ⓙ Ⓐ Ⓝ Ⓘ Ⓣ Ⓞ Ⓡ.

Answer key begins on page 220.

Mix and Match!

People use different items to do their jobs. Draw a line to connect each person with the item needed to do his or her job.

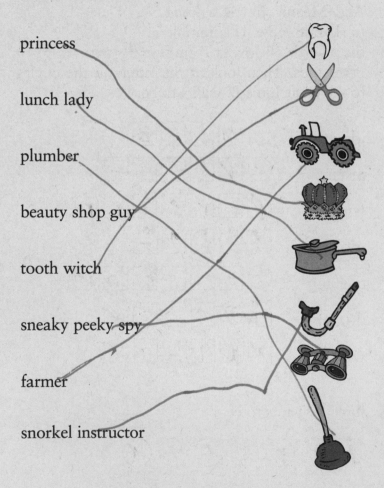

princess

lunch lady

plumber

beauty shop guy

tooth witch

sneaky peeky spy

farmer

snorkel instructor

Answer key begins on page 220.

Triangle Puzzler

On Job Day, Junie B. picks the bestest job in the whole wide world! When she grows up, she would like to be the janitor at her school! The janitor gets to paint and sweep and carry keys. He even has a key to Principal's office! What are two things Junie B. will need for her janitor job? Color in each three-sided shape to find out.

Answer key begins on page 220.

Junie B. Who?

There are lots of other jobs Junie B. could do, too. She could be Junie B.—Ice Cream Truck Guy, or Junie B.—Dog Walker, or Junie B.—Toilet Repairman. Or maybe, Junie B.—Boss of the World! Draw a picture of Junie B. doing one of these jobs in the space below.

Gus Vallony's Closet

Gus Vallony is the janitor at Junie B.'s school. Junie B. drew this picture of his supply closet. She put some extra stuff in there for him. Can you circle two things that don't belong?

Spy Games!

Junie B. is an excellent spier. That's because she has sneaky feet. Are you an excellent spier like Junie B.? Test your sneaky peeky spying skills by looking at these two pictures. Can you circle six differences in the second picture?

"Secret Mystery Guy" Maze!

Mother says *no more spying*. But Junie B.'s real, actual teacher named Mrs. is at the grocery store!!! And so Junie B. just *has* to peek at her! Can you help Junie B. find her teacher?

START

Answer key begins on page 220.

Sneaky Peeky Code Breaker!

Junie B. has a secret! But she can't tell anybody. That's how come there's pressure in her head and it's going to blow! Use the reverse alphabet code (A = Z, B = Y, C = X, and so on) to find out Junie B.'s secret.

MRS. ATE a grape!
NIH. ZGV Z TIZKV!

A	Z
B	Y
C	X
D	W
E	V
F	U
G	T
H	S
I	R
J	Q
K	P
L	O
M	N
N	M
O	L
P	K
Q	J
R	I
S	H
T	G
U	F
V	E
W	D
X	C
Y	B
Z	A

Test Your Sneaky Peeky Spying Skills!

Junie B. wears attractive bows in her hair. Use your super-spying skills to look at the bows below. Circle the two that are exactly the same.

Answer key begins on page 220.

Crossword Puzzle

Spies use clues to solve mysteries! Can you figure out the answers to the clues and solve this crossword puzzle?

Across:
5. Junie B.'s pet, Tickle, is a _____
6. The boss of school
8. Junie B.'s grampa's name

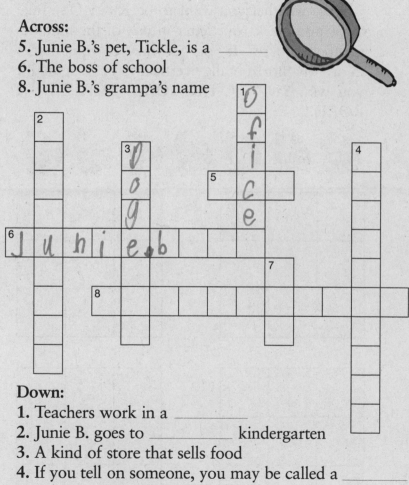

Down:
1. Teachers work in a _____
2. Junie B. goes to _____ kindergarten
3. A kind of store that sells food
4. If you tell on someone, you may be called a _____
7. A boy Junie B. doesn't like

Tic-Tac-Toad! Three in a Road!

Junie B. and her best kindergarten friend "that Grace" play "tic-tac-toad" on the school bus. Challenge a friend to a game of tic-tac-toad. Choose whether you want to be X's or O's. Take turns and mark your letter in one of the nine tic-tac-toad squares. If you get three of your marks in a row horizontally, vertically, or diagonally, you win! Say "TIC-TAC-TOAD! THREE IN A ROAD!"

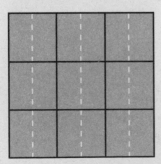

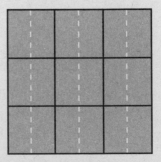

"All About Carnivals" Word Search

It's Carnival Night at Junie B.'s school. But Junie B. thinks carnivals are rip-offs. They have scary clowns and cotton candy that rots your teeth. But carnivals also have fun games and prizes. Can you find and circle the carnival words? Words can go horizontally, vertically, diagonally, or backward.

bullseye • Cake Walk • clown • dumb comb • fake duck • Moon Walk • Penny Toss • Ring Toss

D	R	I	N	G	T	O	S	S	F
K	B	O	A	N	B	U	W	I	A
L	D	U	M	B	C	O	M	B	K
A	C	L	O	O	N	F	C	I	E
W	G	L	R	O	N	D	F	N	D
E	G	P	O	I	L	S	G	L	U
K	Z	E	P	W	L	R	T	M	C
A	P	M	O	O	N	W	A	L	K
C	P	E	N	N	Y	T	O	S	S
P	N	B	U	L	L	S	E	Y	E
D	R	C	M	S	J	D	L	C	G

Goonie Bird Art!

Meanie Jim calls Junie B. Goonie Bird Jones. Is a goonie bird *really* a bird? What do you think it would look like? Draw it!

"Putting the Golf Ball" Maze!

Junie B. has been waiting for this exciting evening her whole entire career! When she gets to Carnival Night, she runs and runs until she finds her favorite game. Its name is Putting the Golf Ball. Help Junie B. make a hole in one!

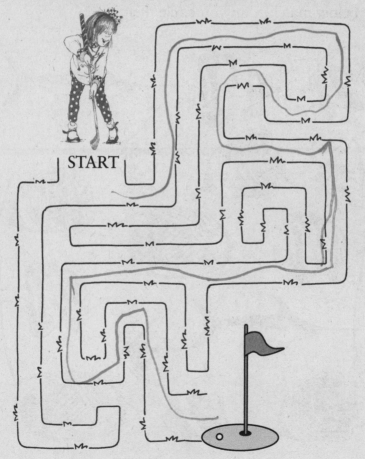

START

"Gone Fishing" Matching

Carnival Night is turning out to be the "worstest" night of Junie B.'s life. First, she lost at Penny Toss. Then she lost at Ring Toss. And yikes! She *even* lost at the stupid fishing booth! See if you have better luck. Only two of the fish below match. Can you circle them?

Answer key begins on page 220.

"Back Off, Clown" Maze!

Junie B. thinks that clowns are not normal people. Their teeth are yellowish. And their feet are too big. Help Junie B. get away from the scary clown and find her way to a prize.

START

Pat-and-Leather Tangle!

Uh-oh! Junie B. lost one of her shoes named Pat and Leather, and Daddy is getting "grumpity." The lost shoe is shiny and black with a strap that buckles. One of the lines below leads to the missing shoe. Can you help Junie B. find it? Remember, stay on one path—don't be fooled by intersections!

Answer key begins on page 220.

Take the Cake!

Yay! Junie B.'s carnival luck has changed! She won a cake at the Cake Walk. And you can help her celebrate! Challenge a friend to a cake-off. Take turns drawing lines connecting the cakes, one line at a time, to make a square. Lines can go horizontally or vertically, but not diagonally. The player who completes a square gets to put his or her initials inside it and take another turn. The player with more squares wins. (Junie B. has made the first move here!)

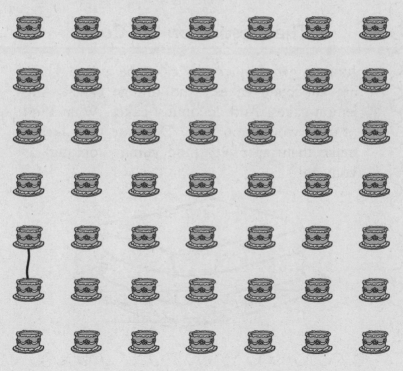

The Frosting on the Cake!

Junie B. gets to pick any cake she wants. There are chocolate cakes. And orange cakes. And lemon cakes. And coconutty cakes. What kind of cake would you pick? Decorate the cakes—make them as pretty (and yummy-looking) as you can!

Spot the Differences!

Today there was a birthday party in Room Nine! Paulie Allen Puffer got all wound up and he put cake on his head. Then he laughed till milk came out of his nose. Look at the two pictures. Can you circle seven differences in the second picture?

Clowning Around

Meanie Jim has *cool* birthday parties. Last year his party was named Clowning Around, and he had two real, actual clowns from the circus. Look at all the circus clowns below. Can you circle the one that's different?

Answer key begins on page 220.

"Old MacDonald's Farm" Scramble

This year Meanie Jim's birthday party is named Old MacDonald's Farm. A real farmer is bringing a petting zoo right to Jim's front yard! Unscramble the words below. (Hint: They're all things that might be at the Old MacDonald's Farm birthday party.) Then look at the letters in the birthday presents to find out what Junie B. gets Jim for his birthday.

gato *goat* `g` `o` `a` `t`

bruor *ruorb* `☐` `☐` `☐` `☐` `☐`

nopy `P` `o` `n` `y`

balnool `☐` `☐` `☐` `☐` `☐` `☐` `☐`

rbabit `r` `a` `b` `b` `i` `t`

ekac `☐` `☐` `☐` `☐`

mbal `☐` `☐` `☐` `☐`

gfit `☐` `☐` `☐` `☐`

Junie B. gets Jim a

`F` `o` `o` `t` `☐` `☐` `☐` `☐` .

A Puzzling Story By Junie B. Jones and

_____

(your name)

Can you help Junie B. finish the story? Fill in the word list BEFORE you read the story. Then transfer the words you wrote for each number to the spaces for that number in the story. Happy storytelling!

1) A living thing: _____

2) A day you celebrate with cake: _____

_____

3) A place to keep clothes: _____

4) A small animal: _____

5) An item of clothing: _____

6) A verb (an action word, like _jump, jiggle,_ or _squawk_): _____

7) An adjective (a word that describes something, like _nutty, silly,_ or _loony_): _____

8) A jungle animal: _____

9) A liquid: _____

10) Something delicious to eat: _____

_____

Once there was a little (1) _____
who didn't get invited to a meanie kid's
(2) _____ . That made the little
(1) _____ annoyed, of course.
And so, late one night, she sneaked into the
meanie kid's (3) _____ .
And she put a prickly (4) _____
in his (5) _____ . And so the
next morning, the meanie kid got up and put on
his (5) _____ . And then
YEOWIE! He started to itch and scratch and
(6) _____ like a (7) _____
(8) _____ . And he couldn't stop
scratching the whole entire day! Not even at his
own (2) _____ party! And so
finally, all the guests hosed him down with
(9) _____ until the prickly
(4) _____ ran away. And hurray!
The itching stopped! And then the meanie kid
called the little (1) _____ , who
was hiding at home. And she came over and ate
(10) _____ .
And they all lived happily ever after!

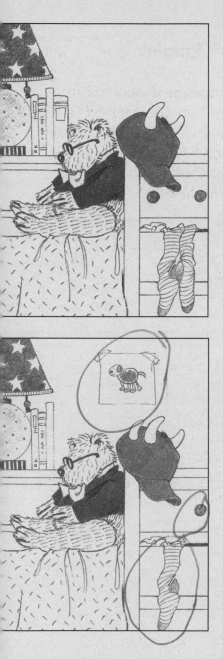

"Bad Day!" (What's the Difference?)

Junie B. is having a bad day. She goes to her room and crawls underneath her covers. It is very muffly down there. You can say mean stuff and no one can hear you. These two pictures of Junie B. under her covers aren't the same, though. Look at the pictures. Can you circle nine differences in the bottom picture?

Answer key begins on page 220.

"It Takes Two" Tangle!

Oh no! That Meanie Jim brought invitations to every single person in Room Nine! Except NOT to Junie B.! She's the *only one* in the whole class who's not invited. But hurray! One of the lines below leads to an invitation! Can you help Junie B. find it? Remember, stay on one path!

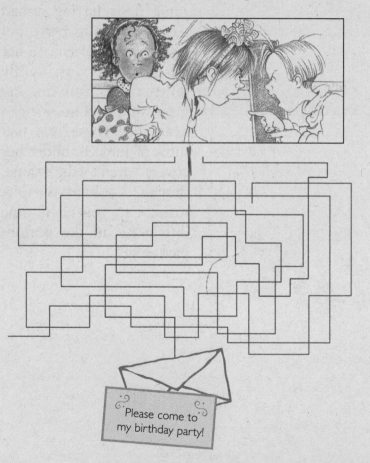

Please come to my birthday party!

Answer key begins on page 220.

Take the Plunge!
Crack the Code!

If Junie B. goes to Meanie Jim's birthday party, she will have to take a bath. And that doesn't even make sense! Because Junie B. doesn't even *like* that meanie kid. So how come she has to get clean for him? That boy is ruining

her whole entire Saturday! What would Junie B. like to do instead of going to Jim's birthday party? Cross out any letters in the word *grampa* to find out, and write the remaining letters on the lines below.

GFRIX TPHMER
TGORIAPRLMEPATA

Junie B. would like to

F̶ix t̶h̶e t̶oilet̶.

Another Puzzling Story
By Junie B. Jones and

_____

(your name)

Can you help Junie B. finish this story? Fill in the word list BEFORE you read the story. Then transfer the words you wrote for each number to the spaces for that number in the story. Have fun!

1) A friend who is a girl: _____

2) A type of relative: _____

3) A farm animal: _____

4) Something that flies: _____

5) A piece of clothing: _____

6) An occupation: _____

7) Things that are soft to land on: _____

_____

Do NOT ask me WHY . . . but my friend

(1) _____ 's (2) _____

brought a bucking (3) _____ to her

56

house for us to ride in the living room. This did
not seem like a good idea. But we are very good
sports. And so (1)_____ went upstairs
to put on her bucking (3) _____
riding outfit. But as she was getting dressed,
a hugie big (4)_____ flew in
her window. And it got all tangled up in her
(5) _____ . So yikes! Then her
(2)_____ had to call 911! And
YAY! A real-life (6)_____ came
to her house. And he carefully cut the
(4)_____ out of her
(5)_____ with the safety
scissors. And so (1)_____
and I took a deep breath. And we spread softie
(7) _____
all over the living room floor. And we rode the
bucking (3) _____
perfectly perfect! It was a delightful day.

"What a Chunk!" Triangle Puzzler

Wowie wow wow! What a chunk! There's a new boy at school and he's as handsome as a movie star. Junie B. would like him for her new boyfriend. That's why she dresses up for him in a very special outfit. (But Mother says you don't make friends by wearing new clothes. You make friends by being fun to be with.) What does Junie B. wear? Color in each three-sided shape to find out!

Answer key begins on page 220.

"Mirror, Mirror" Princess Match-Up!

Junie B. finds all sorts of princess clothes in her house. She finds a lovely collar of jewels where Mother keeps the dog food. Also, she finds long white gloves. They are the same kind of gloves that Cinderella wears! (And Cinderella is a real, actual princess!) Below, only two of the Princess Junie B. pictures match. Draw a line to connect them.

Answer key begins on page 220.

Find the Fake!

Junie B. has a real, actual Dairy Queen crown. But oh no! One of the crowns below is a fake! It's the only one that's different. Can you find and circle it?

Answer key begins on page 220.

Connect-the-Dotties!

It's Picture Day at school! Picture Day is when you wear your bestest dress. And you go to the cafeteria. And a "cheese man" is there. He makes you say *cheese* when he takes your picture. (Cheese makes you smile, apparently.) Start at 1 and connect the dots to see what the picture is on Junie B.'s new dress.

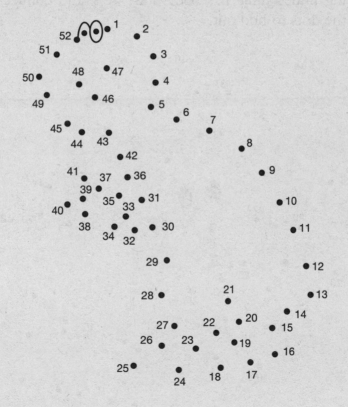

Spooky and Scary Connect-the-Dots

Yikes! The cheese man took a picture while Junie B. was making a terrible face. Then, to ruin her day even more, Paulie Allen Puffer told her something super scary! What did he say was hiding under Junie B.'s bed? Start at 1 and connect the dots to find out.

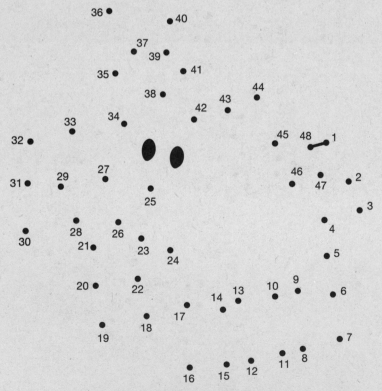

Answer key begins on page 220.

Monster Scramble!

Paulie Allen Puffer's brother says the monster waits until you're asleep. Then he crawls up next to you. And he lies down on your pillow. And he practices fitting your head in his mouth. Paulie Allen Puffer can even *prove* it! Unscramble the words below. (Hint: They're all things that might be in your bedroom.) Then look at the letters in the circles to find the proof.

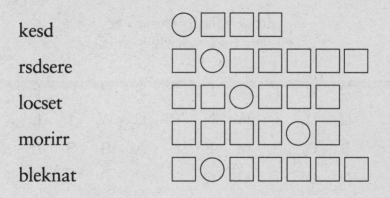

kesd

rsdsere

locset

morirr

bleknat

When you wake up,

there is monster

◯◯◯◯◯

on your pillow!

Answer key begins on page 220.   63

"I'm Not Thinking About That Monster" Word Search!

Junie B. takes her mind off the scary monster by doing a happy dance. It is called the Happy Feet Popcorn Dance. Find and circle some of the things that Junie B. is trying not to think about. Words can go horizontally, vertically, or diagonally.

drool • flatso • monster
• piggy toes • snarly • snuffly

```
D  L  I  S  R  A  S  G  O  F
Q  D  I  A  N  B  U  W  I  L
S  O  R  M  F  U  A  B  S  A
N  D  I  O  O  N  F  G  A  T
A  G  G  R  O  N  D  F  K  S
R  G  S  G  I  L  S  G  L  O
L  Z  R  P  S  L  R  T  M  Y
Y  P  I  G  G  Y  T  O  E  S
F  B  N  K  B  B  L  E  Y  R
P  N  B  L  I  G  V  N  X  W
```

Answer key begins on page 220.

Monster Munchie Connect-the-Dots!

Gulp! Junie B. is worried that the monster under her bed might be getting hungry. What does she think the monster might want to munch on? Start at 1 and connect the dots to find out. Ick!

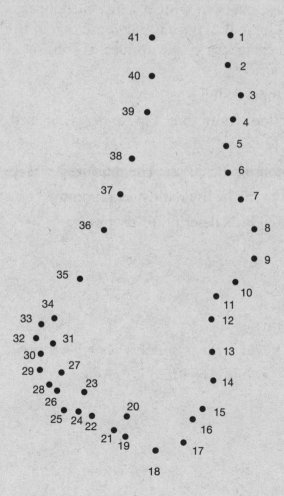

Monster Story Starter!

Do you think the monster under Junie B.'s bed is a nice monster or a mean monster? How do you think the monster got under Junie B.'s bed? Does he like it there? Pretend you're the monster. Then use these pages to write a letter introducing yourself to Junie B. (Hint: You can use one of the suggested choices or create an idea of your own!)

Dear Junie B. Jones,
Don't look now, but I'm under your bed. My name is _____ . I am in the monster business. The business was passed down to me by my daddy and mommy monsters. Here is a little description of myself: _____

_____

_____ .

I like my: _____ .
* *tangly fur* • *stickly hair* • *head horn*
* *four ears* • *two noses* • *hairy feet*

But I'm not crazy about my:

_____.

• *pointy toenails* • *longish nose hairs*
• *crooked teeth* • *serious drooling problem*

The reason I'm under your bed is because:

_____

_____.

• *it's an assignment from Monster School*
• *Daddy is making me*
• *I got lost on my way to Meanie Jim's house*
• *I just like you*

The best part of being a monster is: _____

_____.

The worst part of being a monster is: _____

_____.

I like your room, Junie B. I am not actually that cramped under your bed.

Thank you for letting me be your monster.

Sincerely,

_____

The Invisiblest Guy! Draw-It

Junie B. doesn't know what the monster under her bed looks like. That's because that Grace says monsters turn invisible when you look at them. And so that's how come nobody ever actually sees them. (Gulp. That news gave Junie B.'s stomach the shakies.) What do *you* think the monster under Junie B.'s bed looks like? Draw it!

Monster Matching

Grandma Miller tells Junie B. there's no such thing as monsters. But, of course, Junie B. knows better. Below, only two of the monsters are the same. Draw a line to connect them.

Monster Maze!

Junie B. can't sleep. Daddy is helping her look for the monster. First, he looks under her bed. Then he looks in her closet, and in her drawers, and in her trash can. Plus he even looks in her crayon box! But Daddy can't find a monster anywhere. Can you?

START

Answer key begins on page 220.

"Who's Her Hero?" Connect-the-Dots

Junie B. has a special friend who says he will save her from the monster. He says he will squirt water in the monster's face! And then he will stomple him with his giant feet! Start at 1 and connect the dots to find out who her hero is.

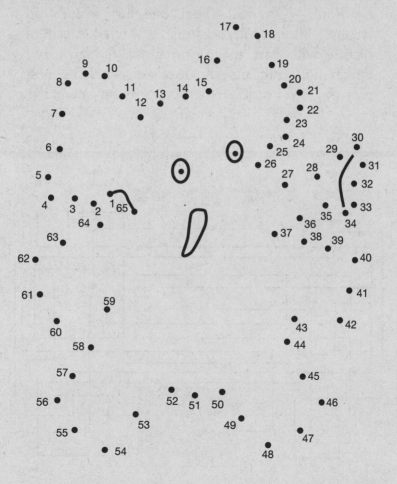

Monster Buster Tangle!

Junie B. doesn't think Philip Johnny Bob is strong enough to save her. That's because he is just made of "fluffy." But wait! Maybe she could suck the monster up in the vacuum cleaner! Or maybe Mother can get a broom and "bash the monster's head in!" (Oh dear. That one just sounds all wrong.) Hmm. Maybe Junie B.'s terrible school picture will scare the monster away! Figure out which line connects the monster with the best way to get rid of it. Remember, stay on one path!

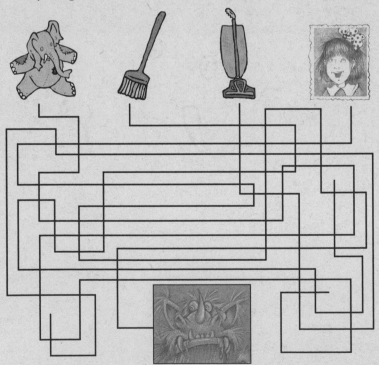

Answer key begins on page 220.

Happy Triangle Mystery

Junie B. has a happy new gift. It fills her with glee. *Glee* is when you run and jump and skip and laugh and clap! Plus also, you dance on top of the dining room table! Color in each three-sided shape to find out what made Junie B. so happy.

Winter Scramble!

Junie B. is not actually allowed to dance on the dining room table. So her glee doesn't last for long. Unscramble the *winter* words below. Then look at the letters in the mittens to find out what kills Junie B.'s glee.

aht □□🧤

eci 🧤□□

tmel 🧤□□□

edls □□🧤□

oswn □□🧤□

uslsh □□🧤□□

cato □□□🧤

🧤🧤🧤🧤 - 🧤🧤🧤 kills the glee.

Answer key begins on page 220.

Mitten Match-Up!

Junie B.'s lovely new mittens are made out of black furry fur. But mittens come in all kinds of different colors and patterns. Look at the mittens below. Circle the two that are exactly the same.

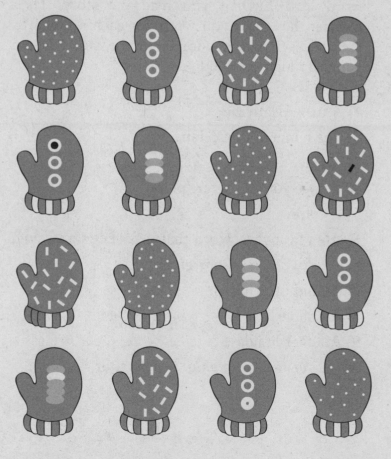

Puzzling Tale #3
By Junie B. Jones and

_____
(your name)

Can you help Junie B. finish the story? Fill in the word list BEFORE you read the story. Then transfer the words you wrote for each number to the spaces for that number in the story. Make yourself laugh out loud!

1) A male relative: _____

2) The name of that relative: _____

3) A place you go: _____

4) Things you can wear (plural): _____

5) A color: _____

6) An adjective (a word that describes something, like *fluffy, scratchy,* or *ugly*): _____

7) A kind of material: _____

8) A holiday: _____

9) Another holiday: _____

10) A talent (like *singing, yodeling,* or *bowing*):

_____

Once upon a time my (1)_____
named (2)_____
went to the (3)_____
and he brought me home some
(4)_____.
They are made out of (5)_____
(6)_____ (7)_____.
And guess what? It was not even my birthday!
Or (8)_____!
Or (9)_____!
(1)_____ (2)_____
just bought them for no good reason! And that is
the bestest reason I ever heard of! That's how
come I love that guy very much. Plus also he is
good at (10)_____.
And that makes me proud of him. I am a lucky
duck!

A	Z
B	Y
C	X
D	W
E	V
F	U
G	T
H	S
I	R
J	Q
K	P
L	O
M	N
N	M
O	L
P	K
Q	J
R	I
S	H
T	G
U	F
V	E
W	D
X	C
Y	B
Z	A

Lost and Found Code Breaker

52835338

911! 911! Junie B. is heartsick because somebody stole her mittens! *Heartsick* is the grown-up word for when your heart is sick. Mrs. takes Junie B. to the Lost and Found box. There is a poem on the front of the box. Use the reverse alphabet code (A = Z, B = Y, C = X, and so on) to complete the poem.

> If you find stuff,
> Bring it in.
> All day long,
>
> ’
>
> ____ ____ __ ____.
>
> BLF'OO DVZI Z TIRM.

Lost and Found
Word Search

The Lost and Found box at Junie B.'s school is filled with the "wonderfulest" items Junie B. has ever seen! Find and circle the things Junie B. sees in the box. Words can go horizontally, vertically, diagonally, or backward.

backpack • baseballs • caps • gloves • lunch box
• scarfs • sunglasses • sweaters • watch

```
S  B  A  S  E  B  A  L  L  S
Q  U  U  A  N  B  U  W  I  L
S  O  N  M  S  C  A  R  F  S
N  D  C  G  O  N  F  C  Y  W
A  W  H  R  L  N  D  M  K  E
B  A  C  K  P  A  C  K  C  A
G  L  O  V  E  S  S  T  M  T
Y  S  D  G  C  A  P  S  E  E
F  B  W  A  T  C  H  E  E  R
P  X  O  B  H  C  N  U  L  S
```

"Junie B. Jones Is Not a Crook" Code

Wowie wow wow! On her way back from the office, Junie B. sees something she loves on the floor. It is a pen that writes in four different colors! And a pen like that makes scribbling a pleasure! Someone lost it. But Junie B. really wants to keep it! So now she remembers a *different* poem. Cross out the letter J for *Junie* and the letter B for *Beatrice* to read the poem Junie B. remembers. Write the remaining letters on the lines below.

JFBIJNBJDJBEBRJSJ

BKJEBEBPJEBRJSJB

JJLBJJBOJSBEJRBSB

BBJWJEJEJPBEJRBS

_____

_____

_____

_____

Answer key begins on page 220.

"Missing Mitten" Tangle

Oh dear! Only one of these paths leads to Junie B.'s missing mittens! Can you help her figure out which one? Remember, stay on one path!

Packing My Party Bag!

Yippee! Yippee! Richie Lucille has invited Junie B. and that Grace to spend the night! And Mother and Daddy said yes! But Mother says Junie B. has packed waaaay too much stuff. Help Junie B. get ready by circling the things that don't belong in her bag.

Answer key begins on page 220.

Connect-the-"Cattle-Act!"

Lucille's richie nanna is picking up Junie B. in her big, expensive "cattle-act." Junie B. has been waiting for her the whole livelong day! Start at 1 and connect the dots to find out what a "cattle-act" looks like.

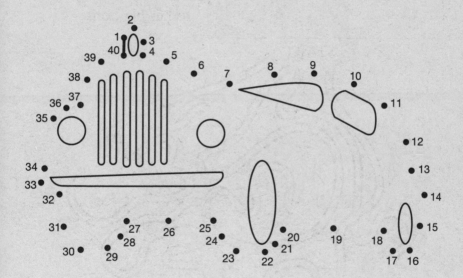

"Ooh-la-la" Mansion Maze!

Lucille's family lives with her richie nanna in a big, giant house with a million rooms in it. (Junie B.'s nanna just owns a plain old, regular house. And that Grace's nanna just owns a condo

in Florida.) Can you help the richie nanna's expensive car find the way to her big house?

START

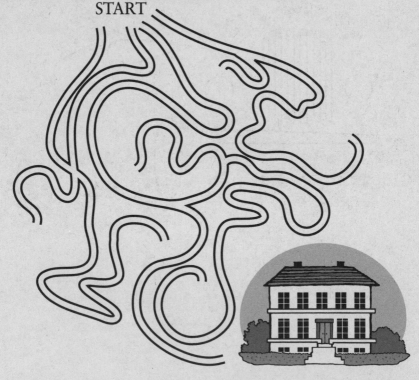

Answer key begins on page 220.

"Party Animal" Crossword Puzzle

Junie B. thinks Lucille's mansion is even "beautifuller" on the inside than it is on the outside. Use the clues for Down and Across to fill in the puzzle spaces with some of the things Junie B. sees at Lucille's.

Across:
2. Sparkly dinner glasses made of
6. A place where you swim
7. A place where you find books

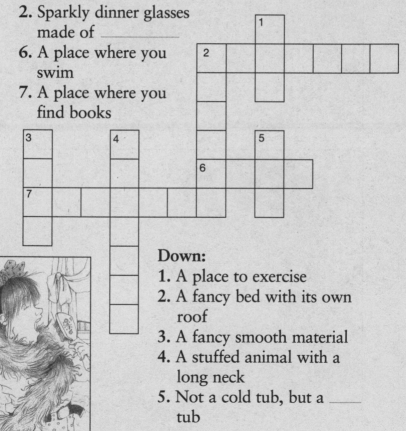

Down:
1. A place to exercise
2. A fancy bed with its own roof
3. A fancy smooth material
4. A stuffed animal with a long neck
5. Not a cold tub, but a _____ tub

"Double the Fun" Differences!

Sleepovers are fun! But these sleepovers aren't exactly the same. Look at the top picture. Then look at the picture on the bottom and circle the five differences.

"Bull in a China Shop"
Triangle Mystery

Oh no! Lucille's nanna tells Junie B. she's a "bull in a china shop"! That's because Junie B. spills things, and breaks things, and makes a mess. Color in each three-sided shape to find out what Junie B. broke.

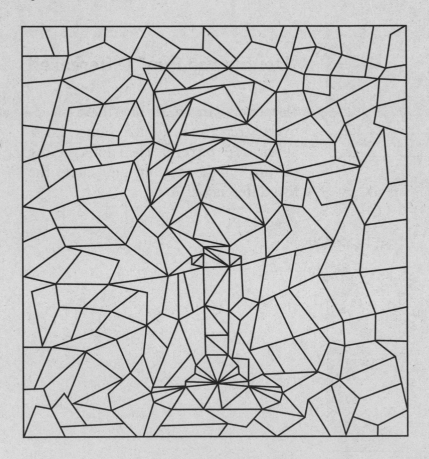

Answer key begins on page 220.

Pancake Tangle!

Yum! Grandma Miller makes blueberry pancakes every Sunday morning. And blueberry pancakes are Junie B.'s favorite breakfast in the whole entire world! Help Junie B. figure out which car goes to Grandma Miller and her delicious pancakes. Remember, stay on one line—no sharp turns!

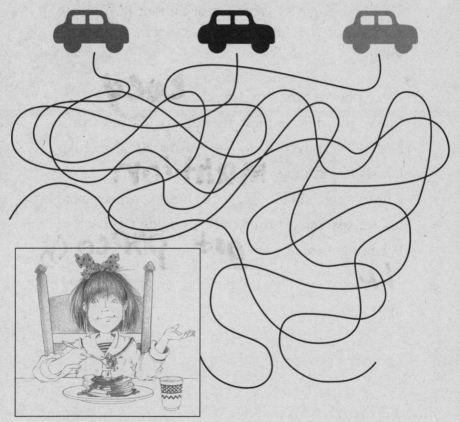

The Bestest Sleepover Ever
By Junie B. Jones and

_____

Oh boy! Imagine you are going to the bestest sleepover ever! Where would it be? Who would you like to go with you? What would you do? Use these pages to write a story about it. You can use one of the suggested choices or create your own.

Once upon a time, my friend **Lucy**

(name of your funniest friend) invited me to the bestest sleepover ever. It wasn't at a regular house. It was in a: **Mantion**

(circus tent, dollhouse, tree house, gingerbread house, spaceship, toy store). I couldn't believe it! When I got there, we: **got popcochn**

iL _____

_____

_____

_____

_____

_____

_____

_____

_____

_____

_____

_____

_____

Name Game!

Junie B.'s daddy is named Robert. Also he has other names, too. 'Cause some people call him Bob. And other people call him Bobby. Junie B. would like to be named Pinkie Gladys Gutzman. That's because "pinkie" is the loveliest color she ever saw. Write your name or nickname below, going from top to bottom, with one letter on each line. Add more lines if you need them. Then write a word that describes you that starts with each letter. Decorate each line with stars, balloons, and other happy shapes.

"Are We There Yet?" Tangle!

Hurray! Hurray! Junie B. is going to the beauty shop with her daddy. She really enjoys that place! But Junie B. and Daddy have been driving in the car a real long time. And now Junie B. is worried that they're lost. Can you help Daddy pick the right road to get to the beauty shop? Remember, stay on one path!

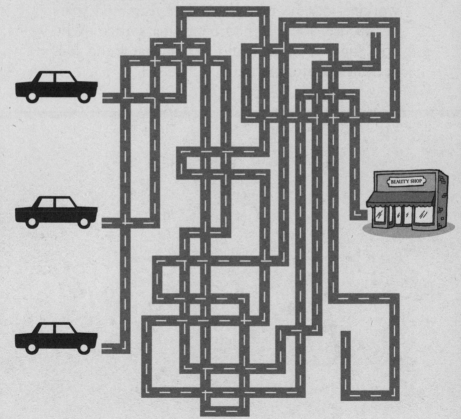

Answer key begins on page 220.

Snipping, Snipping, Snipping

Junie B. would like to be a beauty shop guy. She already has a name tag and a towel and a broom and some scissors. She thinks she is all set to go to work, probably. But then Daddy tells her that working in a beauty shop takes years and years of practice. Junie B. had better get started! Who does Junie B. practice on first? Start at 1 and connect the dots to find out.

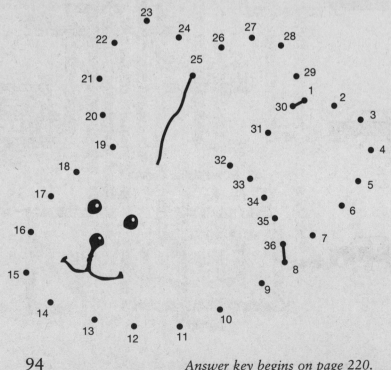

Answer key begins on page 220.

You Be the Beauty Shop Guy!

Yikes! Junie B. cut her own hair! And now she has sprigs! (Sprigs are "little shortie sticklets." And they are *not* attractive.) Now it's your turn to be the beauty shop guy. Can you help Junie B. give the people below new hairstyles?

Matching Hats!

Junie B. has a good idea! If she wears her hat with the devil horns to school, no one will even see her hair sprigs. Hmm . . . but what if somebody steals the devil horn hat off her head? Maybe she'd better wear *three* hats. 'Cause that will give her two whole extra hats of protection! Look at the hats below. Only two of them match. Can you circle them?

Answer key begins on page 220.

Beauty Shop Word Search

Junie B. loves *everything* about beauty shops! Can you find and circle the beauty shop words? Words can go horizontally, vertically, diagonally, or backward.

blow dryer • broom • comb • fluffy towel
• hair gel • scissors • shampoo

B M O C Z L R O Y F P
Q L I R I L T E X L S
P S O G S Y L N M U E
L C O W G B V O O F R
E I P G D G G I O F G
G S M K I R W S R Y U
R S A L A U Y U B T V
I O H R B S C E O O Y
A R S N O B V L R W N
H S H U Y A G R S E K
L I Z H A Y R B L L W

Pet Day Triangle Puzzler

Yay! Yay! Hurray! It's Pet Day in Room Nine! Color in each three-sided shape to find out what Junie B.'s bestest friend named that Grace is going to bring to school.

Answer key begins on page 220.

Pet Day Connect-the-Dots!

Junie B.'s other bestest friend named Lucille can't wait for Pet Day, either! Start at 1 and connect the dots to see what Lucille wants to bring in.

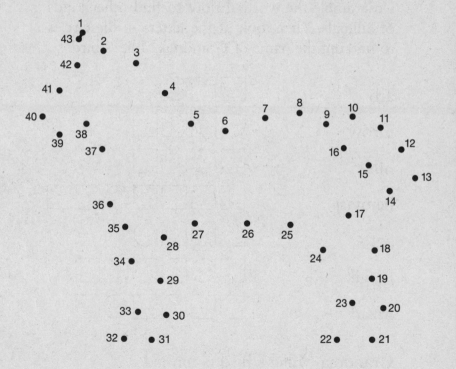

Scrambled Pets!

Junie B. has a dog named Tickle. But Mrs. says no cats or dogs on Pet Day. The only animals the children can bring in are small pets in cages. Grandma Miller says Junie B. can bring in her pet bird. Unscramble the words below to find other kinds of animals. Then look at the letters in the circles to find out the name of Grandma Miller's bird.

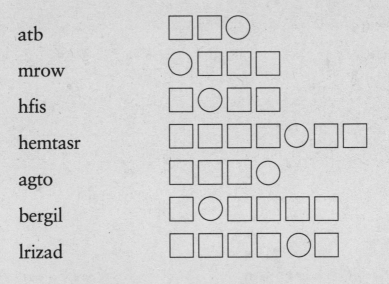

atb

mrow

hfis

hemtasr

agto

bergil

lrizad

Grandma Miller's bird is named

◯◯◯◯◯◯.

Answer key begins on page 220.

Junie B. Has a Secret

Junie B. tells Grandma Miller a secret about her bird. (Warning: It is not a pleasant secret.) Cross out any letters in the word *NO* to find out why Junie B. doesn't want to take that bird to school. Write the remaining letters on the lines below.

NSOHNEO NNHOONAONTONEONSO

TNNHOANTO NNDNUOMNBO

NBONINROND

___ ____

____ ____

____

Catching-Friends Maze

Oh dear! A crazy old raccoon keeps breaking into Grandma Miller's garbage can! And now Junie B. wants to catch it so she can bring it in for Pet Day. Can you help Junie B. catch the raccoon? (P.S. Do NOT try this at home. Raccoons have sharp claws and teeth.)

START

Answer key begins on page 220.

Ooey Gooey Pet Puzzle

Grandma Miller says Junie B. can bring a baby worm to Pet Day. At first, Junie B. thinks worms cannot be pets. She says that pets have to have fur so you can *pet* them. And worms just have "ooey gooey skin." But then she changes her mind. Start at this worm's head and cross out any letters in the word *fur* to find out what Junie B. names her new worm. Write the remaining letters on the lines below.

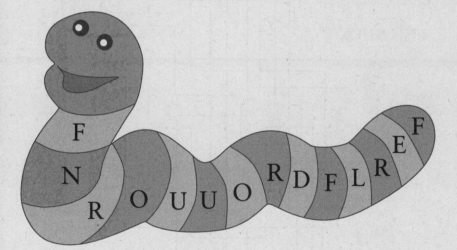

Junie B.'s worm is named

—— —— —— —— —— ——.

"My Proudest Honor" Tangle

Junie B. wants to find the perfect pet for Pet Day. She has lots of ideas. But she can only bring one pet to school. Can you pick the pet that will win her a prize? Remember, stay on one path!

SPARKLE

FISH STICK

NOODLE

TICKLE

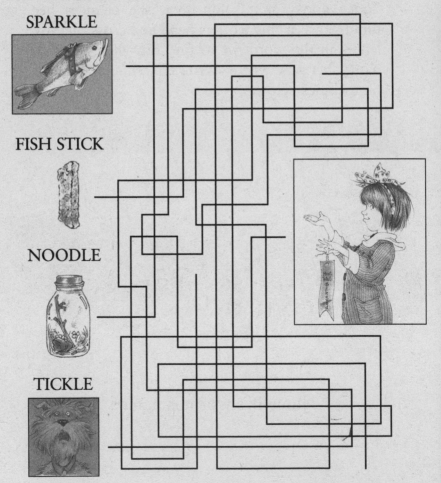

Answer key begins on page 220.

Pet Picture!

Pet Day in Room Nine is very exciting! There are all *sorts* of animals there! Crybaby William brings his bullfrog named Wendell! And Charlotte brings her bunny named Slippers! And Paulie Allen Puffer brings his parrot named Pirate Pete! Draw a picture of your pet or the pet you'd like to have. You can be in the picture, too!

Your Perfect Pet!

Now use the space below to write about your pet. If you don't have a pet, write about an imaginary pet you would like to have.

My pet is the cutest _____
you ever saw!
I named my pet _____
because _____
_____.

The thing about my pet that makes me giggle is
when she/he _____
_____
_____
_____.

The thing that my pet loves best about me is
when I _____
_____
_____
_____.

My pet is "specialer" than every other pet
because _____

_____

_____

_____ .

If my pet could talk, his/her voice would sound
like _____

_____

_____ .

If I took my pet to Pet Day in Room Nine, my
pet would win the prize for most _____

_____ .

My pet made me laugh out loud when

_____

_____

_____ .

If my pet could have a pet, it would have a
_____ , probably.

A	1
B	2
C	3
D	4
E	5
F	6
G	7
H	8
I	9
J	10
K	11
L	12
M	13
N	14
O	15
P	16
Q	17
R	18
S	19
T	20
U	21
V	22
W	23
X	24
Y	25
Z	26

"Worstest Day" Number Code!

Today was the worstest day of Junie B.'s life. That's because her boyfriend named Ricardo wanted to chase other girls on the playground! But Mother says Junie B. is *way* too young to have a boyfriend. Use numbers to solve the code below. Each problem gives a number. Each number equals a letter in the alphabet (A = 1, B = 2, C = 3, and so on). Use the letters to fill in the blanks and find out what Mother says little girls are supposed to be.

3 + 3 = _____

14 + 1 = _____

10 + 5 = _____

10 + 10 = _____

2 + 4 = _____

15 + 3 = _____

2 + 3 = _____

4 + 1 = _____

Little girls are supposed to be

_____ _____ _____ _____ loose and fancy _____ _____ _____ _____.

Answer key begins on page 220.

Wedding Word Search!

Good news, people! Junie B.'s aunt Flo is getting married, and Junie B. is going to her first wedding ever! Can you find and circle the wedding words? Can you find a word that *doesn't* belong in weddings? Words can go horizontally, vertically, or diagonally.

bells • bouquet • bride • cake • flower girl • groom • love • potato • ring • veil

```
D  L  P  S  R  A  S  G  O  F
Q  B  O  U  Q  U  E  T  I  X
S  R  T  M  H  O  A  B  S  E
G  I  A  C  A  K  E  C  K  T
R  D  T  R  O  N  D  D  U  S
O  E  O  G  L  L  R  G  L  B
O  O  R  P  O  L  I  V  M  E
M  M  I  G  V  Y  N  E  E  L
F  L  O  W  E  R  G  I  R  L
P  K  O  Z  P  T  A  L  X  S
```

Match the Bouquet!

Oh my! Oh dear! Junie B. has a LOT to learn about being in a wedding. Carrying flowers can be a real problem! Below, only two of the bouquets match. Can you help Junie B. find the matching bouquets? Draw lines to connect them.

110

Answer key begins on page 220.

Philip Johnny Bob

Poor Junie B.! She is SO disappointed! Aunt Flo asked someone *else* to be the flower girl. Thank goodness Junie B. has her favorite stuffed animal, Philip Johnny Bob, to talk to. And he always gives her good advice. What do you think Philip Johnny Bob is thinking in this picture? Write it in the thought bubble.

Don't worry, Junie B. When I get married, you can be *my* flower girl! Plus there are LOTS of other things you're good at, too! Like you're good at _____

_____

and _____

_____

and you're *really* good at _____

_____!

Big-Day Triangle Puzzler!

Here comes the bride! All dressed and wide!
Her name is Clyde! And she reads *TV Guide*!

Aunt Flo's big day is finally here! Color in each three-sided shape to reveal something she'll need when she walks down the aisle.

Answer key begins on page 220.

Rings 'n' Things!

Oh no! Aunt Flo lost her engagement ring!
And it is a beauty! This is what it looks like:
But only one of the rings below is Aunt Flo's.
Can you help her find the right ring? Circle it.

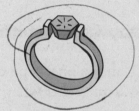

Big-Day Connect-the-Dots!

Now start at 1 and connect the dots to see something Aunt Flo *won't* need when she walks down the aisle.

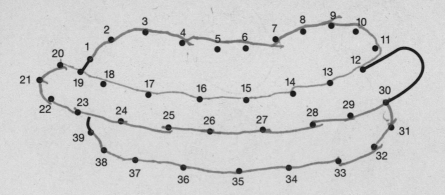

Answer key begins on page 220.

"A Little Tussle" Tangle

Oh my! This is NOT good. The *real* flower girl, Bo, is walking down the aisle. But Junie B. *still* wants to carry the wedding flowers! That is why she quick reaches for Bo's flower basket. And she and Bo get into a "little tussle." (*Little tussle* is

the grown-up word for *Bo just won't let go of the darned thing!*) Who will end up with the basket? Follow the paths to find out! Remember, stay on one line—no sharp turns!

"Tic-Tac-(Loose) Toe" Tussle

"Loose feet" feel very "freeish." Sometimes "loose feet" are even funner than "grown-up feet." Challenge a friend to a friendly tic-tac-(loose) toe tussle. Choose whether you want to be X's or O's. Take turns and mark your letter in one of the nine tic-tac-toe squares. If you get three of your marks in a row horizontally, vertically, or diagonally, you win! Wiggle your toes and enjoy!

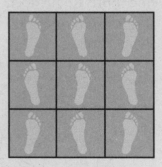

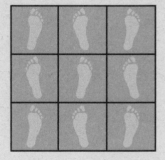

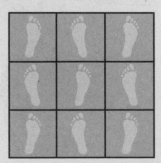

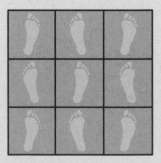

Flower Power Face-Off!

Now challenge a friend to a flower face-off. Take turns drawing lines connecting the flowers, one line at a time, to make a square. Lines can go horizontally or vertically, but not diagonally. The player who completes a square gets to put his or her initials inside it and take another turn. The player with more squares wins. (Junie B. has made the first move here!)

Spot the Differences!

Mother and Daddy were right! Junie B. feels better with "loose feet." 'Cause now she can wiggle her piggy toes! Look at the pictures below. Can you circle seven differences in the second picture?

"Valentime's" Day Party Ideas!

Fun! Fun! Fun! Room Nine is planning a "Valentime's" Day party, and everyone has ideas! Junie B. would like to have cake and doughnuts. Plus also, she'd like cheese popcorn and cotton candy and pretzels and candy apples. And, of course, they'll need red licorice and peanut butter cups! Circle the items below that DON'T belong at a "Valentime's" Day party.

Answer key begins on page 220.

Give Your Puzzled Brain a Rest

Valentines are special cards about friendship. Junie B. has to bring them for everyone in Room Nine. (She even has to bring cards to the "big, fat stinky heads.") Give your puzzled brain a rest and cut out these special Junie B. "valentimes." Then give them to *your* friends. It doesn't even have to be Valentine's Day!

Zzzt! You make everything sparky!

To:

_____

From:

_____

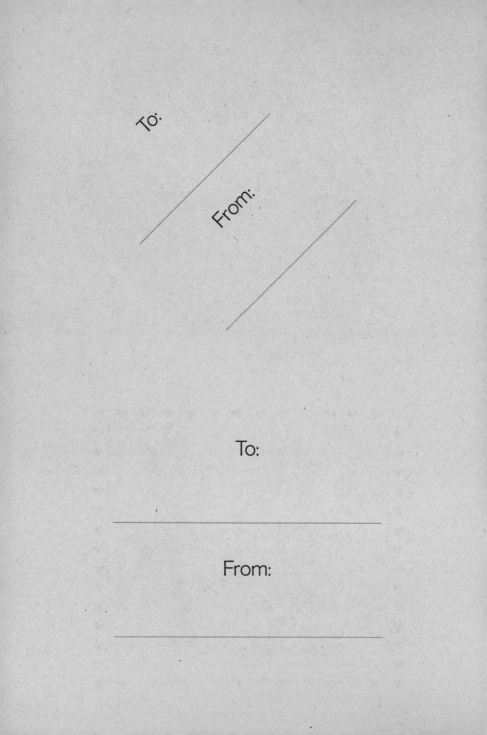

To:

From:

To:

From:

Mushy Gushy Match-Up

All the children in Room Nine are cutting out hearts. But Junie B. and Meanie Jim got in trouble. And so their cutting days are over. (And their pasting days never even got started!) Look at the valentine hearts below. Can you circle the two that match?

Missing-"Valentime" Maze!

Yahoo! It's time to pass out the "valentimes"! But oh no! Junie B. is *missing* one! Can you help Junie B. find her way to her missing card?

START

Be Mine!

Answer key begins on page 220.

Secret-Admirer Secret Code!

Yippee! Junie B. found her missing "valentime" card. It was the "mushy gushy" kind. And it was signed, *From Your Secret Admirer.* Now Junie B. just has to figure out who her secret admirer *is* and she will be in business! Use the reverse alphabet code (A = Z, B = Y, C = X, and so on) to find out the name of Junie B.'s secret admirer.

MEANIE Jim

NVZMRV QRN

A	Z
B	Y
C	X
D	W
E	V
F	U
G	T
H	S
I	R
J	Q
K	P
L	O
M	N
N	M
O	L
P	K
Q	J
R	I
S	H
T	G
U	F
V	E
W	D
X	C
Y	B
Z	A

Unscramble Junie B.'s Secret Message!

Junie B. wrote her own secret "valentime" message. Unscramble the words below. (Hint: They're all things you might have on Valentine's Day!) Then look at the letters in the hearts to find out who Junie B.'s valentine is for!

nyacd   ☐ ☐ ☐ ☐ ♡

eøvl   ☐ ♡ ☐ ☐

fnu   f ♡ n

My bestest friend is
Y O U !
Love,
Junie B. Jones

    Answer key begins on page 220.

"What's Junie B. Scared Of?" Scramble!

Surprise! Surprise! Room Nine is going on a field trip. They're going to a real, actual farm! But Junie B. doesn't want to go. Farms are *not* her favorites. (And she has a good reason, too!) Unscramble the *animal* names below. Then look at the letters in the circles to find out why Junie B. doesn't want to go.

ipg   Ⓟ i Ⓖ

ocw   c Ⓞ w

enh   h Ⓔ Ⓝ

kcihc   c h Ⓘ c k

sehpe   s h Ⓔ e P

gsooe   g Ⓞ o Ⓢ e

Junie B. is afraid of ◯◯◯◯◯◯.

Triangle Puzzler!

Mother says ponies won't actually stomple you into the ground and kill you, like Junie B. heard on TV. But now Junie B. is worried about something else. Color in each three-sided shape to find out what she's afraid of.

Answer key begins on page 220.

And on This Farm There Was a . . . What?!

Lucille wants to go to a flamingo farm. But Mrs. says no. They are just going to a plain old, regular farm with plain old, regular farm animals. Can you circle the things below that don't really belong on a plain old, regular farm?

⋈ Cockle-Doodly-Doo Differences! ⋈

Uh-oh! Bad news! Mother is *actually* going to make Junie B. go on the field trip! And look! Everyone from Room Nine is already on the school bus and ready to go. But the two bus pictures aren't the same. Can you circle six differences in the second picture?

Old MacDonald Maze

Farmer Flores shows the children pigs and goats and lambs and a black-and-white cow. He even shows them how to *milk* the cow! (Junie B. believes that he used a *demo cow*.) Can you help Junie B. find her way to an animal on the farm that she will love? (Hint: It's fluffery, and softie, and light as feathers.)

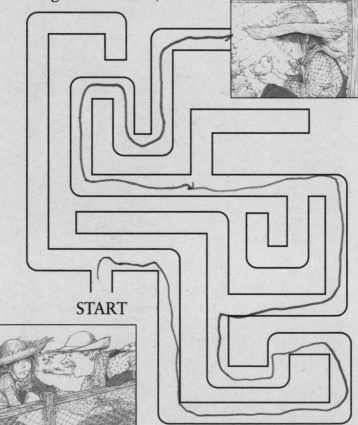

START

Answer key begins on page 220.

Confusion Number Code!

The baby chick's name is Spike. Junie B. thinks Spike is not a good name for a fluffery baby chick. But Farmer Flores says Spike won't be a little chick forever. Use numbers to solve the code below. Each problem gives a number. Each number equals a letter in the alphabet (A = 1, B = 2, C = 3, and so on). Use the letters to fill in the blanks and find out what Spike will grow up to be.

17 + 1 = _18_

12 + 3 = _15_

10 + 5 = _15_

15 + 4 = _19_

10 + 10 = _20_

3 + 2 = _5_

16 + 2 = _18_

Spike will be a
_r o o s t e r_.

A	1
B	2
C	3
D	4
E	5
F	6
G	7
H	8
I	9
J	10
K	11
L	12
M	13
N	14
O	15
P	16
Q	17
R	18
S	19
T	20
U	21
V	22
W	23
X	24
Y	25
Z	26

"Peep in Her Pocket" Word Search

Junie B. has a "peep" in her pocket! If her pockets were "HUGIE BIG," she could put lots of other things from the farm in there, too! Can you find and circle the farm things that would need "HUGIE BIG" pockets? Words can go horizontally, vertically, or diagonally.

chicken • corn • duck • eggs • farmer • hay • horse • pig • rooster • sheep • tractor

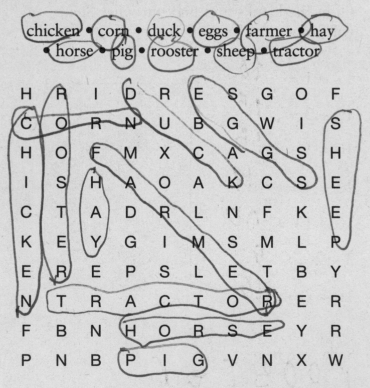

H R I D R E S G O F
C O R N U B G W I S
H O F M X C A G S H
I S H A O A K C S E
C T A D R L N F K E
K E Y G I M S M L P
E R E P S L E T B Y
N T R A C T O R E R
F B N H O R S E Y R
P N B P I G V N X W

Answer key begins on page 220.

Captain Field Day Warm-Up!

Yay! Yippee! Hurray! It's Field Day at school! Junie B. and her bestest friends that Grace and Lucille are running and skipping all over Room Nine. That's because they have to warm up their muscles! Use the reverse alphabet code (A = Z, B = Y, C = X, and so on) to find out what Junie B. *thinks* will happen if you don't warm up.

    Your muscles will get

CLAMS!

XOZNH!

Answer key begins on page 220.   137

A	Z
B	Y
C	X
D	W
E	V
F	U
G	T
H	S
I	R
J	Q
K	P
L	O
M	N
N	M
O	L
P	K
Q	J
R	I
S	H
T	G
U	F
V	E
W	D
X	C
Y	B
Z	A

Superhero Word Power!

How many different words can you make from the letters in CAPTAIN FIELD DAY? Try to make at least ten. Write them on the lines below. Junie B. wrote down two to get you started!

CAPTAIN FIELD DAY

pie

cape

Answer key begins on page 220.

Captain Field Day!

Hurray! Hurray! Junie B. is Captain Field Day! Mrs. says a team captain supports the team. But Junie B. thinks *captain* means the same thing as *boss*. Also, Captain Field Day sounds like the name of a superhero! Imagine you were a superhero. Tell about your super self here. (Hint: You can circle one of the suggested choices or create an idea of your own!)

My superhero name is: _____
_____ .

My special superpower is: _____
_____ .

1. *Super Smelly Breath*
    (breath that is so bad it can melt a monster)
2. *Super Expando-Feet (feet that can inflate*
    to stomple out evil robot lizards)
3. *Super Screechy-Whistle Lips*
    (lips that can whistle for police and hurt
    bad guys' ears . . . but they don't harm dogs)

Super Me to the Rescue
By Junie B. and

_____

(your name)

Now use the space below to write a story about the time superhero Y-O-U saved your school. (Hint: You can circle one of the suggested choices or create an idea of your own!)

It started out as a regular morning in school. No one knew I was really a superhero. But then, out of the blue, _____

_____

1. *Mega Monster, "Ghoulbert Droolbert"*
2. *Robot Lizard, "Scaly-Skin Larry"*
3. *Library Crook, "the Big Book Schnook"*
appeared out of nowhere! And I knew he

wanted to: _____

_____

_____.

1. *drip gooey monster drool on the sliding board.*
2. *eat the swing set with his scaly jaws of steel.*
3. *steal all the easy-reader books from the library,*
   leaving only thick books with no pictures.
So ha! I used my: _____

_____.

1. *Super Smelly Breath.*
2. *Super Expando-Feet.*
3. *Super Screechy-Whistle Lips.*
And I saved the day. This is how I did it: _____

_____

_____

_____

_____

_____

_____

_____

_____

Event Number One!

The first event between Room Eight and Room Nine is a team relay race. "On your mark, get set, go!" shouts Mrs. Then, boom! That Grace goes first! She is fast as a rocket! Now it's Junie B.'s turn! Can you help Junie B. run the relay race?

START

Answer key begins on page 220.

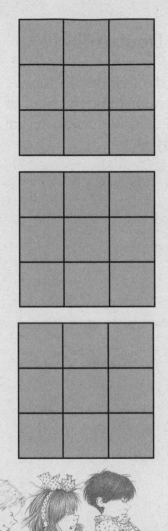

Tic-Tac-Toe
Tug-of-War

Have your own Field Day contest! Remember, Mrs. says Field Day is not about who wins or loses. It's about having FUN! So find a friend and play tic-tac-toe tug-of-war! Choose whether you want to be X's or O's. Take turns and mark your letter in one of the nine tic-tac-toe squares. If you get three of your marks in a row horizontally, vertically, or diagonally, you win!

Happy Birthday Double Take!

Junie B. was named after the month of "Junie." That's because she was born on Junie the first, of course! Can you circle eight differences in the second happy-birthday party picture?

Graduation Connect-the-Dots

Lucille thinks she knows some wonderful news! Gus Vallony brought Room Nine a big stack of boxes. And everyone is getting a box for kindergarten graduation. Start at 1 and connect the dots to see what Lucille thinks is inside each box.

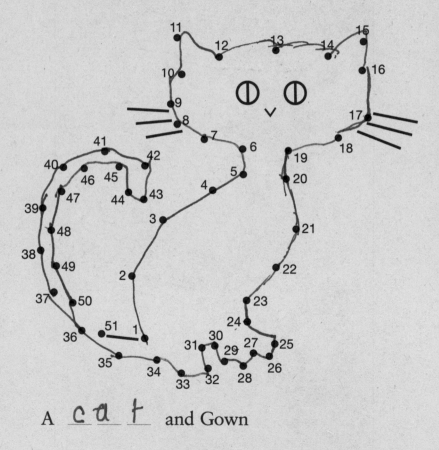

A __c a t__ and Gown

Answer key begins on page 220.

"Cats and Gowns" Puzzler

Oh dear! Lucille misunderstood, apparently. And now all the children are disappointed in their boxes from Gus Vallony. Color in each three-sided shape to find out what's *really* inside the boxes.

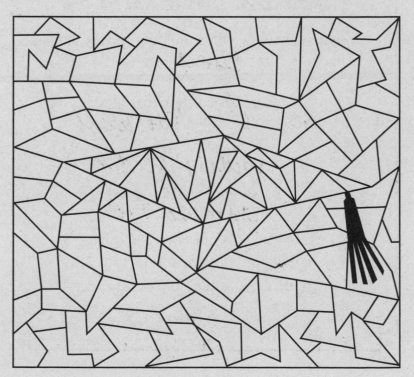

Congratulations, Graduate!

A diploma! A diploma! Junie B. loves diplomas! Mrs. says a diploma is a certificate that says you've completed part of your education. Fill out the diploma that Junie B. made for you. Cut it out and hang it somewhere special.

JUNIE B. UNIVERSITY

Wowie wow wow! This diploma means that

Lucy

(your name)

has learned how to

do a kartweel

and

multiplecatin

and has also gotten pretty good at

gymnastis .

Learning stuff is not easy, I tell you!
Keep up the good work!
Your friend and diploma maker,

Junie B. Jones

Graduation Rhymes

Room Nine is writing a poem about graduation. So far, they only have three lines. Can you complete the last line? (Hint: Mrs. would like it to rhyme with the word *blue*. So Lucille suggests: "My dress will be new!" And Lynnie suggests: "We made it! Woo-hoo!" And Paulie Allen Puffer suggests: "The zoo is P.U.!") How would *you* finish the poem to make it your own? Remember, the last word has to rhyme with *blue*.

> *Roses are red,*
> *Violets are blue.*
> *Graduation is here*
> cows Say moo .

Juice-Splotchie Scramble

Whoops! Junie B. has had a very terrible grape juice spill! And now her graduation gown has juice driblets soaked into its front! BUT HA! She colored purple splotchies all over her gown. So maybe no one will notice the grape juice spots!

What does Grampa Miller say about Junie B.'s splotchies? Unscramble the *color* words below. Then look at the letters in the circles to see what Grampa says.

slivre

pelrup

orgaen

hiwte

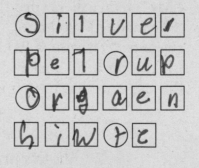

She'll be easy to Ⓢ Ⓟ Ⓞ Ⓣ .

Answer key begins on page 220.

Spot the Same Spots!

Wowie wow wow! Junie B.'s friends colored spots on their gowns, too. So now she won't feel bad. *That* is called friendship, I tell you! Two of the gowns below are exactly the same. Can you SPOT the matching pair and circle them?

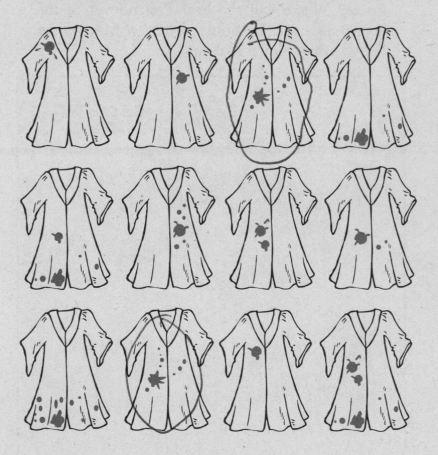

Graduation Story Starter!

Mrs. tells the children that as they go through school, they'll get several diplomas. Take a minute to imagine Junie B. graduating from college! What do you think she'll be like as a grown-up? Will she still be friends with Lucille and that Grace? Where will she live? Pretend you're the grown-up Junie B. Write a letter to Mrs. telling her what your life is like now.

Dear Mrs.,

My name is Junie B. Jones. You might remember me from kindergarten. Or maybe not. Some of my teachers have blocked me out of their heads, I believe.

I am all grown up now. Here are some things you might be surprised to know about me:

_____

_____

_____

_____

_____

_____

_____

_____

_____

_____

_____

_____

Love,
Junie B. Jones, grown-up lady

"The Time of Your Life" Tangle!

Kindergarten has been the time of Junie B.'s life!
Now she is finally ready to get her diploma! But
only one of the lines below leads to the diploma.
Can you help Junie B. find it? Remember, stay on
one path—don't be fooled by intersections!

154

Answer key begins on page 220.

"Junie B., First Grader" Words

At last! At last! Junie B. is finally in first grade! How many different words can you make from the letters in JUNIE B., FIRST GRADER? Try to make at least ten. Write them on the lines below. Junie B. wrote down two to get you started!

JUNIE B., FIRST GRADER

read

fun

Junie

first

grader

Dear

Deer

fist

June

rist

grand

grade

Puzzling Words

Some children get to school by carpooling. Carpooling is one of the biggest disappointments of Junie B.'s whole entire school career. Because there's no actual *pool* in the *car*! This is what Junie B. *thought* her car pool would look like:

Here are some other words that may sound different from their actual meaning. Pick one (or think of your own) and illustrate what it might look like if it looked exactly the way it sounded.

book bag • bookworm • catfish • cupcake • doggy bag • eggplant • football • housefly • junk mail • swordfish

First-Grade Word Search

Junie B. meets lots of new friends in first grade. There are *so* many new things to remember! Can you find and circle the first-grade names and words below? Words can go horizontally, vertically, or diagonally.

Camille • Chenille • glasses • Herb • José • journal • Lennie • May • Mr. Scary

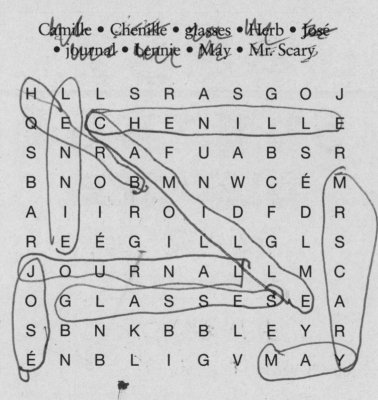

```
H L L L S R A S G O J
Q E C H E N I L L E E
S N R A F U A B S R
B N O B M N W C É M
A I I R O I D F D R
R E É G I L L G L S
J O U R N A L L M C
O G L A S S E S E A
S B N K B B L E Y R
É N B L I G V M A Y
```

The Fuzzy-Smudgie
Eye Game!

Oh dear! Junie B. is having trouble reading the board. It looks like it's filled with fuzzy smudgies and smearballs. Cross out the fuzzy smudgies. Write the remaining letters in the circles below. Unscramble them to find out what Junie B. needs.

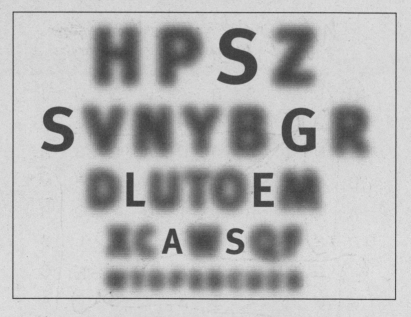

Junie B. needs ⓖⓘⓐⓢⓢⓔⓢ **Glasses**.

Answer key begins on page 220.

Looking for Lunch!

Hurray! Hurray! Junie B.'s new lunch box finally came in the mail! Can you find and circle the things that she can put in her lunch box? Words can go horizontally, vertically, or diagonally. Draw a star next to the things that do NOT belong in a lunch box.

apple • banana • cheese • cookie • forklift • mattress • milk • raisins • sandwich • seal

D V I S R A M G O U
Q M I C H E E S E O
C I M B F G K B S F
O L I A P P L E E R
O K G N T N D F A A
K G S A I T S G L I
I U R N S L R T M S
E J N A L H T E E I
F O R K L I F T S N
S A N D W I C H U S

Ho-Ho-Hoagie Match

It's Hoagie Day at school! Hoagies are a very popular lunch item. (Except Sheldon is not actually *allowed* to eat hoagies, because he's allergic to "fake meat and cheese.") Can you draw lines to connect the matching hoagies below?

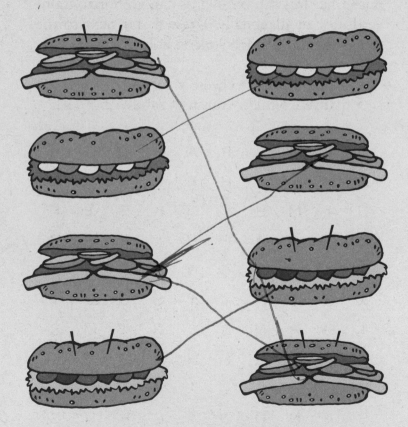

Answer key begins on page 220.

Look at the Lunch Boxes!

Junie B. thinks "brought" lunches are way better than "bought" lunches. (May does not agree, of course. May does not agree with *anything*.) Look at the lunch boxes below. Only two of them are the same. Can you find and circle them?

Answer key begins on page 220.

Illustrate It!

Gladys Gutzman is one of Junie B.'s very favorite people. She used to be the Boss of Cookies. But this year, she's the Boss of *the Whole Entire Kitchen Operation*!

Here is a picture Junie B. drew of Gladys Gutzman. She made her out of sugar cookie shapes.

Junie B. also drew a picture of the school nurse using Band-Aid shapes.

Now you try it.
Can you draw
a person using
just circles?

Now try drawing
someone using
only triangles!

Cookies!

One of Mrs. Gutzman's jobs is to bring sugar cookies to the children. Sugar cookies are Junie B.'s favorite! Look at the cookies below. Can you find and circle the two that match?

Answer key begins on page 220.

Junie B., Boss of Lunch

Good news! Gladys Gutzman invited Junie B. to be her kitchen helper. And *more* good news! Mother and Daddy said Y-E-S! Junie B. will even get to wear a *real professional apron*! Draw a line connecting Junie B. to the things she might need in the cafeteria kitchen. Draw an X over the things that don't belong in the kitchen.

Answer key begins on page 220.

A	Z
B	Y
C	X
D	W
E	V
F	U
G	T
H	S
I	R
J	Q
K	P
L	O
M	N
N	M
O	L
P	K
Q	J
R	I
S	H
T	G
U	F
V	E
W	D
X	C
Y	B
Z	A

Cafeteria Secret Code!

Yuck! When Junie B. works in the cafeteria kitchen, something does NOT smell delicious. And yuck! She has to serve it for lunch! What is Junie B. smelling? Use the reverse alphabet code (A = Z, B = Y, C = X, and so on) to complete the menu and find out what's for lunch.

Today's Menu

carrots   peas

GFMZ

MLLWOV

HGRMPOV

Answer key begins on page 220.

Stinkle Strike!

Being a kitchen helper is not a breeze. Junie B. tells her friends she has to keep the "hair and germs" out of the tuna noodle stinkle. And so bluck! Who wants to eat *that*? Help the children in Junie B.'s class get away from the stinkle and find their way to something delicious instead.

START

Stinkle Scramble

What do the children end up eating for lunch instead of the tuna noodle stinkle? Unscramble the *food* words below. Then look at the letters in the circles to see what Mrs. Gutzman brings them.

abnana

aplep

likm

arrcot

sneab

ceehes

yugrot

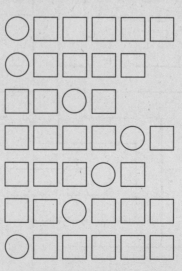

○○○○○○○ SANDWICHES

Answer key begins on page 220.

Connect-the-Teeth!

Yikes! Junie B. is losing her top front tooth. And she thinks she knows the truth about the tooth fairy. She is (almost) positive that the tooth fairy is really someone *else*. Start at 1 and connect the teeth to find out who Junie B. thinks is really collecting her teeth!

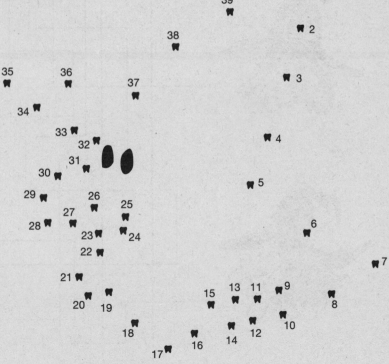

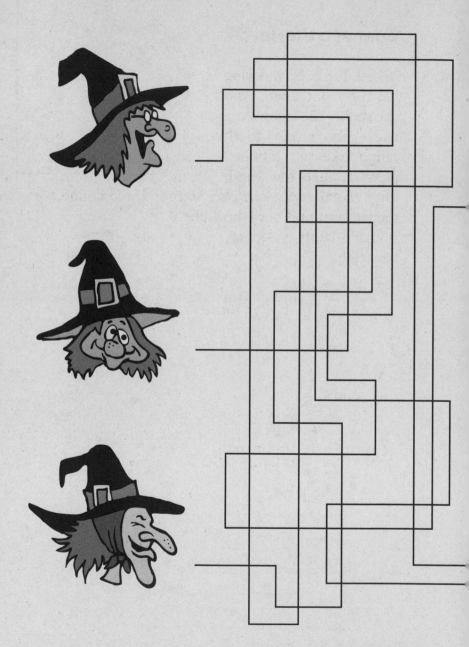

Which Witch Tangle

Gulp! What if Junie B. is right? What if there really *is* a tooth witch? Surely, she would be a nice little witch, though . . . correct? One of the lines below leads to a tooth. But only one of the witches has the right path. Can you find *which* witch? Remember, stay on one path!

"Toothless Wonder" Words

Junie B. is a toothless wonder! How many different words can you make from the letters in TOOTHLESS WONDER? Try to make at least ten. Write them on the lines below. Junie B. wrote down two to get you started!

TOOTHLESS WONDER

one

hoot

Answer key begins on page 220.

A Stumper

Wowie wow wow! Last night was a good tooth night for Ollie *and* Junie B.! First, Junie B. got CASH for her *old* baby tooth! Then HA! Ollie got a brand-*new* baby tooth! Whoa! Wait a minute! Hold the phone! What if the tooth fairy gave Junie B.'s old baby tooth to Ollie? That would be a great plan! Use the reverse alphabet code (A = Z, B = Y, C = X, and so on) to find out why.

Because

———————————————————————

IVXBXORMT

———————————————————————

NZPVH   XVMGH

A	Z
B	Y
C	X
D	W
E	V
F	U
G	T
H	S
I	R
J	Q
K	P
L	O
M	N
N	M
O	L
P	K
Q	J
R	I
S	H
T	G
U	F
V	E
W	D
X	C
Y	B
Z	A

Those Puzzling Cinquains

Mr. Scary shows Junie B.'s class how to write cinquains. A cinquain is a poem that has five lines. Each line has its own special rule.

1st line: One word (title)
2nd line: Two words that describe the title
3rd line: Three action words about the title
4th line: Four words that express a thought or feeling about the title
5th line: One word that means the same thing as the title

Here are some of the poems that Mr. Scary and Junie B.'s class writes:

Pickle.
Bumpy, lumpy,
Crunching, munching, lunching,
Cucumbers makin' you pucker,
Gherkin.

Me.
Richie Lucille.
Shopping, buying, spending.
Everyone's jealous of myself.
Princess.

Pallies.
Chummy, happy,
Joking, gelling, sharing.
Four amigos all together.
Friendship.

Junie (B.)
Bubbly, bouncy.
Learning, growing, glowing.
Your HONESTY is awesome!
Trusted.

Now it's your turn! Use the five lines below to write your own cinquain. Remember to follow the rules on the opposite page!

1. _____

2. _____

3. _____

4. _____

5. _____

Hiding Maze

Uh-oh! Junie B. did something bad at school today. And Mr. Scary sent home a "tattletale note" to her parents! Junie B. quick gave the note to Mother and Daddy. Then she and Philip Johnny Bob ran to hide. Can you find them?

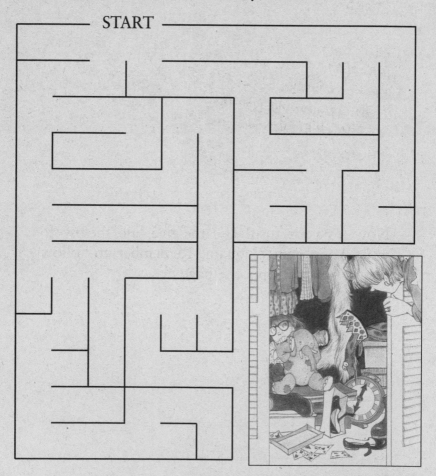

START

Answer key begins on page 220.

Kicking the Cow

A kickball tournament! A kickball tournament! The whole entire first grade is going to have a kickball tournament! Junie B. has been practicing her kicking every day. She can kick high and low. And fast and slow. And to and fro. But oh no! Junie B. hurts her toe when she kicks something she shouldn't. Start at 1 and connect the dots to find out what it is.

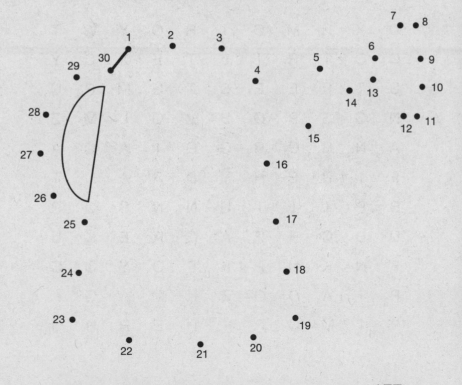

Kickball Tournament Word Search

Junie B. can't play in the kickball tournament because of her sore toe. The other children know just how she feels. That's because some of them have accidentally kicked things that didn't feel good, either. Can you find and circle some things you *shouldn't* kick? Words can go horizontally, vertically, diagonally, or backward.

brick • cow • fire hydrant • hippo • rock
• tree stump • truck

D	X	R	M	O	I	R	O	Y	W	T
Q	O	I	R	I	L	T	E	X	C	Y
S	T	R	E	E	S	T	U	M	P	U
N	G	S	P	G	B	V	O	L	M	Z
A	N	B	G	B	G	G	I	A	Q	A
F	I	R	E	H	Y	D	R	A	N	T
B	P	I	I	I	U	N	N	S	O	R
U	B	C	R	P	A	C	A	E	K	U
F	N	K	N	P	K	F	O	Y	C	C
P	I	A	D	O	Z	K	M	W	O	K
L	I	M	O	P	I	H	E	R	R	U

Answer key begins on page 220.

Spot the Differences!

Even though Junie B. can't play kickball, maybe she can juggle in Sheldon's halftime show. Then everyone will clap and cheer! And she will be the star of that whole production! Junie B. is practicing in the pictures below. Can you circle six differences in the pictures?

Answer key begins on page 220.

Fun with Me and Sheldon

Junie B. and Sheldon practice for the halftime show at recess. Mr. Scary gives Junie B. a drumstick and a woodblock to hit. Then all three of them practice marching around the playground. Now it's almost time for the real show. Can you help them find their way to the field?

START

Answer key begins on page 220.

Junie B. Jumble!

Oh dear! The halftime show is not going that well. First, Sheldon ran away. Then Junie B. tried to play the cymbals, and children threw food at her from lunch! (That is just rude.) So ha! Junie B. picked up the food and started to juggle! Unscramble the words below. (Hint: They're all things you find in school.) Then look at the letters in the circles to find out what kind of food Junie B. juggles.

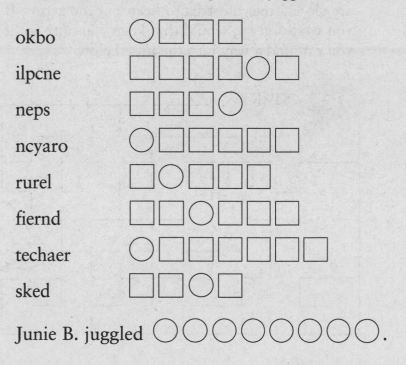

okbo

ilpcne

neps

ncyaro

rurel

fiernd

techaer

sked

Junie B. juggled ◯◯◯◯◯◯◯◯.

The Most "Disgustingest" Maze Ever

SPLAT-O! A boy named Roger "threwed up" on the floor. Sheldon says that whenever someone throws up, their germs shoot out in the air all over the place. Then, if somebody else breathes that air, those germs can get sucked right up their nostrils. Now all the children in Room One are closing their nostrils to keep out the germs. If you were a germ, would that keep you out? See if you can find a way into the nose below.

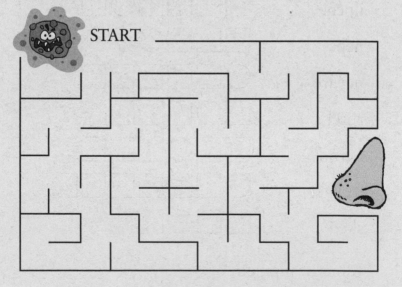

START

Answer key begins on page 220.

Triangle Puzzler!

Room One is putting on a play for Parents' Night. It is going to be about Christopher Columbus. And Junie B. gets to pick her favorite part! Color in each three-sided shape to find out which part Junie B. chooses.

Answer key begins on page 220.

Columbus Day Tangle

Christopher Columbus had three ships: the *Niña,* the *Pinta,* and the *Santa María.* Junie B. wants to be the *fastest* ship. Because the fastest ship is the winner ship. And the winner ship is the *star* ship! Help Junie B. pick the ship that gets to America first! Remember, stay on one line—no sharp turns!

LAND!

Answer key begins on page 220.

Niña

Pinta

Santa María

Spot the Differences!

Junie B., Sheldon, and May are all going to be
ships in the play. They are very busy making
their costumes. But guess what? The pictures on
these two pages are not the same. Can you circle
six differences?

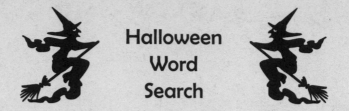

Halloween Word Search

Halloween is coming! (Unfortunately, Junie B. doesn't like Halloween. But she will just have to get over that!) Can you find and circle the Halloween words below? Words can go horizontally, vertically, diagonally, or backward.

bats • boo • candy corn • costume • ghost • monster • mummy • pumpkins • trick • witch

C	L	I	M	O	N	S	T	E	R
A	C	E	P	M	W	I	T	C	H
N	O	R	M	U	U	A	A	S	L
D	S	I	O	M	Q	F	C	T	T
Y	T	P	U	M	P	K	I	N	S
C	U	R	G	Y	L	S	G	L	O
O	M	R	I	S	L	T	T	O	Y
R	E	Y	G	C	Y	A	O	E	P
N	B	N	R	B	K	B	E	Y	R
P	G	H	O	S	T	V	N	X	W

Answer key begins on page 220.

Paulie Allen Puffer's Scary-Secrets Code

Junie B. is actually scared of Halloween. That's because last year, Paulie Allen Puffer told her five scary secrets about that day. Secret #1 is that real, "alive" creepy things will be trick-or-treating on Halloween. Use the reverse alphabet code (A = Z, B = Y, C = X, and so on) to find out what creepy things he was talking about.

IVZO   NLMHGVIH

ZMW   DRGXSVH

will be trick-or-treating.

A	Z
B	Y
C	X
D	W
E	V
F	U
G	T
H	S
I	R
J	Q
K	P
L	O
M	N
N	M
O	L
P	K
Q	J
R	I
S	H
T	G
U	F
V	E
W	D
X	C
Y	B
Z	A

Jack-o'-Lantern Matching

Secret #2 is that you shouldn't carve pointy, sharp teeth in your pumpkin. If you do, it could roll into your room while you are sleeping and eat your feet. Look at these jack-o'-lanterns. Can you help Junie B. find the two that match? Circle them when you do.

Answer key begins on page 220.

Spooky Connect-the-Dots

Paulie Allen Puffer has three more scary secrets about Halloween. Secret #3 is that there are spooky flying things that can land on your head and live in your hair. Start at 1 and connect the dots to find out what they are.

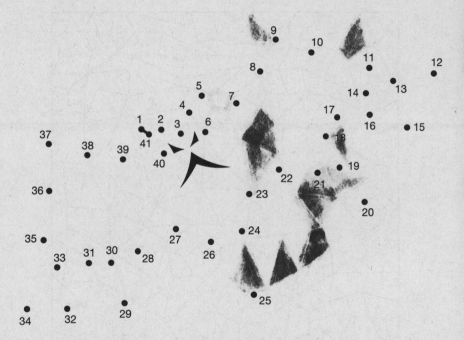

Spooky Triangle Mystery

Secret #4 is that there are scary things with sharp claws that can claw you into a shreddle. Color in the three-sided shapes to find out what it is.

Answer key begins on page 220.

Scary-Secret Scramble!

Paulie Allen Puffer's fifth Halloween secret is just plain shocking. Unscramble the words below. (Hint: They're all things you can dress up as for Halloween!) Then look at the letters in the pumpkins to find out the most surprising secret of them all!

cwnlo

gshto

ripate

picrness

Candy corn is not really 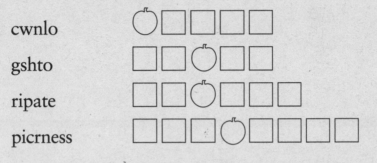.

"Trick or Treat!" Words

How many different words can you make from the letters in TRICK OR TREAT? Try to make at least ten. Write them on the lines below. Junie B. wrote down two to get you started!

TRICK OR TREAT

kite

rock

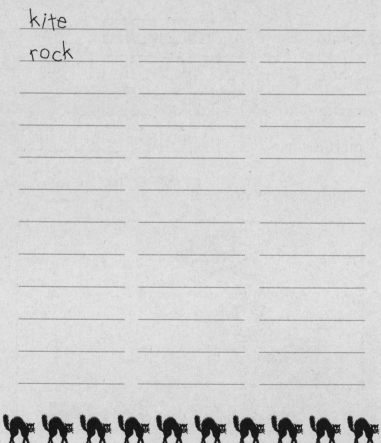

Answer key begins on page 220.

HA HA Halloween Code

Good news, people! Junie B. has an idea for a costume that will out-scare even the creepiest competition. So HA HA on monsters! And HA HA on witches and bats and cats! And HA HA on scary Halloween! Cross out any letters in the word *BOO* to find out what Junie B.'s going to be. Write the remaining letters on the lines below.

BSOCORBEABMOY

__ __ __ __ __ __ the clown

Trick-or-Fruit Maze

Now that she's picked out a costume, Junie B. can go trick-or-treating. Only here's the problem. Grouchy Mrs. Morty gives her an apple! What kind of treat is that? Plus other neighbors give Junie B. raisins! And a pencil! And (bluck!) a box of trail mix! Can you help Junie B. find her way to some *real* treats?

START

Answer key begins on page 220.

Holiday Sing-Along Connect-the-Dots

It's the last week before winter break, and Room One is having a Holiday Sing-Along! Start at 1 and connect the dots to see what the children will be wearing.

Laughing All the Way!

The first song at the Holiday Sing-Along is "The Twelve Days of Christmas." Junie B. thinks "The Twelve Days of Christmas" is about a guy who gives his girlfriend a bunch of silly presents. Look at the presents below. Circle the two that are exactly the same.

Answer key begins on page 220.

The children also sing "Frosty the Snowman."
(That one is a classic!) Look at the snowmen
below. Circle the one that is different.

"Jingle Bells" Word Search

Junie B. sees *lots* of things she loves at the holiday gift shop. (And that includes all the tattoos a kid could ever dream of!) Can you find and circle some of the tattoos and other fun things Junie B. sees there? Words can go horizontally, vertically, or diagonally.

barrettes • candy canes • crayons • dinosaurs
• dragon • kitty cat • pirate

D	K	C	S	R	A	S	G	P	R
Q	B	R	A	N	B	U	W	P	D
D	R	A	G	O	N	A	B	I	I
N	I	Y	R	O	N	F	C	R	N
A	G	O	R	R	N	D	F	A	O
R	G	N	U	I	E	S	G	T	S
L	Z	S	P	S	L	T	T	E	A
K	I	T	T	Y	C	A	T	B	U
F	B	N	K	B	B	L	E	E	R
C	A	N	D	Y	C	A	N	E	S

Answer key begins on page 220.

Giving

Uh-oh! Junie B. and Blabbermouth May are arguing in the gift shop. May says it is nicer to give than receive. Use the reverse alphabet code (A = Z, B = Y, C = X, and so on) to find out what *else* May tells Junie B.

Some people are born to be givers.
And *others* are born to be

_____ .

HSVOOURHS

Spot the Differences!

Room One is having a happy holiday party! It is getting festive in there! Look at the two pictures. Can you circle seven differences in the second picture?

Peace-and-Goodwill Secret Code

Junie B. picked Blabbermouth May's name in a drawing, and now she has to buy her a Secret Santa gift. (This was *not* on purpose.) Junie B. thinks that meanie girl doesn't even *deserve* a

Secret Santa gift. If Junie B. were the real Santa Claus, she would give May *coal* in her stocking. But will Junie B. *really* get May coal for her Secret Santa gift? Or will she choose a gift that May will like? Cross out any letters in the word *goodwill* to see what Junie B. gets for May. Write the remaining letters on the lines below.

GSOQOUDEGEWZLEL-AI-DBOUWRLPI

___ ___ ___ ___ ___ ___ - ___ - ___ ___ ___ ___ ___ ___

Answer key begins on page 220.

"The Bestest Gift" Scramble

Yay! Yay! Hurray! It's the moment everyone's been waiting for! Mr. Scary is delivering the Secret Santa gifts. Unscramble the words below. (Hint: They're all holiday words.) Then look at the letters in the Christmas trees to see what Junie B. finds in her gift sack.

ceape ☐☐☐△☐

eret ☐△☐☐

asnta ☐△☐☐☐

yjo ☐☐△

sonwamn ☐☐☐△☐☐☐

soctikng ☐☐☐☐☐☐△☐

lelbs ☐☐☐☐△

Junie B. finds △△△△△△△.

Vacation Triangle Puzzle

Vacation! Vacation! Junie B. is going on a vacation to Hawaii! And that's not even the most exciting part! 'Cause guess how she's getting to Hawaii? Color in each three-sided shape to find out.

Answer key begins on page 220.

Amazing-Adventure Tangle!

That's right! Junie B. is going to be flying in a real, actual airplane! But only *one* of these airplanes is heading to Hawaii. Help Junie B. pick the airplane that will take her there. Remember, stay on one path!

HAWAII!

Pair-o-Dice Word Search

The travel booklet says Hawaii is a real, actual paradise. (And that is not the same as a "pair-o-dice.") Can you find and circle some things Junie B. might see on her trip to paradise? Words can go horizontally, vertically, or diagonally.

beach • birds • fish • flowers • lei • volcanoes

```
D  L  I  S  R  A  S  G  O  Z
Q  D  B  A  N  V  U  L  I  S
U  F  R  E  F  O  A  B  E  A
N  L  I  O  A  L  J  E  Q  I
U  O  G  S  O  C  D  F  K  S
A  W  S  G  H  A  H  G  L  O
L  E  R  P  S  N  R  T  M  Y
J  R  I  T  H  O  B  L  U  H
F  S  N  K  B  E  L  E  Y  R
P  B  I  R  D  S  V  N  X  W
```

Answer key begins on page 220.

Hello-and-Goodbye Scramble

When Junie B. gets to Hawaii, she learns a Hawaiian word that means *hello* and *goodbye*. Unscramble the words below. (Hint: They're all things Junie B. might see in Hawaii.) Then look at the letters in the flowers to find out what the Hawaiian word is.

becha ☐☐❁☐☐

aulh ☐☐❁☐

vanlooc ☐☐☐☐☐☐❁

shlle ☐❁☐☐☐

sdan ☐❁☐☐

The word is ❁❁❁❁❁.

Answer key begins on page 220.

"The Happiest Part of All"
Connect-the-Dots

Yippee! Yippee! Here is the happiest part of all. On the way to the pool, Junie B. spots something wonderful in a gift-shop window. Start at 1 and connect the dots to find out what Junie B. wants to buy.

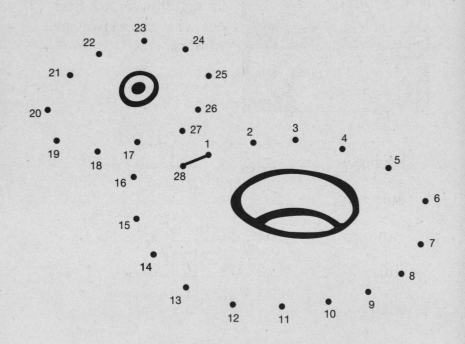

Answer key begins on page 220.

Swim Ring Match-Up

Junie B.'s new swim ring looks exactly like a colorful parrot. She names it Squeezer. That's because it is too tight and it squeezes her insides in half. Look at the swim rings below. Can you circle the two that match?

Aloha-ha-ha Code Breaker!

Hurray! Junie B. is ready to go in the ocean! She even has her swim fins! (Swim fins look exactly like frog feet. Except they are not on an actual frog.) What is she going to do? Use the reverse alphabet code (A = Z, B = Y, C = X, and so on) to find out.

HMLIPVO

Junie B. is going to

—— —— —— —— —— —— —— .

Eely Squealy Maze

Snorkeling is like being in a fish zoo. Except Junie B. keeps getting scared. Because YIKES! First, she spots an eel! Then WHOA! WAIT! HOLD THE PHONE! Something even worse floats her way. And it's called . . . JELLYFISH! Can you help Junie B. find her way back to shore?

START

"Bye-Bye, Birdie" Maze!

Bird! Bird! 911! 911! A little Hawaiian bird is tangled in Junie B.'s hair! Help the little bird find its way out of her hair and back home.

START

Answer key begins on page 220.

Richie Lucille's Connect-the-Dots

Richie Lucille is having an Easter-egg hunt at her big, giant house. And all the children in Room One are invited! A very famous celebrity will be there to meet them. Start at 1 and connect the dots to find out who Lucille's special guest is.

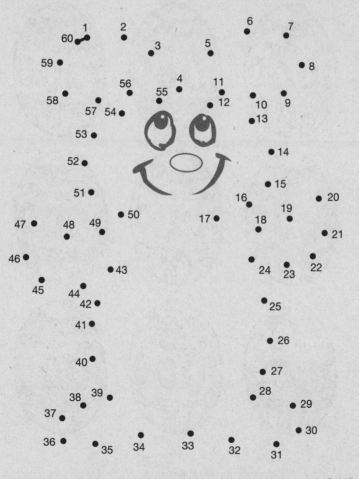

Egg Hunt

There are lots of beautiful eggs at Lucille's egg hunt. But Lucille's daddy hid one extra-special pretend *golden egg*. Can you circle it below? (Hint: It's the one that's not like any of the others.)

Answer key begins on page 220.

Egg-stra-Special Art!

Everything at Richie Lucille's house is egg-stra fancy. Decorate your own *egg-stra*-special eggs below!

Golden-Egg Maze

Whoever finds the golden egg will win the Grand Prize of the Day. And that is a fabulous playdate swimming with Lucille in her indoor heated

swimming pool! Junie B. would LOVE to take a closer peek at that pool! Can you help her find it?

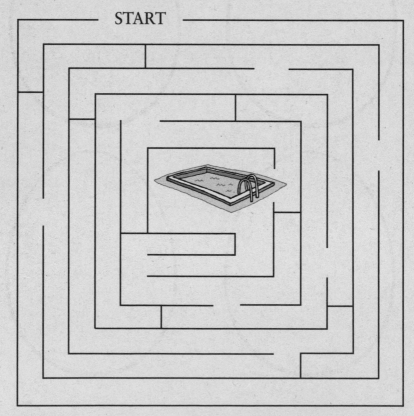

START

Answer key begins on page 220.

Lucky-Bunny Tangle!

The golden egg! The golden egg! Junie B. sees the golden egg. But May and Sheldon see it, too. So *OOMPHFF! FOOMFF! PHIFFOOPHFF!* They all dive for it at once! But only one of them can get it. Can you pick the line that leads to the golden egg?

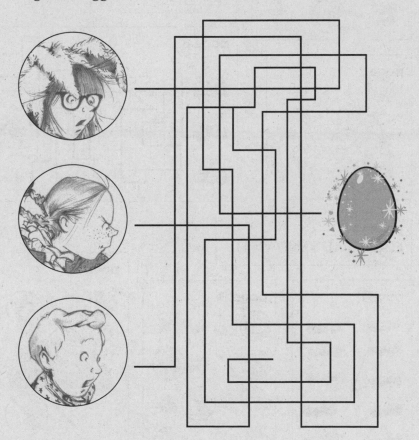

Answer Key

page 5

page 6
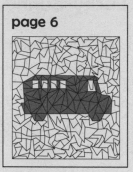

page 7
Piggyback

page 8
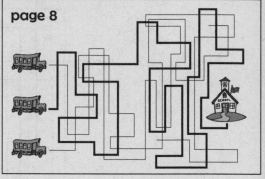

page 10
EGG SALAD SANDWICH

page 11

page 13

page 14

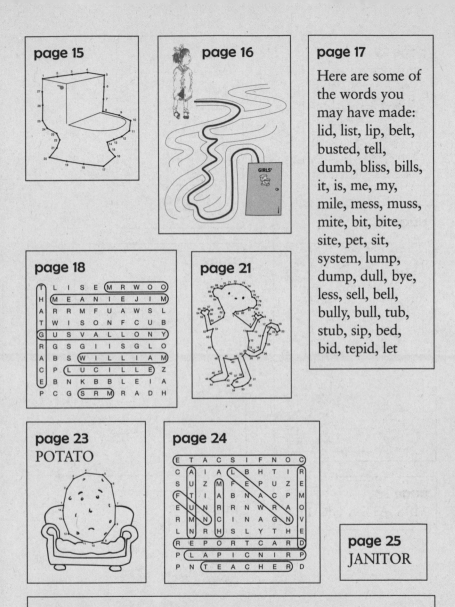

page 15

page 16

GIRLS'

page 17

Here are some of the words you may have made: lid, list, lip, belt, busted, tell, dumb, bliss, bills, it, is, me, my, mile, mess, muss, mite, bit, bite, site, pet, sit, system, lump, dump, dull, bye, less, sell, bell, bully, bull, tub, stub, sip, bed, bid, tepid, let

page 18

T	L	I	S	E	M	R	W	O	O
H	M	E	A	N	I	E	J	I	M
A	R	R	M	F	U	A	W	S	L
T	W	I	S	O	N	F	C	U	B
G	U	S	V	A	L	L	O	N	Y
R	G	S	G	I	I	S	G	L	O
A	B	S	W	I	L	L	I	A	M
C	P	L	U	C	I	L	L	E	Z
E	B	N	K	B	B	L	E	I	A
P	C	G	S	R	M	R	A	D	H

page 21

page 23
POTATO

page 24

E	T	A	C	S	I	F	N	O	C
C	A	I	A	L	B	H	T	I	R
S	U	Z	M	F	E	P	U	Z	E
T	I	U	R	R	N	W	R	A	M
E	U	N	N	C	I	N	A	G	O
R	M	N	C	I	N	A	G	N	V
L	N	R	H	S	L	Y	T	H	E
R	E	P	O	R	T	C	A	R	D
P	L	A	P	I	C	N	I	R	P
P	N	T	E	A	C	H	E	R	D

page 25
JANITOR

page 26
Princess with crown; lunch lady with saucepan; plumber with plunger; beauty shop guy with scissors; tooth witch with tooth; sneaky peeky spy with binoculars; farmer with tractor; snorkel instructor with snorkel

page 27

page 29

page 31

page 32

page 33
MRS. ATE A GRAPE

page 34

page 35

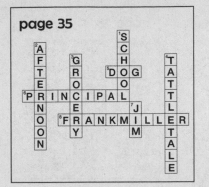

page 37

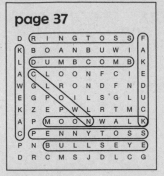

page 39

page 40

page 41

page 42

223

page 47

page 48

page 49
TOOL BELT

page 52

page 54

page 55
FIX THE
TOILET

page 58

page 59

page 60

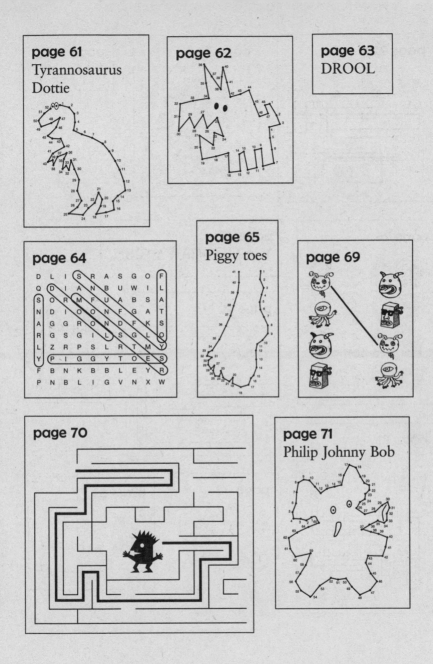

page 61
Tyrannosaurus
Dottie

page 62

page 63
DROOL

page 64

page 65
Piggy toes

page 69

page 70

page 71
Philip Johnny Bob

225

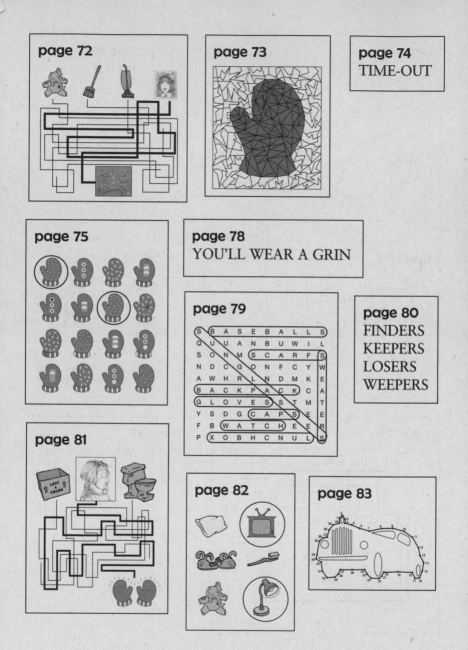

page 72

page 73

page 74
TIME-OUT

page 75

page 78
YOU'LL WEAR A GRIN

page 79

S	B	A	S	E	B	A	L	L	S
Q	U	U	A	N	B	U	W	I	L
S	O	N	M	S	C	A	R	F	S
N	D	C	G	O	N	F	C	Y	W
A	W	H	R	L	N	D	M	K	E
B	A	C	K	P	A	C	K	C	A
G	L	O	V	E	S	S	T	M	T
Y	S	D	G	C	A	P	S	E	E
F	B	W	A	T	C	H	E	E	R
P	X	O	B	H	C	N	U	L	S

page 80
FINDERS
KEEPERS
LOSERS
WEEPERS

page 81

page 82

page 83

page 84

page 85

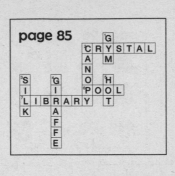

```
          G
     C R Y S T A L
     A   M
   S A N O   H
   I   P O O L
  L I B R A R Y   T
   K   A
     F
     F
     E
```

page 86

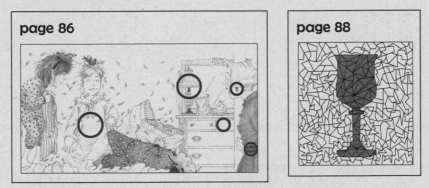

page 88

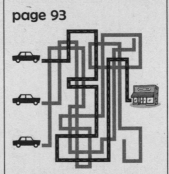

page 89

page 93

227

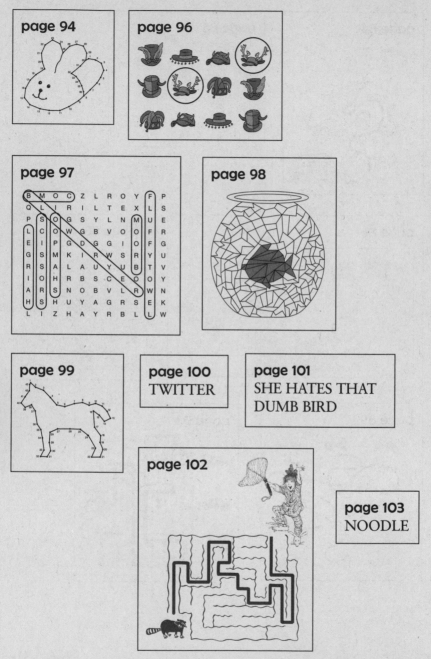

page 94

page 96

page 97

page 98

page 99

page 100
TWITTER

page 101
SHE HATES THAT
DUMB BIRD

page 102

page 103
NOODLE

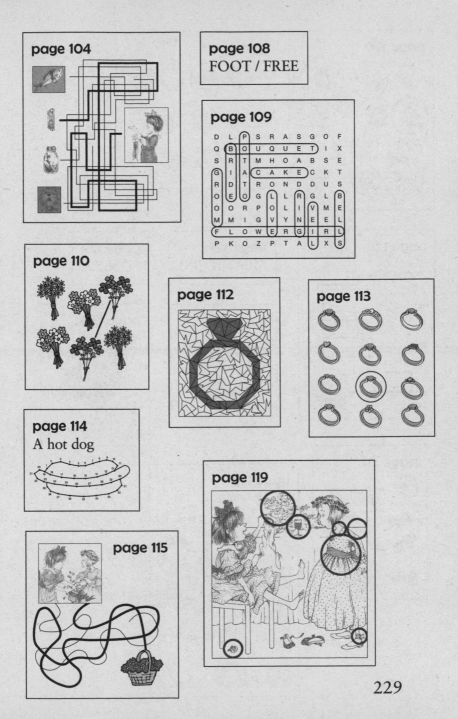

page 104

page 108
FOOT / FREE

page 109

```
D  L  P  S  R  A  S  G  O  F
Q (B  O  U  Q  U  E  T) I  X
S  R  T  M  H  O  A  B  S  E
G  I  A (C  A  K  E) C  K  T
R  D  T  R  O  N  D  D  U  S
O  E  O  G  L  L  R  G  L  B
O  O  R  P  O  L  A  V  M  E
M  M  I  G  V  Y  I  E  E  L
(F  L  O  W  E  R  G  I  R  L)
P  K  O  Z  P  T  A  L  X  S
```

page 110

page 112

page 113

page 114
A hot dog

page 115

page 119

229

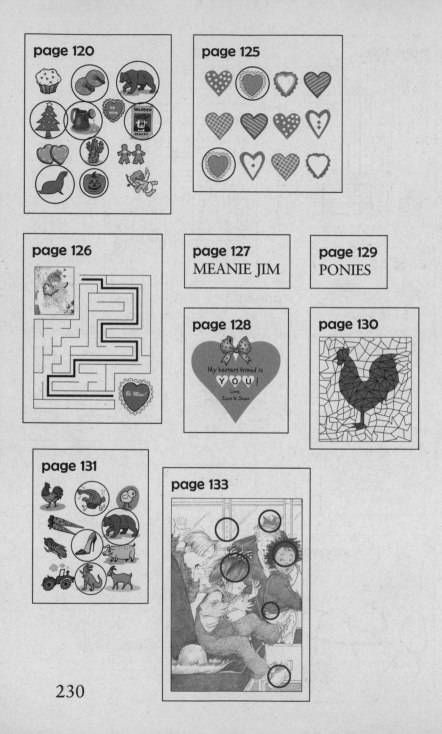

page 120

page 125

page 126

page 127
MEANIE JIM

page 129
PONIES

page 128
My bestest friend is
Y O U !
Love,
Junie B. Jones

page 130

page 131

page 133

230

page 134

page 135
ROOSTER

page 137
CLAMS

page 136

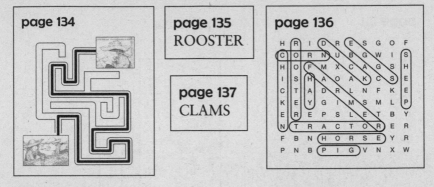

page 138
Here are some of the words you may have made: at, an, in, cap, tap, pat, nap, tin, can, if, pin, pen, pad, lap, dip, fat, fit, cat, late, flea, clap, clip, flip, yap, yet, file, pile, dine, date, fate, pay

page 142

page 145

page 146

page 147

page 150
SPOT

231

page 151

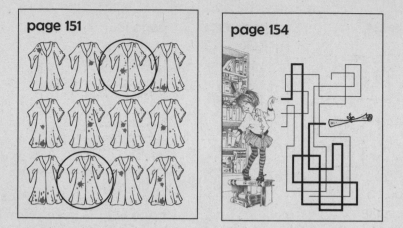

page 154

page 155

Here are some of the words you may have made: in, an, it, at, ad, jab, badge, grade, dare, fire, bite, bit, nag, nab, near, budge, dear, find, site, sit, fan, grab, bag, bat, tag, tab, rat, fast, drain, grain, fair, fudge, brat, burst, bun, under, burn, drift, rain, sat

page 157

```
H  L  L  S  R  A  S  G  O  J
Q  E  C  H  E  N  I  L  L  E
S  N  R  A  F  U  A  B  S  R
B  I  O  B  M  N  W  C  É  M
A  I  I  R  O  I  D  F  D  R
R  E  É  G  I  L  L  G  L  S
J  O  U  R  N  A  L  L  M  C
O  S  G  L  A  S  S  E  S  A
S  B  N  K  B  B  L  E  Y  R
É  N  B  L  I  G  V  M  A  Y
```

page 158
GLASSES

page 159

```
D  V  I  S  R  A  M  G  O  U
Q  M  I  C  H  E  E  S  E  O
C  I  M  B  F  G  K  B  S  F
O  L  I  A  P  P  L  E  E  R
O  K  G  N  T  N  D  F  A  A
K  G  S  N  A  I  T  S  G  I
I  U  R  S  L  R  T  M  S
E  J  N  A  L  H  T  E  E  I
E  F  O  R  K  L  I  F  T  N
S  A  N  D  W  I  C  H  U
```

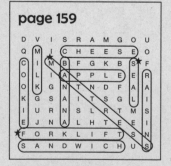

page 160

232

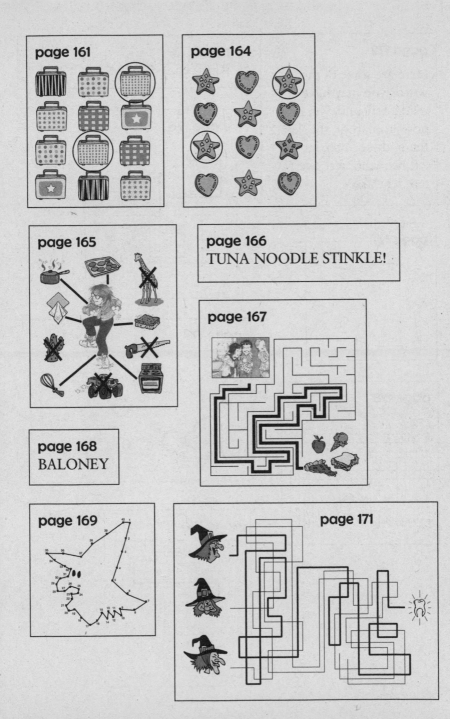

page 161

page 164

page 165

page 166
TUNA NOODLE STINKLE!

page 167

page 168
BALONEY

page 169

page 171

page 172

Here are some of the words you may have made: tone, no, we, now, nose, tool, root, the, less, there, these, then, lent, let, her, who, wet, west, ten, tent, tree

page 173
RECYCLING MAKES CENTS

page 176

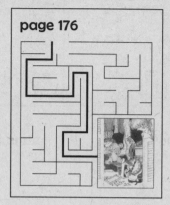

page 177

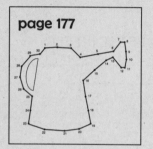

page 178

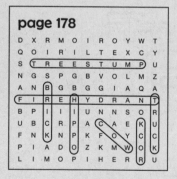

page 179

page 180

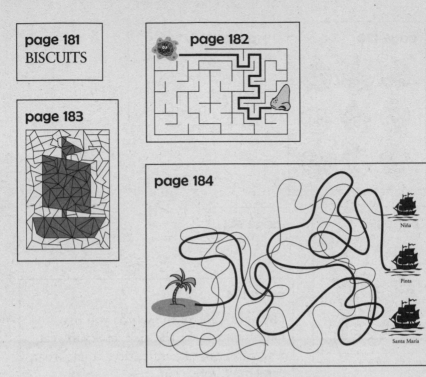

Niña

Pinta

Santa María

C L I M O N S T E R
A C E P M W I T C H
N O R M U U A A S L
D S I O M Q F C T T
Y T P U M P K I N S
C U R G Y L S G L O
O M I S C Y T O E Y
R E Y G C A B E P R
N B N R B K B E Y R
P G H O S T V N X W

235

page 190

page 191

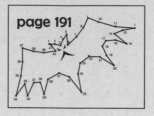

page 192

page 193
CORN

page 194

Here are some of the words you may have made: it, or, ick, tick, tock, are, eat, tear, care, car, rat, crate, rice, at, ate, roar, cat, croak, tote, coat

page 195
SCREAMY

page 196

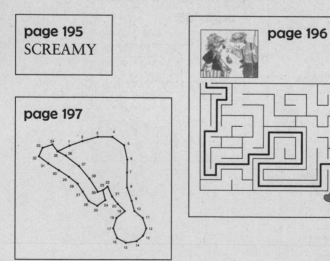

page 197

236

page 198

page 199

page 200

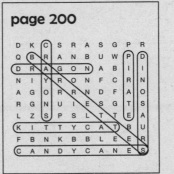

page 201
SHELLFISH

page 204
SQUEEZE-A-BURP

page 203

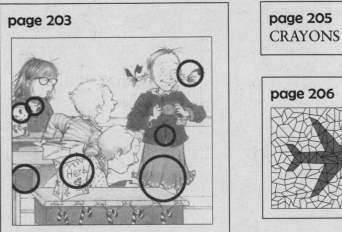

page 205
CRAYONS

page 206

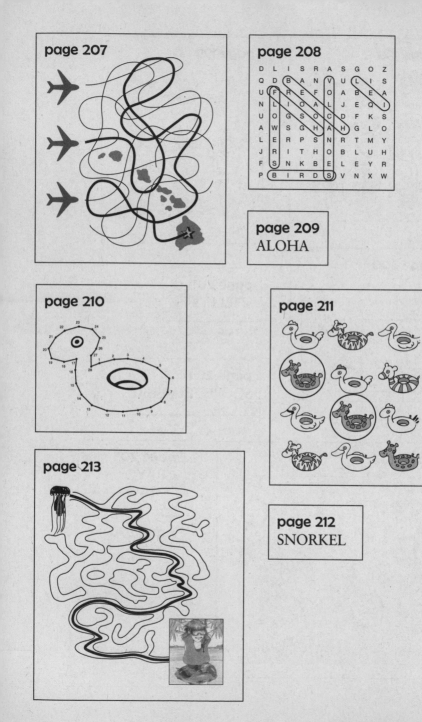

page 207

page 208

D	L	I	S	R	A	S	G	O	Z
Q	D	B	A	N	V	U	L	I	S
U	F	R	E	F	O	A	B	E	A
N	L	I	O	A	L	J	E	Q	I
A	O	G	S	O	C	D	F	K	S
A	W	S	G	H	A	H	G	L	O
L	E	R	P	S	N	R	T	M	Y
J	R	I	T	H	O	B	L	U	H
F	S	N	K	B	E	L	E	Y	R
P	B	I	R	D	S	V	N	X	W

page 209
ALOHA

page 210

page 211

page 213

page 212
SNORKEL

page 214

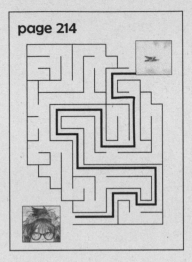

page 215

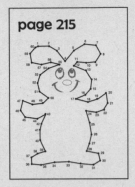

page 216

page 218

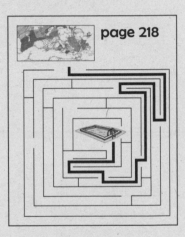

page 219

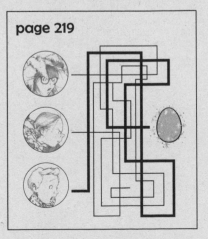